BLUE REVOLUTION

BLUE REVOLUTION
Unmaking America's Water Crisis

Cynthia Barnett

BEACON PRESS, BOSTON

Beacon Press
Boston, Massachusetts
www.beacon.org

Beacon Press books
are published under the auspices of
the Unitarian Universalist Association of Congregations.

20 19 18 17   8 7 6 5 4 3 (pbk.)

This book is printed on acid-free paper that meets the uncoated paper
ANSI/NISO specifications for permanence as revised in 1992.

Text design and composition by Wilsted & Taylor Publishing Services

Library of Congress Cataloging-in-Publication Data

Barnett, Cynthia.
Blue revolution : unmaking America's water crisis / Cynthia Barnett. p.
cm.
Includes bibliographical references and index.
ISBN 978-0-8070-0317-6 (hardcover : alk. paper)
ISBN 978-0-8070-0328-2 (paperback : alk. paper) 1. Water-supply—
Government policy—United States. 2. Water-supply—Case studies.
3. Water resources development—Moral and ethical aspects. I. Title.
TD223.B37 2011
333.9100973—dc23   2011012334

FOR WILL & ILANA

Contents

CHAPTER 1

The Illusion of Water Abundance

During America's retreat to the suburbs in the 1950s, large home lots, disposable incomes, and a nifty concrete spray called gunite gave families a new marker of success: the backyard swimming pool. For the rest of the twentieth century, residential pools symbolized upward mobility and offered a sense of seclusion not possible at city pools or even private clubs.[1]

The following decades redefined our relationship with water itself—from essence of life to emblem of luxury. By the time of the twenty-first-century housing run-up, even the plain blue pool had lost its luster. Adornments were needed. Aquatic affluence meant floating fire pits, glass portholes, and vanishing edges, which create the illusion of never-ending water.[2]

The amenity to envy was no longer the diving board. The must-have, now, was the waterfall.

No community glorified the trend like Granite Bay, California.

Granite Bay is nestled on the north shores of Folsom Lake, commuting distance east of Sacramento. The upscale suburb is named for the Cretaceous age rock that underlies this region in the foothills of the Sierra Nevada. But during the housing boom, Granite Bay's developers were determined to upstage the area's natural geologic outcroppings.

In Granite Bay's best backyards, rocky waterfalls cascade artfully into boulder-lined swimming pools, set off with grottoes, swim-up

bars, and built-in hot tubs. Thick bushes and trees bearing flowers and fruit adorn the watery wonders, making a place naturally
dominated by needlegrass and sedge look more like Fiji. Precisely
groomed lawns, a quarter acre and larger, complete the sublimely
unnatural tableau.

On Waterford Drive, a beige ranch home with a trim green carpet
out front only hints at the tropical excess out back: a pair of waterfalls
flow into a clear-blue lagoon, with large rocks positioned for sunning
and for diving. This is one of the more subdued motifs. Sacramento
landscape architect Ronald Allison tells of a two-and-a-half-acre residential design in Granite Bay with a waterfall, a grotto, a cave, six
fountains, a pool with a bridge and an island, *and* a ninety-foot water
slide: "It's fun for the grandkids."[3]

Such fun has helped push average water use in Granite Bay to
among the highest on Earth. Its residents use nearly five hundred
gallons of water a person every day—more than three times the
national average.[4] Even when drought conditions cut federal water
deliveries to California farmers and closed the state's salmon fisheries, Granite Bay residents continued to consume water as if it
were as plentiful as air. After three consecutive years of California drought, Folsom Lake—actually a reservoir created by a dam
on the American River—was so dry, it looked like a moonscape.
As water levels plummeted in summer 2009, officials from the U.S.
Bureau of Reclamation, which manages the lake, ordered all boats
removed from the Folsom Marina.[5] Yet the San Juan Water District,
which supplies Granite Bay from the reservoir, informed its customers that summer they would have to endure no mandatory water
restrictions.[6]

Spectacular squander in the middle of a water crisis is not much
of a shock in the United States, where we use about half our daily
household water bounty outdoors. The dryer the conditions, the
more we tend to pour. What is surprising, however, is to find some of
the world's worst waste in the Sacramento metropolitan area. That's
because Greater Sacramento has become a national leader in finding solutions to America's energy and climate challenges—and in
working to solve other problems brought about by suburban growth.

Sacramento glitters with all things green. But when it comes to water, the city represents a national blind spot.

Somehow, America's green craze has missed the blue.

California's capital likes to call itself "Sustainable Sacramento." The progressive municipal government is spending heavily on light rail and constructing only green city buildings. The utility generates solar, wind, biomass, and hydro power for customers willing to pay more for renewable energy. Sacramento's citizens choose to do so at some of the highest rates in the nation.[7]

The city is so green, it provides organic food to public school children, bike racks to businesses, and free trees to residents who want to cool their homes with natural shade.

But with water, Sacramento isn't so enlightened. The metropolitan area, which lands regularly on lists of top green cities, smart cities, and livable cities, also has earned this startling ranking: it squanders more water than anywhere else in California. That distinction makes it one of the most water-wasting places in the United States. And that makes it one of the most water-wasting places on the planet.[8]

Residents of the metro region use nearly 300 gallons of water per person every day—double the national average.[9] By comparison, the equally affluent residents of Perth, Australia, use about 75 gallons per day. Londoners tap about 42 gallons per day. The water-rich Dutch use about 33 gallons daily.[10]

Grottoed communities such as Granite Bay aren't solely to blame. Some of the same politicians who forged the new path for energy in Sacramento fought for the city's right to keep to the old road for water. The city is one of the last major metro areas in the nation to hold on to flat rates that charge residents the same no matter how much water they use.[11] In 1920, Sacramento had amended its charter to declare that "no water meters shall ever be attached to residential water service pipes." Only an act of the state assembly, which requires the measuring of water use statewide by 2025, has the city installing meters these days.[12]

Sacramento is by no means unique. Even as our green consciousness evolves, we often manage to ignore water not only on a global
level but also in our own backyards. The Copenhagen climate accord,
negotiated by the United Nations in 2010, did not mention the most
immediate threat from a changing climate—the worldwide freshwater crisis.[13] Across the United States, we give little thought to our
water use even as we replace lightbulbs with compact fluorescents
and SUVs with hybrids.

The conscientious consumer who plunks down $25,000 for a
Prius may still wash it every weekend in the driveway. The office
manager who rallies every department to recycle paper is unaware
of the millions of gallons of water a year that could be recycled from
the building's air-conditioning system.

How is that?

One part of the answer is the illusion of water abundance. When
we twist the tap, we're rewarded with a gush of fresh, clean water. It's
been that way since the turn of the twentieth century, when Americans perfected municipal waterworks, indoor plumbing, and wastewater disposal as a response to diseases like cholera or typhoid fever.

Water is also our cheapest necessity. Four-dollar-a-gallon gasoline helped drive consumers to cars that cost them less to operate.
Lower fossil fuel consumption and reduced carbon emissions are
fringe benefits to protecting our pocketbooks. No equivalent economic incentive makes us think about our water waste. In fact, our
water is so subsidized that many Americans pay less than a tenth of
a penny a gallon for clean freshwater delivered right into our homes.

"As a society, from a water standpoint, we're fat, dumb, and
happy," says Tom Gohring, executive director of the Sacramento
Water Forum, a coalition of business, environmental, and other
competing water interests that work together to find solutions to the
region's water woes. "In the history of our country, we've had some
serious water shortages, but very, very seldom have people been told
that they cannot turn on the taps but for an hour in the afternoon,
or that they must boil water.

"Water is just too easy to take for granted," Gohring says. "It's
always there."[14]

This is true in Sustainable Sacramento, and it's true in the scorched Southwest. The most conspicuous water consumption in America is often found in those parts of the country where water shortages are most serious. Nationwide, we use an average of 147 gallons each day. In wet Florida, the average hits 158 gallons. In Las Vegas, it's 227 gallons per person—in one of the most water-scarce metro areas of the United States, where water managers lose sleep at night thinking about what will happen when the level in Lake Mead drops below the intake pipes that carry water to the city.

Vegas swimming pools—with their glass walls, underwater sound systems, sushi bars, and stripper poles—make Granite Bay's look like they came from the Kmart garden department. But in both locales, the extreme illusion of abundance makes it all but impossible for people who live and play there to notice their personal connection to the nation's water crisis—to understand how wasteful water use in one house, in one backyard, multiplied by 310 million Americans, equals trouble for the generations to come.

Profligate water use today will imperil future generations, the same as profligate use of oil, destruction of forests, and other environmental tipping points will. But water is much more important to our future than oil. That's because there are no alternatives to it, no new substitute for life's essential ingredient being cooked from corn, french fry grease, or algae.

Like our other great, national illusions—say, the unending bull market, or upward-only housing prices—the illusion of water abundance is a beautiful bubble doomed to pop. With petroleum, those $4 gas prices sparked a collective "Aha!" moment for Americans. But there's been no "Aha!" in the case of water, even though the largest of our waterworks are beginning to show a few cracks.

Let's put it this way: It will not be fun for the grandkids.

Rising 726 feet above the Colorado River between Arizona and Nevada, Hoover Dam stands as a breathtaking marvel of U.S. engineering. Its mammoth hydraulic turbines generate energy for hundreds of thousands of homes. Its reservoir, Lake Mead, supplies water to millions of Americans and another million acres of farmland. The dam's iconic symbolism makes a study by the University of California's Scripps Institution of Oceanography that much more unsettling. In a grim paper titled "When Will Lake Mead Go Dry?," marine physicist Tim Barnett (no relation to this book's author) and climate scientist David Pierce say there's a fifty-fifty chance it will happen by 2021. By 2017, they say, there's an equally good chance water levels in the reservoir will drop so low that Hoover Dam will be incapable of producing hydroelectric power.[15]

Most Americans, including the millions who visit this popular tourist spot each year, don't yet seem to fathom that the largest reservoir in the United States is in danger of drying up, that the famous dam's turbines could cease to hum. Even the Scripps scientists say they were "stunned at the magnitude of the problem and how fast it was coming at us."

A dried-up Lake Mead is only the most dramatically visible of the collapses that scientists say could play out in the seven states— Arizona, California, Colorado, Nevada, New Mexico, Utah, and Wyoming—that rely on the Colorado River and its tributaries as ever-increasing water use, ever-growing population, and a changing climate shrink its flow. Scientists who study tree rings to learn about long-ago climate now say that the twentieth century, when America built its grand waterworks and divvied up its rivers, was the wettest in a thousand years.[16] Now, the wet period is over; the National Academy of Sciences reports it unlikely that the Southwest will see its return. Instead, the region is expected to become dryer, and to experience more severe droughts, than in the twentieth century.[17] Trees in the West are already showing the strain, dying off and burning at unprecedented rates.[18] Now, people must adjust, too, conclude Barnett and Pierce, to forestall "a major societal and economic disruption in the desert southwest."[19]

This dry, dusty American future is not confined to the desert. In the Great Plains, farmers are depleting the enormous High Plains Aquifer, which underlies 225,000 square miles of Colorado, Kansas, Nebraska, New Mexico, Oklahoma, South Dakota, Texas, and Wyoming, far faster than it can recharge. We pump an average of one million acre-feet from the High Plains every day. (That's the equivalent of one million acres covered to a depth of one foot.) If that rate continues, scientists say, this ancient aquifer responsible for nearly one-third of all agricultural irrigation water in the United States will dry up within the century.[20] We've even managed to tap out some of the wettest parts of the United States. Florida has so overpumped its once abundant groundwater that the hundred-thousand-square-mile sponge known as the Floridan Aquifer, one of the most productive aquifers in the world, can no longer supply the state's drinking-water needs. The Atlanta region has come within ninety days of seeing the reservoir Lake Sidney Lanier, primary water source for five million people, dry up.

But here's the confounding thing: practically every scientific study that describes these catastrophes and the gloomy future they portend also concludes that it doesn't *have* to be this way. In the Southeast and in the Great Plains, and even in the arid states supplied by the Colorado River, it's possible to reverse the parched path we've set out for our grandchildren and their grandchildren, not to mention ourselves. Conserving water and changing the way we manage water would "play a big part in reducing our risk," says Kenneth Nowak of the University of Colorado at Boulder, coauthor of a recent study that shows the likelihood of depleting the Colorado River's massive reservoirs depends on human actions.[21]

America needs nothing less than a revolution in how we use water. We must change not only the wasteful ways we consume water in our homes, businesses, farms, and energy plants but also the inefficient ways we move water to and away from them. This revolution will bring about the ethical use of water in every sector. Such an ethic is as essential—and as possible—as past awakenings to threats against our environment and ourselves: on the large scale, the way we halted use of DDT and other deadly chemicals; in our communities, the way we stopped tossing litter out car windows and trashing public parks; and at the family level, the way we got used to setting out recycling bins alongside the garbage.

Using water ethically isn't difficult. It's revolutionary only because it's so different from the way modern America relates to water. But this revolution isn't big, costly, or bloody. It's a revolution of small technologies over mega-waterworks. It's a savings of billions of dollars in infrastructure and energy costs. It's as painless as floating on your back in an azure spring. Call it a blue revolution.

America's Big Gulp

In all, America guzzles about 410 billion gallons of water per day.[22] That's more than the daily flow of the entire Mississippi River. Power plants drink up more than any other sector of the economy, and while much of what they use is returned, it is often at higher temperatures that can change the ecology of the source. Agricultural irrigation, which accounts for about 40 percent of all freshwater sucked up in the United States each day, is by far the largest drain on our aquifers and rivers.

Throughout the twentieth century, farmers and energy suppliers were the mightiest wizards behind the illusion of abundance. Farmers turned the driest grassland states in the nation into the most heavily irrigated to raise corn, wheat, and cattle (chapter 5, "Taproot of the Crisis"). Energy companies tapped the nation's rivers first for hydropower, then to cool coal and nuclear plants, never imagining that someday Hoover Dam's turbines could stop spinning or that the Tennessee Valley Authority would have to shut down a nuclear reactor due to declining river levels (chapter 4, "Powerful Thirst").

But even for the wizards, the illusion is beginning to evaporate. Population growth has fueled residential competition for the shrinking aquifers and rivers long tapped by farms and energy plants. Our sprawling growth is also physically pushing urban America into those parts of the country that farms and power facilities once had to themselves. In recent years, water-scarcity worries have fallowed cropland in the West and halted or held up new thermal power plants in every region of the United States.[23]

In both the energy and agricultural sectors, the green sweep of the nation has not only missed water; it is also aggravating scarcity. It can take ten times as much water to generate power for a plug-in electric vehicle as to produce gasoline for the family car. Biofuels are worse. The production cycle can consume twenty or more times as much water for every mile traveled than for producing gasoline. When scaled up to the 2.7 trillion miles Americans travel each year by car, scientists say, water could become the limiting factor for our biofuels craze.[24]

Many Americans seem resigned to the notion that agriculture and big industries require a ton of water, and there's not much we can do to change that. This is an especially common refrain in California, where agricultural irrigation accounts for three-fourths of water use.[25] Farmers pump so much, what impact could citizens possibly have on the water crisis? But this is like throwing up our hands and concluding that because coal plants are the nation's top emitters of greenhouse gases, there's nothing we can do about climate change.

It is time, now, to turn our attention to water. Since the turn of the century, Americans have not been involved in the workings of water; we haven't had to be. The conveyance of clean water to homes was one of the most successful feats of technology and engineering in modern times. But occasionally, we've gotten fed up with the nation's direction on water—when pollution-plagued rivers led to the Clean Water Act, for example, and when fed-up ordinary citizens joined environmentalists more than thirty years ago to help bring an end to the era of mega-dams.

Now, the overtapping of nearly every large river and aquifer in the nation, and the inability of our political institutions to change course, call for our involvement once more. In his best seller *Hot, Flat, and Crowded: Why We Need a Green Revolution—and How It Can Renew America*, Thomas Friedman writes that citizens were way ahead of politicians when it came to energy efficiency and green living.[26] The same will be true of water. The citizen involvement and creativity now driving innovation in the green economy will eventually build a blue one.

The blue revolution will require deliberately different choices and the political backbone to make them: No wasted water in agriculture. No subsidies for crops that are irreparably harming aquifers. Water-efficient power plants. Restoring floodplains rather than building taller and taller levees. Planting trees and installing green roofs on the grand scale, rather than expanding sewers and costly new wastewater-treatment plants. Reusing water and harvesting rain to irrigate our lawns and to cool commercial air conditioners. Replacing wasteful, outdated fixtures in our homes and businesses rather than building expensive new reservoirs.[27]

Though the driest coastal cities will still build desalination plants and the largest ones, like New York City and Los Angeles, will still import water from outside their regions, the blue revolution is a turn from the vast waterworks of the twentieth century toward local solutions. It's an appreciation for local water in much the same way we're embracing local produce (chapter 12, "Local Water").

In that spirit, the blue revolution begins in our own backyards. Just as it's no longer possible to give all large water users as much as they want, any time they want, it's no longer possible for every one of us to use 150 gallons a day from our ailing aquifers and rivers. It's a lot like America's bank accounts: we are seriously overdrawn for luxuries we didn't even need.

So, how much of that daily 410 billion–gallon Big Gulp is just *us* watering our lawns, flushing our toilets, and washing our dishes? Coming in third after power plants and agriculture, about 43 billion gallons a day, or 10.5 percent of the total, goes to public and private utilities. That's where the majority of us get our household water. For the most part, this water comes from aquifers (groundwater) or from surface waters (rivers and lakes). Water managers like to accentuate the difference between groundwater and surface water, but those terms simply refer to the location of water at a given moment. Water is often moving between the two. After falling as rain, water percolates into the soil, then flows underground to river channels. Evaporation and transpiration from plants pick it up again to cycle back into the atmosphere.[28]

To satisfy the Big Gulp, we pump this freshwater from underground, or from a reservoir or river, filtering and treating it at great cost so it meets state and federal drinking-water standards. Then, we move water through a network of millions of miles of pipes under our cities and highways—some the diameter of a small pizza, some wide enough to drive a Volkswagen Beetle through. All of this takes a remarkable amount of energy. About 13 percent of all electricity generated in the United States is spent pumping and treating water and moving it around.[29] That's nearly double the most generous estimate of U.S. electricity spent powering computers and the Internet. (This means a good way to save energy is to save water, and vice versa.)

And then, the vast majority of this painstakingly purified drinking water is never drunk. Some of it goes down our toilets. But the lion's share is soaked, sprayed, or sprinkled on grass. Waterfalls and grottoes aside, the distance between Americans and their global neighbors who use less than 50 gallons of water per person each day is about one-third of an acre. That's the average size of the American lawn.[30]

The Fifty-First State

California State University research scientist Cristina Milesi grew up in northeast Italy and moved to the United States to pursue a PhD in ecosystem modeling. When she arrived, she was struck by the size of lawns compared with those in Italy and wondered how much they contributed to Americans' super-sized water consumption.

In the early 2000s, Milesi, a remote-sensing expert, wanted to design computer systems that use weather and climate information to help homeowners make better decisions about when and how much to water their lawns. But no one had ever figured out how much lawn actually carpeted the United States. There were no Google Maps for lawns to overlay with rainfall, soil moisture, and other data. So Milesi, who works at the NASA Ames Research Center at California State University, Monterey Bay, began to create her own using satellite imagery.

The findings so surprised her that she repeated her calculations over and over to make sure they were accurate. Her satellite analysis showed that, between our homes and our highway medians, our golf greens and our grassy sports fields, lawns are America's largest crop. We're growing far more grass than corn—with 63,240 square miles in turfgrass nationwide. That's larger than most individual American states.

To irrigate this "fifty-first state," Milesi estimates that we use as much as nineteen *trillion* gallons of water per year. That's more than it takes to irrigate all the feed grain in the nation. "People don't believe their water use makes a difference, especially because agricultural consumption is so high," Milesi says. "But water is probably the most important issue facing urban areas in the future—and the primary pressure point on urban water use is the lawn."[31]

It's not that we don't have enough water. It's that we don't have enough water to waste. And we definitely don't have enough to pour off nineteen trillion gallons a year, most of it drinking water created at high cost to both wallets and wetlands. Sure, some of our lawn water, now spiked with pesticides and fertilizers, percolates back underground. But much of it becomes so-called stormwater, which local governments then have to handle through an entirely different network of drains, storm sewers, pipes, and treatment to make it safe enough to flow back to streams and rivers. Sometimes, the stormwater never makes its way back to its source; in the coastal United States, hundreds of millions of gallons of freshwater shoot out to sea every day.

Landscaping and sod soak up about half of all household water drawn in the United States. Scientists report that Americans who live in cooler climates use up to 38 percent of their water outside, and those who live in hotter, drier climates use up to 67 percent of theirs outdoors.[32] Water managers say this pattern persists despite multimillion-dollar public-education programs to convince Americans that they need not water their grass every day—or even every other day—to keep it green.

We don't have heroes for saving the planet's blue, the way we do other environmental causes. You can find climate celebrities all along the political spectrum and from Hollywood to Washington. Water is harder. Who in the world would be willing to stand up against watering the lawn or filling the swimming pool?

Maybe Donald Trump could fire water hogs—but he'd have to start with himself. The same year he proclaimed himself a water-loving environmentalist in his bid to build a luxury golf resort and community on a breathtaking oceanfront site in Aberdeen, Scotland, Trump's estate on a breathtaking oceanfront site in Palm Beach, Florida, was the most water-wasting on the entire island.

Trump's Maison de l'Amitié, viewed from the air, looks barren compared to the surrounding estates and hotels. It takes a moment to realize that's because the property has been razed of trees; most of its seven acres is solid grass that stretches all the way to the sea. In 2007, during the worst drought in the history of the southeastern United States, Trump gulped an average of two million gallons of water a month for his outsized lawn and twenty-two bathrooms. He racked up a $10,000 average monthly bill.[33] By comparison, even thirsty Palm Beach looks frugal; the average family there uses about 54,000 gallons of water per *year*.

The '07 drought was dire along the southeast coast of Florida. Lake Okeechobee, primary water supply for Palm Beach and other cities and backup water supply for more than five million Floridians, began to dry up. The grassy lakebed was so parched that it caught fire and burned for weeks. To try to save precious freshwater, local governments in Palm Beach County slapped a 30 percent surcharge on customers who used more than 6,000 gallons a month, enacted lawn-irrigation restrictions, and imposed fines on anyone who didn't follow the rules. But the oceanfront dwellers found a loophole. Residents with new landscaping were allowed to water three days a week instead of one for a month after planting. After the month was up, if they planted more new vegetation, they could again water three days a week. The *Wall Street Journal* found that residents were putting in new trees and turf, at the cost of tens of thousands of dollars a home, just to avoid the water restrictions. "We're all just ripping out the old lawn and shrubs and putting in new ones," one Palm Beacher told the *Journal*.[34]

It may not be all that surprising that Donald Trump and some other Ocean Drive residents (or nonresidents, as is more often the case in summer) would have the highest water consumption in the land. But water hogs come from all corners. Golfer Tiger Woods used nearly 4 million gallons a year at his Jupiter Island, Florida, home during the region's devastating drought.[35] Pierre Omidyar, the founder of eBay, consumed 13.8 million gallons of water in one year at his Las Vegas mansion.[36]

Canadian pop singer Céline Dion has the dubious distinction of being called out as one of the largest water users in two states—both Florida and Nevada.[37] In 2010, she spent $20 million on her Jupiter Island, Florida, backyard water park with two swimming pools, two water slides, and a lazy river, all of which use 500,000 gallons a month.[38] Then there's Lance Armstrong, who makes his home in Austin, Texas. During an intense dry spell, the local daily newspaper reported that the seven-time Tour de France winner was the city's worst water guzzler. Armstrong used 330,000 gallons in one month at his Spanish-colonial home with its swimming pool, grass, and gardens, according to the *Austin American-Statesman*.[39]

There's not a more perfect picture of the American dream than Lance Armstrong swimming laps in his pool or doing crunches on his lawn. Grass brings the healthy enticements of the outdoors to America's doorstep. It's been associated with physical health in the United States since the nineteenth century, when our fore-families created the first suburbs to escape pollution and disease in the cities.

In recent years, environmentalists have drawn a bead on high-maintenance turfgrasses, not only for their intense water use but also for the pesticides and fertilizers that run off and pollute rivers and estuaries. Lawn lovers—and the $60 billion turfgrass industry—are arming up to defend their turf. But it doesn't have to be all grass, or no grass. There's nothing wrong with a little, especially if it's of a native variety able to thrive in local conditions. We've simply gone way over the top.

Moms and dads with small kids will tell you it's better to play and picnic on grass than, say, gravel or smelly recycled tire treads—the lawn substitutes showing up on urban playgrounds. Life is good with a patch of grass to spread a picnic blanket and let your kids run. But should it really be America's No. 1 crop? Irrigated at more than double the rate needed?

Grass is not the root of our country's water problems; it's a symptom. A 63,240-square-mile indicator of the real ailment—our lack of an ethic for water in America. The illusion of abundance gives us a false sense of security, a deep-down belief that really, there's enough water for anything, anytime. Grottoed new subdivision in the desert? We'll find the water. Sprinklers leaking down the sidewalk? We'll get to it.

Kids bugging you to take them to the nation's largest water park, with its 1.2 million–gallon wave pool that holds more than 20,000 bathtubs full of water?

Jump right in.

Aldo Leopold and the Big Kahuna

When they hear the names of rivers like the Mississippi, the Ohio, the Missouri, and the Delaware, most people assume they were named for the states. It just goes to show how much closer we've gotten to our artificial systems than our natural ones. The river names came first in almost every case, reminding us that rivers were the lifeblood of both Native Americans and colonists.

Mississippi is an Ojibway word for "big river." *Ohio* is derived from an Iroquois word for "great river." The Alabama, Arkansas, Iowa, and Missouri rivers were all named for Native American tribes before the states existed. The Connecticut River came from a regional tribe's description of its waters, and the state came later. Same with Wisconsin, although historians and linguists still argue over the origin of the word. Most have come to agree that it's a rough iteration of a Miami Indian phrase that meant something like "This stream meanders through something red."[40]

The 430-mile Wisconsin River traverses the middle of the state, northeast to southwest, through forests, glacial plains, and hills before it meets up with the Mississippi just south of a historic French fur-trading town called Prairie du Chien. About three-quarters of the way through its journey, the river winds through striking cliffs, canyons, and sandstone rock formations—the likely "something red." This sand-plain region of Wisconsin was both muse and refuge for Aldo Leopold, whose *A Sand County Almanac* has inspired our evolving ecological awareness ever since it was published posthumously in 1949. Leopold thought through many of his ideas about people and ecology at what he called his "humble shack"—actually, a rehabbed chicken coop—on eighty acres near the Wisconsin River. He, his wife, Estella, and their five children drove up from Madison, where he was on the faculty at the University of Wisconsin, to spend weekends and vacations here in the 1930s and '40s.

Leopold was trained as a forester and founded the field of wildlife ecology. But he was intensely interested in people, specifically in figuring out how to help them see their connection to and responsibility for the natural world. Leopold believed that the answer was "an extension of the social conscience from people to land"[41]—or, put simply, a "land ethic."

If people could see how closely their children's and grandchildren's well-being is tied to the health of the land, personal ethics would drive them to cooperate not only on behalf of their families and communities but also for the natural world they inhabit. The land ethic, wrote Leopold, "enlarges the boundaries of the community to include soils, waters, plants, and animals, or collectively: the land."[42] By *land*, he meant the entire web of life, from climate to water, says his biographer, Curt Meine: "The water is a constant."[43]

Leopold died of a heart attack while fighting a grass fire on his Wisconsin River land in 1948, just a week after the manuscript for what became *A Sand County Almanac* was accepted for publication. Had he lived, he surely would have been thrilled: First, that he sold a few books—more than 2 million. Second, that his credo, what we've come to call sustainability, has become all the rage.

Well, it isn't *exactly* the rage in Leopold's own backyard. Leopold's land and shack are preserved in quiet posterity by the Aldo Leopold Foundation, housed nearby in a showcase carbon-neutral building the U.S. Green Building Council has pronounced the greenest in the nation. Visitors can tour the building and then walk through the pine forest and prairie the Leopold family restored and along the sandy banks of the Wisconsin River.

Visitors can, but not many do. Thousands a day, though, flock to a tourist strip that lies exactly ten miles from Leopold's shack. They come to worship water, although not the sort in the river. For here is the largest concentration of water parks on the planet, including the one at the Hotel Rome at Mount Olympus, where a gargantuan fake Colosseum and wooden Trojan horse loom over a highway choked with miniature golf courses, haunted mansions, and saltwater taffy shops.

The sandstone bluffs that gave the Wisconsin River and the state their names began drawing nature-loving tourists in the mid-1800s to see "the dells"—from the French *dalles*, or flagstone. The town bisected by the river and the dells changed its name in 1931 to the Wisconsin Dells to capitalize on its scenic draw. In the 1950s, a show-man named Tommy Bartlett added a water-skiing "thrill show" to the natural water wonders and marketed it like P. T. Barnum would have. In the ensuing decades, one attraction after another opened along the tourist strip. Most were small time, featuring the likes of bumper boats and go-karts. Then, in 1994, Stan Anderson, owner of a Polynesian-themed resort, decided to shore up foul-weather business by building an indoor kids' water park. Children went nuts, and so did their parents.

Fifteen years later, the Wisconsin Dells are no longer the main attraction in the Wisconsin Dells.

Today, the town overflows with twenty water parks that slosh around about 20 million gallons of water. The biggest indoor water park in the world is here. So is the biggest outdoor water park—Noah's Ark. The biggest attraction in the biggest park is called—what else?—the Big Kahuna, a 1.2 million–gallon wave pool. My kids and I found it right next to the fried Twinkies. We had a blast leaping up over fake waves in time with the pop music thumping out of the Big Kahuna's loudspeakers.

The waves build up from the back of the Big Kahuna, roll forward, and crash on concrete beaches. Behind the scenes, a balance tank makes the mega–swimming pool work, a lot like the tank in a toilet. The Big Kahuna is always losing water, so the park uses what are called autofill pipes to constantly pull new water into the tank. To make the waves, a centrifugal fan blower pushes air at high pressure down onto the tank water. An air valve alternately opens to fill the balance tank and closes to push waves out. The electricity bill just to produce the Big Kahuna's waves: $1,500 a day.[44]

During operating hours, the twenty parks of the Wisconsin Dells constantly pump groundwater from an aquifer that scientists say is robust. Madeline Gotkowitz, a hydrogeologist with the Wisconsin Geological and Natural History Survey who's done extensive ground-water modeling throughout the region, foresees a day when water-intensive industries like microchip plants flee America's arid regions to build a blue economy in places like Milwaukee. The counties with some of the highest unemployment rates in the Midwest happen to sit atop the healthiest water reserves in the nation (chapter 9, "The Business of Blue").

So, maybe the Big Kahuna isn't hurting anyone. Not like Geor-gia's Stone Mountain theme park would have, if public shame hadn't iced its ill-timed plan to make an entire mountain of artificial snow during Atlanta's 2007 drought emergency, which threatened the city's drinking-water supply. But the surfer-themed wave pool is a 1.2 million–gallon homage to America's illusion of water abundance— particularly to the children exposed solely to the chlorinated wonders of the Wisconsin Dells.

If children's love for water is cradled only within the bright-colored resin sides of a thrill ride, never the wondrous red sides of a sandstone bluff, future Americans will have ever less understanding of, and value for, our freshwater resources.

American kids are often the household nudges who make sure bottles, cans, and newspapers get tossed into the recycling bin. Kin-dergartners come home singing a song about turning off lights to save energy. But most don't know anything about the watershed they live in, where their house water comes from, or where it goes when they flush. Early on, America had a water ethic. We lost it to indoor plumbing. When we relied on a stream to run a grist mill for the fam-ily farm, we understood the value of water. Even the littlest members of families knew that water was worth its weight in gold—because they're the ones who had to lug it in buckets. Another Wisconsin native, Laura Ingalls Wilder, devotes a chapter of *Little House on the Prairie* to "Fresh Water to Drink." She remembers in vivid detail the moment Pa finished digging the family well and the Ingalls had the luxury of hauling water from their yard instead of the creek: "Laura thought she had never tasted anything so good as those long, cold drinks of water."[45]

In summer 2009, one of the Midwest's most famous natural waterfalls, fifty-three-foot Minnehaha in Minneapolis, dried to a trickle because of drought.[46] But at Noah's Ark, children could still whiz down Bahama Falls. They could ride the Black Anaconda water coaster instead of looking for black snakes, play at Tadpole Bay instead of dipping for tadpoles in the sandy banks of the Wisconsin River. In fact, they could no longer see the river from the Wisconsin Dells strip. The town's water parks, with their tall slides, tubes, and coaster tracks, blocked all views of the river and its sandstone walls that drew tourists here in the first place.

The overwhelming popularity of parks like Noah's Ark proves that humans love water. We begin life in water, and we're drawn to it from the day we're born: plop a chubby-legged nine-month-old down on a riverbank, or even on a concrete beach, and the response is usually a huge, gummy smile and a splash attack. Somehow, we have to figure out how to harness that natural affinity to create a shared water ethic: an aquatic revival of Leopold's land ethic that would help Americans see that our future ecological—and economic—prosperity depends on how well we take care of the water flowing under our feet, down our rivers, and through our wetlands.

It's not complicated, especially compared with our climate-change challenge. The easiest, and cheapest, thing we can do is use less. At its most basic, the blue revolution means no one uses more than they really need. Individuals wouldn't pour potable water on the grass. Our agricultural subsidies would help farmers transition to efficient irrigation, rather than give them incentive to deplete aquifers and their grandchildren's ability to farm. With a shared water ethic, we live well, with much less water. Not just a lot less in our own backyards, but a lot less across industries—in much the same way that the smallest households and the largest corporations are evolving a mind-set for releasing less carbon into the atmosphere. Industrial and agricultural engineers are showing us how in ways that increase crop yields for farmers and save companies millions of dollars in water and energy bills (chapter 9, "The Business of Blue").

Sixty years after Leopold's call for a land ethic, most of us take some personal responsibility for the planet. Think of what's changed in that time: Anglers now catch and release. We recycle our cans at home, our paper at work. And no one with a conscience tosses garbage out the car window anymore.

But when it comes to water, we've gone in the opposite direction. Our homes and lawns are bigger, and so is our thirst: We use quadruple the amount of water today, per person, than we did in 1950.[47] We no longer pay attention to where our water comes from or where it goes. Adults and children alike are disconnected from the nation's rivers and streams. And the nation's illusion of water abundance blinds us from seeing how our own backyard garden hose connects to the bigger picture—a concept we are starting to grasp when it comes to energy use, recycled materials, and other green issues.

In 2010, I went in search of a water ethic for America. The journey took me halfway around the world, but also to some unexpected places closer to home, like the Texas Hill Country, where residents have figured out new ways of living with water based on their own unique cultures and watershed. The water ethic will look a little different from place to place. Some regions, like the Hill Country, will embrace rainwater catchment en masse. Older metropolitan areas will transform as they replace aging water infrastructure, sending water to rain gardens and nature's filters—wetlands—rather than stormwater drains. Philadelphia has switched out even the kids' basketball courts with pervious concrete, allowing water to percolate underground rather than run off to expensive stormwater-infrastructure systems. (An added benefit, say the kids, is that water dries from the courts much faster instead of pooling.)[48]

Although there were some hopeful signs, my search led me to another, harder truth about a water ethic: Americans will embrace it only if it's also supported by the people who make decisions about our water, from private companies to utility managers to governors. Although the blue revolution may start in our own backyards, it can't stop there. It doesn't make sense for local government to require citizens to lay off the lawn sprinklers, then approve a new subdivision atop the community's most important water-recharge area—no matter how green the new homes are. It's unprincipled for water utilities to fight lawn-watering restrictions, as a group of them did during Florida's last big drought. The fundamental belief in water as a national treasure to be preserved has to catch on at every level of society, including what I'll call America's water-industrial complex.

The American illusion of water abundance follows a long and peculiar tradition. Throughout modern history, humans flaunted water as a symbol of power, wealth, and control of nature—especially, it seems, in places where there is not nearly enough water to control.

In seventeenth-century France, Louis XIV built some of the greatest water features in the world at the gardens of Versailles, spread across both sides of the mile-long Grand Canal (complete with sailing ships and the secondary ships that followed them with violinists and other entertainers). The sumptuous gardens were home to 1,400 water splendors when Versailles was the seat of French political power. The colossal fountains, pools, and waterfalls—and grottoes, too—were positioned so that the sovereign and his visitors would never lose sight of water during exhausting garden tours that lasted from morning until night.

But here's what the royal visitors didn't know: There wasn't enough water at Versailles to keep all those fountain jets soaring, pools overflowing, and waterfalls cascading. They were built in careful groups so they could be turned on and off according to the king's progress around the gardens. A secret palace staff would scurry ahead of the king's touring parties, signaling their whereabouts with an elaborate system of flags and whistle blasts to convey when it was safe to shut down one group of fountains and turn on the next one.[49]

Like Versailles, the American illusion of water abundance is also carefully maintained—not by palace staff, but by the water-industrial complex. These are the professionals who make sure water gets to agriculture, to energy plants, to the utilities that make our faucets flow—to every interest group that has come to expect large amounts of water. The water-industrial complex includes the $680 billion U.S. construction/engineering industry; thousands of technocrats who populate the nation's mind-boggling array of water agencies; scientists, lawyers, and lobbyists who work for large water users; and the public relations professionals who work for them and for government agencies—often hand-in-hand—to spin the latest water narrative.[50]

America's agriculture, energy, and real estate industries have been built on a water-supply model that no longer works. So have the profits of the water-industrial complex—all of which makes it difficult to change course. The sector's revenues are directly proportional to the size of the water projects they build or land for local communities. In general, the higher the number of gallons captured for our growing thirst, the bigger the profit. Until recently, few companies saw the profitability in saving water, although that is beginning to change, in the same way we've seen corporations like GE and BP increase revenues by creating more energy-efficient products, from small lightbulbs to giant wind turbines.

Up to now, the water-industrial complex has been so good at harnessing water and moving it around cities and regions, even up and over mountains, that Americans, like the visitors to Versailles, have never had to think about how it all works. Most of us never fret about how we use water, where it comes from, where it goes—or whether it is wise to drain so much from our aquifers, rivers, and lakes.

The constant reengineering of those natural systems, from the dammed-up rivers of the West to the canal-dissected Florida Everglades, bolsters the illusion of abundance. Two mighty rivers, the American and the Sacramento, run through the middle of California's capital city. How can it be water stressed? The same can be said of south Florida, surrounded by the Everglades and pummeled regularly by rains that flood the streets. Yet, astonishingly for the amount of water you see when you're standing in Sacramento or south Florida, these watersheds on opposite coasts of America have been manipulated to the point of near ruin. The Everglades of Florida and California's Sacramento–San Joaquin Delta were two of the most water-abundant ecosystems on one of the most water-abundant continents. Today, they are among the best arguments for a blue revolution—a water ethic for America. That's because they're both dying of thirst.

CHAPTER 2

Reclamation to Restoration

On opposite coasts of America, the Sacramento–San Joaquin Delta of California and the Everglades of Florida once flowed as two of the greatest water treasures in the nation, their interiors, rivers, and lakes flush with freshwater, their tidal wetlands rich as the sea. Dreams sent early settlers west, to a gold rush, and south, to a land boom, to seek their fortunes in the Delta and in the Glades. But neither gold nor land turned out to be the true mother lode. Ever since California and Florida earned their statehood, the most rewarding quest in both regions has been the control of water.

In 1850, the federal government ceded the waterlogged Everglades to Florida and the Sacramento–San Joaquin Delta to California in what was called the Swamp Land Act. The idea was that states could turn water into land with canals and culverts, dikes and drains.[1] Over the next hundred years, federal and state engineers made wetlands into farmlands, peat into soil, rivers into channels. They built some of the most complex waterworks in the world and engineered them to perform miracles: in Florida, shunting Glades water away from croplands in a place too wet to farm; in California, harnessing the Delta water to irrigate a place too dry.

The stories of water in the Everglades and the Delta followed two divergent plots, but the core narratives, characters, and conclusions are remarkably similar. They also seem to be repeating themselves over and over again: Powerful interest groups have a water problem.

Elected officials send government engineers to the drawing board. The engineers come up with a solution—the biggest and boldest yet. Significant public investment follows. Water users are happy until serious unintended consequences begin to reveal themselves, as they do today: while the natural water systems of the Delta and the Glades are dying, the artificial ones keep the heavily populated regions vulnerable to flood and drought.

This time, it's not just special interests that have a water problem. It's all of us.

Among all its natural resources, America was especially lucky when it came to freshwater—Lotto-winning, born-beautiful lucky. Our supply was abundant, with 3.5 million miles of rivers running across the country and another estimated 60,000 trillion gallons of groundwater stored beneath our feet in aquifers.[2] Beyond that, North America was blessed with the largest numbers of fish and other freshwater species anywhere on the planet.[3]

That's what makes it such a singular shame that freshwater habitats are now the most degraded of all America's major ecosystems. More than any single threat—pollution, overfishing, or any other— tapping too much water for human use, from agricultural irrigation to power production to watering our backyards, is the primary culprit.[4] This is as true for the great waterways of the eastern United States as it is for those in the West. The most widespread human-caused extinction in North America has been the loss of freshwater mussels in the southeastern states, most notably those drowned in Muscle Shoals, Alabama, with the damming of the Tennessee River. Those mussels had lived through the ice age. They survived the Native Americans who made them a staple. The bearded old men of the water even persisted through America's early-1900s pearling and shell-button crazes. But they could not survive the impoundment of their free-flowing, oxygen-rich waters.[5]

Today, nearly 40 percent of all fish species in North America's streams, rivers, and lakes are imperiled, according to the most exhaustive study to date on the conservation status of fishes, completed by the U.S. Geological Survey in 2008.[6] This number includes shimmering salmon blocked from their upriver migration in the Northwest, and the ancient sturgeon that once spawned in thirty-five coastal rivers from Maine to Florida and are now confined to two.[7]

These are the fish that literally fed America's founding and expansion. More than four hundred years ago, Atlantic sturgeon in the James River helped save the colonists at Jamestown from starvation. "Without sturgeon, we may be speaking Spanish now, or French," says Albert Spells of the U.S. Fish and Wildlife Service.[8]

Their disappearance foretells a turning point in America's water history; the waterways that once gave us a staple now barely manage to produce a delicacy. Likewise, the water manipulations that choked the shellfish and the salmon are now squeezing people and businesses.

So it went in the Everglades. This "River of Grass," as Marjory Stoneman Douglas described the Glades in her 1947 book by that name, begins much higher up the peninsula of Florida than most people think, at a chain of lakes near Orlando. Here, the Kissimmee River started its journey south along a wide and twisting path to the second-largest freshwater lake in the lower 48 states, Lake Okeechobee. The lake, in turn, spilled water south to quench a great, wet prairie flowing slowly for eight million acres down the bottom half of Florida to meet the sea. All told, the Everglades ecosystem was once the wettest stretch of the United States.[9]

All this water stood in the way of southeast Florida's burgeoning winter vegetable and sugarcane fields, and crops of another sort—those with rooftops. Indeed, the water represented "the vicious scourge of mankind," according to a black-and-white propaganda film, *Waters of Destiny*, produced by the U.S. Army Corps of Engineers.[10] In the Everglades, the film's narrator cried out in a hydrophobic frenzy, "We've got to control water! Make it do our bidding!"

Then and now, fear of water in south Florida is easy to understand. In 1926, and again in 1928, deadly hurricanes sent Lake Okeechobee bursting through and over its earthen dike, which was originally built to protect crops rather than human lives.[11] The '28 storm killed 2,500 people, most of them poor blacks who drowned in the agricultural fields south of the lake.[12] The storm inspired the title of Zora Neale Hurston's novel *Their Eyes Were Watching God*:

> [The hurricane] woke up old Oke[e]chobee and the monster began to roll in his bed. Began to roll and complain like a peevish world on a grumble. . . . The wind came back with triple fury, and put out the light for the last time. They sat in company with the others in their shanties, their eyes straining against crude walls and their souls asking if He meant to measure their puny might against His. They seemed to be staring at the dark, but their eyes were watching God. . . . The monstropolous beast had left his bed. The two hundred miles an hour wind has loosed his chains. He seized hold of his dikes and ran forward until he met the [worker] quarters; uprooted them like grass and rushed on after his supposed-to-be conquerors, rolling the dikes, rolling the houses, rolling the people in the houses along with other timbers. The sea was walking the earth with a heavy heel.[13]

The Army Corps of Engineers—part of what was then the War Department—began its war on water in the wake of the hurricane, building up old Okeechobee's dike with gravel, rock, limestone, sand, and shell. In 1947, the engineers set out to defeat "the crazed antics of the elements" for good, with the Central and Southern Florida Project.[14] The scheme would protect Floridians and their growing cities and farms from flooding and provide them with freshwater. Today, south Florida's seven and a half million residents live and play, work and farm on lands kept artificially dry by a maze of ditches, dikes, and pumps, all controlled by computers.

The engineers harnessed the southward-flowing prairie with 1,000 miles of canals and 720 miles of levees. They built sixteen pump stations and two hundred gates and other concrete-and-steel structures to control the flow of water. They straightened the sinewy Kissimmee

River into the Dirty Ditch, as it became known, which carried polluted water into Lake Okeechobee. They built towering gates on the
east and west sides of the lake to push the water through canals to
the Atlantic and Gulf coasts when Okeechobee got too high.

In short, they set out to get rid of water, but they got rid of too
much. Before the project was ever finished, government biologists
predicted it would devastate south Florida's ecology.[15] The water that
remained was laden with phosphorus from fertilizers used on farms
and urban landscapes. More than 90 percent of the waterfowl that
once made their home in the Everglades, like the leggy egrets and
wood storks, vanished. Sixty-nine species that lived here, from pan-
thers to manatees, are now endangered. Toxic mercury and other
pollutants make Everglades fish unsafe to eat.[16]

When the lake levels are too high, the system flushes the polluted water west into the Caloosahatchee River and east into the St.
Lucie River.[17] Business leaders say the toxins wreaking havoc on the
Caloosahatchee and St. Lucie estuaries are also doing a number on
their economies.

Most ironically for the wettest place in America, the labyrinthine
waterworks of the Everglades have come to cause structural droughts
that threaten the freshwater supply of millions of people and thousands of acres of farms. But the biggest concern of all remains the risk
to human life if a major hurricane were to wallop Lake Okeechobee
when its waters are high, sending waves bashing through the dike
the Corps of Engineers is working to fortify.

Today, the Corps must delicately balance the often-unpredictable
dangers of flood and drought, a challenge best explained by events in
fall 2005. After a record-breaking hurricane season weakened Lake
Okeechobee's 140-mile dike, the Corps released hundreds of billions
of gallons of freshwater from the lake into the rivers and ultimately
the ocean. The releases seemed like the prudent course to save lives
and property in case of more rain. Instead, that fall marked the start
of a crippling drought. By spring 2007, the lake was so dry that wild-
fires broke out on its weedy bottom.[18] Residents had to slash their
water use by a third; farmers, by nearly half.[19]

"We wouldn't be in this position," said Malcolm "Bubba" Wade, an executive with U.S. Sugar Corporation, "if we still had that water in the lake."[20]

His industry was the leading special-interest group that had been imploring the government engineers to get rid of water for a hundred years.

As the Everglades are to Florida, the Sacramento–San Joaquin Delta is the liquid heart of California. At the confluence of the rivers for which it is named, the low-lying Delta is the largest estuary on the West Coast, stretching from Sacramento eighty miles west to San Francisco Bay, and south for fifty more miles. Just like the Everglades, the Delta's veins are more bionic than mortal. But through them flows the lifeblood of California's largest watershed, draining from the Sierra Nevada in the east to the coastal ranges in the west. For thousands of years, accumulation of sediment from the watershed, which spans nearly half the state's surface area, formed thick peat deposits, inundated and exposed on the rising and falling tides. In the 1850s, farmers discovered that the rich peat islands were ideal for growing crops. For a century and a half, first Chinese laborers with long-bladed knives, and later huge dredges, worked to dry out the islands for agriculture and build up levees to keep out water. They essentially transformed the peat islands into below-sea-level bowls protected by delicate saucers.[21]

Today, driving through the region on Interstate 5, the view is endless, flat farm acreage intersected by narrow channels dotted with recreational boats. At the south end, near the city of Tracy, motorists pass over two major arteries of California's water infrastructure, the Delta-Mendota Canal and the California Aqueduct. These and several smaller aqueducts, built between the 1930s and 1960s, deliver water from northern rivers to cities and farms in coastal and Southern California and the San Joaquin Valley.[22] Almost half the water used in agriculture in California comes from rivers that once flowed to the Delta, and more than 23 million Californians rely on the Delta for their water supply.[23]

But these days, the natural and human-made arteries alike are on life support. The waterworks that supply the farms and the people depend on more than a thousand miles of levees as fragile as those in New Orleans before Hurricane Katrina. In 2010, scientists who study the Delta concluded that "major levee failures are inevitable due to continued subsidence, sea level rise, increasing frequency of large floods, and high probability of earthquakes."[24]

"It is a two-in-three probability that abrupt change will occur in the Delta in the next fifty years," says geology professor Jeffrey Mount, founding director of the University of California at Davis Center for Watershed Sciences, who has modeled the risks of earthquakes, flooding, or a double-punch quake and flood on the Delta's levees. For a 6.5-magnitude quake along the Hayward-Calaveras fault line, which runs north and south along the eastern side of San Francisco Bay, here is what the models predict: the shutdown of all Delta water supplies to people and farms; the loss of two major highways and two ports as well as railroads and gas and oil pipelines; and the flooding of 85,000 acres of farms and 3,000 homes. Mount estimates the five-year costs at a conservative $40 billion. He declines to speculate on the death toll.[25]

The highly engineered water system that now threatens the lives of people was a death trap for fish and wildlife first. The San Joaquin River was once the southernmost salmon river in the world; the Sacramento River used to be the world's second-largest Chinook salmon river. Those superlatives were overtaken by another: the Central Valley Project, the largest irrigation scheme in the United States. California's legislature approved the project in 1933 to export "surplus" water from the northern, wetter half of the state to the dryer and more heavily populated south. In 1935, the federal government took over the project as part of President Franklin D. Roosevelt's New Deal. It called for a series of dams and canals, starting with the Shasta Dam on the Sacramento River and the Friant Dam on the San Joaquin River. Completed in 1944, the 600-foot-tall Shasta Dam blocked salmon and steelhead from their spawning grounds on the upper Sacramento. The San Joaquin lost 98 percent of its water to the project.[26] The sound of salmon swimming upstream, once so loud that residents likened it to a waterfall, was silenced.

A Reverence for Rivers

Aldo Leopold's work as a land manager never brought him to the Everglades, or to the Sacramento–San Joaquin Delta. Nevertheless, he had an intimate and profound impact on the two ecosystems—as father to the river hydrologist Luna Leopold.

Aldo Leopold articulated "The Land Ethic" in his *Sand County Almanac* with these simple words: "A thing is right when it tends to preserve the integrity, stability, and beauty of the biotic community. It is wrong when it tends otherwise."[27] He and his wife, Estella, taught their children to respect the natural world and learn everything they could about it. At the Wisconsin River shack on weekends, the family worked together to plant thousands of white pines, restore native prairie grasses, trap and band birds, cut firewood, canoe, swim, and hunt.[28] All five kids became conscientious and competent observers of nature. Four became professional scientists. Three of them, Starker, Luna, and Estella, were elected to the National Academy of Sciences, a unique achievement for siblings in that organization's history.[29] Luna would come to be known as the father of modern hydrology.[30]

Aldo and Estella named their second child and second son Luna Bergere Leopold, for her side. Estella, whose maiden name was Bergere, was part of the Luna family, prominent ranchers with a Spanish land grant along the Rio Grande in what is now Los Lunas, New Mexico.[31] The Rio Grande ran through the Leopolds' lives, as did the Mississippi River: Aldo was born in 1886 in the same place he was buried in 1948, at the limestone bluffs rising above the Mississippi in Burlington, Iowa.

Luna Leopold trained as a civil engineer and meteorologist before he earned a doctorate in geology at Harvard University. Then, he joined the U.S. Geological Survey, where he began his remarkable riverine career. Leopold, who became USGS chief hydrologist in 1957, is best known for a key theory about the characteristics of streams—involving depth, width, velocity, and how sediments move—that helps scientists predict the behavior of flowing water.[32] Hydrologists used to think rivers slowed as they reached their end and met the sea, as when the Mississippi widens and seems to come to a muddy standstill near New Orleans. Leopold and his colleagues proved that the reverse is true.[33]

He also helped reverse some bad ideas in the Delta and the Glades.

In 1969, toward the beginning of President Richard Nixon's first term, officials in the U.S. Department of the Interior called Leopold away from field research in Wyoming to wade into the political swamp of the Everglades. Miami port officials wanted to build the largest jetport in the world on thirty-nine square miles of wetlands in the Big Cypress Swamp. Leopold's report, written by a south Florida–based federal scientist named Arthur R. Marshall, was a turning point—helping Florida see that paving the Everglades over would drain more of the state's prosperity than it would add. The opening line lacked the equivocation of many government studies: "Development of the proposed jetport and its attendant facilities will lead to land drainage and development for agriculture, transportation, and services in the Big Cypress Swamp, which will inexorably destroy the south Florida ecosystem and thus the Everglades National Park."[34]

Leopold's Everglades report gave the Nixon administration the line it needed to both hang the airport and tie itself to the burgeoning environmental movement. The report had a much longer reach as well, becoming the model for the environmental-impact statements required by former U.S. senator Henry "Scoop" Jackson's National Environmental Policy Act, signed by Nixon in 1970.[35] Nixon had little personal interest in nature, but he saw the extraordinary political capital to be tapped in a new environmental ethic beginning to flow across the country.

The next phase of Luna Leopold's long life and career took him to the University of California at Berkeley, where he was a professor of geology and geophysics. He studied rivers all over America. But he also stayed involved in his local watershed—the Sacramento–San Joaquin.[36]

Like his father, Leopold understood the complexity of human

systems as well as that of nature's. His federal career had put him at the center of furious disputes over not only the Everglades jetport but also allocation of Colorado River water and construction of the trans-Alaska oil pipeline.[37] He could speak to the general public, operate in the political system, and maintain his exacting observations as a scientist. It would all lead him to conclude that what America needed most is an ethic for water, what he called a "guiding belief" for citizens, large water users, and government.[38]

By the time Luna Leopold arrived in Berkeley in 1972, California had almost outdone the federal government in seizing rivers to solve the state's essential quandary: most of the people are in the south, most of the water is in the north. In 1960, Governor Edmund G. "Pat" Brown Sr. had pushed through the huge State Water Project, only slightly smaller than the feds' Central Valley leviathan. Brown's legacy ("I wanted this to be a monument to me," the governor once said of the State Water Project) encompassed the world's tallest earthen dam, the Oroville; the world's longest aqueduct, to carry water 444 miles south; and the world's highest pump lift, to hoist water 2,000 feet up and over the Tehachapi Mountains to the fast-spreading homes and businesses of Southern California.[39]

In 1975, California voters sent Brown's son to Sacramento. Despite same name, they expected a different fish. Environmentalists were thrilled when Edmund G. "Jerry" Brown Jr. took office, with his emphasis on conservation and his catchphrases "Small is beautiful" and "The era of limits."[40] On most issues, Brown "appeared to be under an extraordinary compulsion not to be like his father," writes water historian Norris Hundley Jr. of the University of California at Los Angeles. But, as in every other era in California water history, political pressure from agriculture, and from the thirsty, more heavily populated southern half of the state—not to mention a devastating drought that seared California in 1976 and 1977—proved more compelling than Brown's or his party's ideology.[41]

As drought forced water rationing and killed the state's cherry trees, Brown called an emergency conference in Los Angeles, where he asked Luna Leopold to give the keynote speech. In a style inherited from his father, Leopold began by referring to ancient times, with the historian Herodotus and his writing in 450 BC on the Persian Wars. Herodotus's account was different than anything that came before, Leopold said, because it showed the connections of politics and economics to geography and climate. But over the ensuing 2,500 years, humans had not grasped the concept.

Leopold's first point was that bigger dams—indeed, any technology—would not, in the end, "fix" California's water dilemma. Second, "continued and indefinite expansion" of California's water supply, he said, is "patently impossible." Leopold made this point in the language of his field when he called for "movement toward a steady-state condition"—a cultural acceptance of the reality that water is not limitless.

The third and most important call, and the title of his talk, was for "a reverence for rivers." Of the Persians who dominated Asia Minor in the fifth century BC, Herodotus wrote, "They never defile a river with the secretions of their bodies, nor even wash their hands in one; nor will they allow others to do so, as they have a great reverence for rivers."[42]

Leopold warned the gathered officials that Californians should expect further water deficits in the years to come. Immediate strategies to improve the outlook were large-scale reuse of treated wastewater and governed limits on potable water. The politics of water, he knew, made this last point difficult. But, he added, "I do not consider this politically impossible." Ultimately, he thought, it was "the acid test of leadership" in California and across the country.[43]

Leopold, who died in 2006 at his home in Berkeley at age ninety, lived to see the reverence build in California, Florida, and the rest of the nation. U.S. senator Gaylord Nelson of Wisconsin, who lent his Interior and Insular Affairs Committee clout to the jetport fight, had conceived the nation's first Earth Day celebration, held on April 22, 1970. But although the nation's environmental movement blossomed in that decade, it was not until the 1980s that more of the general public looked up from their Atari consoles to pay serious attention to the devastation of freshwater ecosystems such as the Delta and the Glades.

The California battle over the Stanislaus River helped galvanize public opposition to dams all the way to the Eastern seaboard. One of the largest tributaries of the San Joaquin River, the Stanislaus was among the most-rafted whitewater runs in the United States before it was flooded in the early 1980s. The drowning of the river's deep, petroglyph-filled canyon infuriated Americans who had never even seen it and helped lead to the preservation of the few partially wild rivers left in the nation. Once-sure projects such as the Narrows Dam in Colorado, the Orme Dam in Arizona, and others never got built.[44] (The Yavapai Nation, in Fort McDowell, Arizona, still throws an annual three-day celebration called Orme Dam Victory Days, marking the feds' decision not to build the Orme, which would have flooded two-thirds of the reservation to send more water to Phoenix. The 2011 celebration marks the thirtieth anniversary of Victory Days.)

In Florida, after years of tireless work by environmental advocates Marjory Stoneman Douglas, Art Marshall, Johnny Jones, and many others, the state legislature finally passed the Kissimmee River Restoration Act in 1976. The act was based on Marshall's plan to blow up the Kissimmee dams, buy back surrounding former wetlands that had been filled for agriculture, and turn the inelegantly named C-38 canal back into the meandering river.[45] It would take another quarter century, however, for the river to flow again, for the waterfowl and wading birds to return.

And, as Luna Leopold foretold, Americans from California to Florida began to rely increasingly on recycled water. Where Leopold had stood thirty years earlier to call for a reverence for rivers, the local government in 2008 opened the largest waste-to-drinking-water plant in the world. The Orange County Groundwater Replenishment System, in Southern California, filters sewage until it's cleaner than rain, then returns the water to an aquifer from which local utilities pump it and deliver it to sinks and showers.[46] In Orange County, Florida, meanwhile, two wastewater facilities help Orlando recycle

100 percent of its wastewater, treated to irrigate more than 2,900 acres of citrus; 1,400 acres of golf courses; 2,100 acres of parks; and 3,600 lawns.[47]

As rivers joined other natural wonders as deserving of our protection, the reverence built a powerful political constituency, particularly around recreation. The late western historian Wallace Stegner estimated that about five thousand Americans who were alive in the 1930s had ever floated a whitewater river. By the early 1990s, the number was thirty-five million.[48]

This broader appreciation for rivers, along with the consequences of mega–water projects and pollution, helped lead to the current era of American water management, at least in name: the Age of Restoration.[49] Yet, three decades into the shift away from mega-dams and toward ecologically friendlier water policies, nature is not being restored. And the health of our fish—and our ecosystems—is not much better.

In 2004, routine fish surveys in the Sacramento–San Joaquin Delta registered sharp declines in the numbers of several species, including the Delta smelt, considered an indicator of the health of the larger watershed.[50] In 2008, the U.S. Geological Survey, in its exhaustive study on the conservation status of fishes, reported that the 700 fishes now in jeopardy represent a staggering 92 percent increase over the 364 listed just two decades ago, in 1989.[51]

And remember the greatest human-caused extinction in North America—the freshwater mussels wiped out by large-scale dam construction in the mid-twentieth century? Scientists have found that a second, as-yet-smaller wave of mussel extinctions followed in the late twentieth century, even though the nation's big-dam-building binge had ended. Over time, this second wave, caused by habitat fragmentation, "can be expected to eclipse the first," says mussel biologist Wendell Haag at the U.S. Forest Service's Southern Research Station, in Oxford, Mississippi.[52]

In the same way that fish and shellfish were the whistle-blowers that exposed the destructive nature of big dams for the rest of us, their continued species losses in the twenty-first century says something larger about the Age of Restoration: we can't just keep trying to "fix water" so that all interest groups can have as much as they want. That, as Luna Leopold foretold, is patently impossible. Meanwhile, "restoration" has too often proven to be nothing more than rhetoric. At times, it is simply a code word for the bad old ideas that got us into trouble in the first place.

The Age of Restoration

The Age of Restoration may best be represented by two celebrated federal-state partnerships that aimed to fix past mistakes and assure future water supplies in the nation's two largest estuaries. The accords, years in the making, were built by coalitions of major water users, environmentalists, and government agencies that included sworn enemies. They were known as the CALFED (California-Federal Ecosystem Directorate) Bay-Delta Program and CERP (the Comprehensive Everglades Restoration Plan). Both plans were approved in 2000. Both were touted as the largest ecosystem restoration projects in American history. Both carried remarkably similar multibillion-dollar price tags. The Delta's was $8.7 billion for the first seven-year stage of the plan.[53] The Glades' was $7.8 billion for an estimated thirty-year project.

The two huge projects were head-spinningly complicated. But they could be boiled down to four promises: each would restore the ecosystems, clean up water pollution, ensure a water supply for cities and farms, and improve levees to keep us all safe from floods.

If you're thinking all that is counter to the water ethic Luna Leopold expressed a quarter-century before—when he said water could no longer be everything to everyone, every time—you're right. The CALFED partnership's motto was "Everyone would get better together." Instead, disagreements began to escalate just a few years after the accord. In 2003, parties fought over a proposal to increase water exports from the Delta. During 2004, they couldn't agree over priorities for levees or fish. Come 2005, in a vote of no confidence in the coalition, environmental groups filed lawsuits against the federal government on two biological opinions related to salmon and Delta smelt. Soon after, Hurricane Katrina burst through the levees of New Orleans, bringing out of the Delta newly interested parties who were appalled at what they learned about the safety of their own levees in California.[54]

By then, CALFED was all but over. CERP did not seem far behind.

By 2000, just 2 percent of the original Everglades remained intact. A 42-member commission of former Florida governor Lawton Chiles that included bankers and lawyers, farmers and developers, reached the unanimous conclusion that south Florida's plumb job was "unsustainable," in the parlance of the Age of Restoration.[55] Working with government scientists, the panel outlined sixty-eight separate projects. The big idea was to capture the freshwater now diverted into the Atlantic Ocean and the Gulf of Mexico and send it south into the dying Everglades, with plenty to spare for agriculture and the cities of south Florida.

Congress passed the CERP bill in 2000 with broad bipartisan support. A smiling President Bill Clinton signed it into law that December with Florida governor Jeb Bush by his side in the Oval Office. On the very same day, just on the other side of the Capitol Building, the U.S. Supreme Court was listening to oral arguments in *George W. Bush et al. v. Albert Gore Jr.,* the epic case that would determine the fate of the recount in Jeb Bush's state—and whether the governor's brother or Clinton's vice president would be sitting in the same office come January. The White House press corps dogged Jeb Bush on the recount, but he would talk only of the Glades: "We're here to talk about something that's going to be long-lasting, way past counting votes," Bush said. "This is the restoration of a treasure for our country."[56]

The good will did not last a decade. When Congress did not come through with its share of CERP funding by 2004, Bush announced that Florida would begin building key Everglades restoration projects on its own. Problem was, those projects, dubbed Acceler8, were more about water supply than about restoration. Just like their peers in Northern California, environmentalists and others began to lose faith in the coalition.

In 2008, the National Academy of Sciences reported that CERP was "bogged down in budgeting, planning, and procedural matters," with hardly any progress toward actual restoration of the Everglades. "Meanwhile, the ecosystems that the CERP is intended to save are in peril, construction costs are escalating, and population growth and associated development increasingly make accomplishing the goals of CERP more difficult," the scientists said.[57]

As the coalition of environmental, agricultural, and other interests that had formed to pass CERP began to break apart, lawsuits filled the cracks. As one example, the Natural Resources Defense Council sued over one of Bush's Acceler8 projects—what would have been the world's largest free-standing reservoir, covering an area as big as Manhattan. Bush had dug the first shovelful of dirt with a celebration of its magnitude—"the equivalent of more than five million residential swimming pools," read the press release from the South Florida Water Management District.[58]

Less than three years after the groundbreaking—and after spending nearly $300 million in public funds on it—board members of the district voted to halt construction. Today, at the far western edge of Palm Beach County, the twenty-five square miles of bulldozed, dynamite-pocked earth sits silent, overgrown with weeds.

In the final years of George W. Bush's presidency, the Republican governors of California and Florida became GOP rock stars for fighting climate change, imploring the states in between to reduce greenhouse-gas emissions, increase energy efficiency, and support renewable energy sources when the federal government would not.

California governor Arnold Schwarzenegger and Florida governor Charlie Crist led green revolutions in their states while defiant fellow Republicans, including the one in the White House, still cast doubt on global warming. But as the tanned bicoastal governors were forging a new path for energy, they seemed unwilling to steer California and Florida off the twentieth-century road for water—even though it was getting pretty dusty.

In spring 2007, as Schwarzenegger and Crist joined singer Sheryl Crow in her campaign to curb global warming, drought had shrunk Lake Mead and Lake Powell, the reservoirs that supply water to 30 million people in seven western states, by half. The bed of Lake Okeechobee was burning. The two governors were inspirational leaders on climate, demanding change from energy companies and car manufacturers. Yet when it came to the water crisis, both men generally played the old reel: their state's water problems could be fixed with billions of dollars to create artificial storage, from the Everglades Agricultural Area Reservoir to more aqueducts and canals in the Delta. They took no responsibility for the crumbling CALFED and CERP, insisting the feds were to blame because Congress had not coughed up enough money.

Of the two, Schwarzenegger was the one determined to leave office with a water legacy as big as a Hollywood blockbuster.[59] That must be written somewhere in the job description for California governors. Even the younger Brown, during his first stint as governor, had tried to top off his father's State Water Project monument with a second phase he originally opposed, a forty-three-mile-long addition called the Peripheral Canal to carry Sacramento River water south around the Delta. California voters turned down Brown's canal in 1982 after one of the most hard-fought and expensive ballot campaigns in state history. The defeat was due in part to California's sluggish economy.[60]

That history was often on Schwarzenegger's mind during his last term as governor. He championed an $11 billion water bond that ensured, he said, "a reliable water supply for future generations, as well as restoring the Sacramento–San Joaquin Delta and other ecologically sensitive areas."[61] The largest chunk would build infrastructure including dams, reservoirs, and canals, followed by watershed protection and restoration projects.[62] But it was a tough sell in a state facing a record $20 billion budget deficit.

In 2010, during a presentation on the latest infrastructure options for saving the Delta, I watched slide after slide click by with promises that essentially hadn't changed in fifty years: full ecosystem restoration and a fully reliable water supply for people and farms. Several of the proposals involved drilling a series of tunnels, up to thirty-five miles long and as big around as a small house, underneath the Delta. The idea was to transport water underground, restoring the Delta's surface and giving fish access to the sea.[63]

The six-hundred-foot-long machine that would bore the tunnels looked like the flagship of an alien enemy of the starship *Enterprise*. I wondered about it rattling around under such an earthquake-prone part of the country.

In the world of water, there's a common refrain that water work is very, very complicated. It's hard for citizens to understand. Water managers and elected officials repeat this like a mantra: Doling out water in the West is made difficult by our arcane system of water rights. In the East, it is complex because there can be too much water as often as too little; water management is as much about protecting people from floods as it is about supplying them water. Groundwater is complicated (you can't see it). Surface water is complicated (you have to share it).

All those things are true. But the repeat-loop stories of water in the Delta and the Glades reveal other essential truths that transcend the legal status of water, the source of water, and even the amount available in any one particular watershed. First, there isn't enough water for all interest groups to have all they want, all the time. There isn't enough for every person in Sacramento to use 287 gallons of potable water every day—especially for lawns—when the Delta next door is dying of thirst.

Second, the larger the technical fix, the larger the unintended consequences for the next generation, or even the next fiscal year. The constant reengineering of past engineering mistakes is a costly drain in which America keeps circling, while our most important water treasures go down. (CERP price estimates have stretched from the original $7.8 billion to $30 billion-plus.)[64] The water-industrial complex is not only trying to fix mistakes made in the 1930s with the

Central Valley Project or the 1940s with the Central and Southern Florida Project. It is already working its way through the mistakes of the twenty-first century—like the aborted Manhattan-size reservoir in Palm Beach County.

Finally, our water needs the protection of leaders willing to make tough calls, rather than the impossible promises of those who try to make everyone happy. The Netherlands boasts perhaps the proudest water-engineering history in the world. Yet the Dutch in recent years have made the politically painful call to tear down some dikes and give water a place to go, to avoid much more devastating consequences in the next flood. Dutch farmers are well compensated for sacrificing croplands to rivers and the North Sea. The emotional costs are also high. But ultimately, they are less than either the technical options for keeping the entire country dry—or the lives lost if they don't work.

The stakes are literally that high in some parts of the United States, including the Delta and the Glades. But in most of the country, the water ethic is easier. It's raising the price of water and getting rid of some grass.

CHAPTER 3

The Netherlands:
Deluge, Dams, and the Dutch Miracle

On January 30, 1953, an unremarkable atmospheric depression formed over the North Atlantic Ocean, south of Iceland. As winds blew it east toward Ireland, it bulked up strength and speed. By the next day, it had grown into one of Europe's notorious winter wind-storms.

The tempest roared into the North Channel, which divides Ireland and Scotland, on the morning of January 31. Ship captains had no forewarning of its fierce winds and waves, and so the channel was full of vessels. The weather forecast had been familiar—a mere call for rain.[1]

East of Belfast, the gale sent an enormous wave crashing through the car-deck doors of a popular ferry called the *Princess Victoria*. A half-hour later, the ship was listing on its side, its captain ordering passengers onto lifeboats.[2] Of 177 passengers and crew who'd set out that morning for a short, routine ferry passage, 133 drowned in the icy channel, including the captain, every crew member, and every woman and child on board.[3] More than a quarter of the Scottish fishing fleet was lost that day as well.[4]

In all, the surprise storm killed an estimated 250 souls in the sea that January 31. After its seaward onslaught, the gale raked across England and Scotland, battering the east coast of the island, where it killed another three hundred or more.[5] Then, with the force of a hurricane, the now-huge depression began to churn slowly southeast across the North Sea. It piled up a powerful storm surge. And it drew a bead on the low-lying Netherlands.

At the southwest corner of the Netherlands, a cluster of peninsulas juts from the land, resembling fingers on a hand. The green digits interlace with blue waters to form a province called Zeeland, which lives up to its name: "sea land." Viewed from the air, the fingers appear hooked, as if clawing for the North Sea. But despite a millennium of effort, it's still very much the other way around.

This is a delta where three rivers—the Rhine, which originates in the Swiss Alps, and the Meuse and the Scheldt, with headwaters in northern France—complete their journeys to the North Sea. One thousand years ago, the place was lots of water and a bit of earth, a vast stretch of salt marsh and peat islands so low lying that they could disappear beneath the sea for decades at a time.

Over the centuries, first slowly and then at great pace, humans turned the water into land. Flemish monks began the work of dike building before the Middle Ages, with tools no more complicated than spades and baskets. The artificially dry lands they reclaimed are called polders. Starting in the thirteenth century, settlers created political bodies called, when translated into English, polder boards, or dike-ring boards, to work together to keep dikes maintained and polders drained. Their first drainage systems were simple sluices that sent water out to sea at low tide. Beginning in the 1600s, they built windmills to pump out large lakes and make increasingly bigger polders. Each new century brought bigger pumps that made bigger polders: steam-powered pumps in the nineteenth century, turbines in the twentieth.[6]

But for all those years spent fighting the sea, the people of the southwestern Netherlands were oddly blasé about the weather building off their coastline on that eventful day in 1953. It was a festive Saturday for the Dutch. Princess Beatrix, future queen of the Netherlands, was celebrating her fifteenth birthday. It was stormy, but the rain, wind, and water brought an air of excitement to the southwestern provinces, the kind that often precedes a hurricane in America.

Most people in Zeeland and South Holland went to sleep that night with no worry about the storm. They expected it to blow itself out overnight. They'd heard nothing of the deaths in neighboring countries.[7]

The force of the storm barreled into the southwest Netherlands around midnight on January 31. For an unrelenting twenty hours, it punished the coast with wind speeds between forty-seven and fifty-four miles an hour and waves twenty-two to thirty-two feet tall. The storm pushed seawater over land with so much pressure that waves couldn't roll out again; there was no ebb tide.

By 2 a.m., water was pouring over dikes and wooden barriers "like boiling milk."[8] At 3 a.m., the spring flood tide—an unusually high tide the Dutch call a *giertij*—made its unfortunate appearance. That moment saw the highest water level in Dutch history: ten feet, two inches above normal. That's also when the first dikes began to crumble.[9]

Most dikes were made of clay, with stone on the seaward side and grass on the land side. Many were weakened during World War II, when they pulled double duty as military bunkers, crammed with machine guns and manholes. Those spots proved some of the first to succumb. Overnight and during the following days, the surge breached a hundred sea dikes. But far more failed in the interior, where they stood between the polders and the vast estuaries of the southwestern delta.[10]

Black-and-white photos of the water rushing through and over dikes look like they were snapped at Niagara Falls. The flood gave rise to many heroic acts, like the skipper who steered his river barge into a dike breach, a maneuver believed to have saved central Holland. But in Zeeland, South Holland, and West Brabant, the powerful water sheets swept away homes, businesses, and parts of villages. Very small villages such as Schuring in South Holland and Capelle in Zeeland were obliterated, without a single house left standing.

In other villages, rooftops and dike tops remained for residents to scramble up and wait in terror there for the sun to rise and the water to drop.[11]

"You can't believe what the sea can do and what the waves can do," remembers Jan Luijendijk, a child survivor of the storm who is now head of hydroinformatics at UNESCO-IHE, the global water school in Delft, the city better known for its blue-and-white pottery. "The world looks completely different in that instant, and you can't imagine that it will ever be the same again."[12]

When the morning of February 1 finally dawned, survivors could see only "an incredible expanse of water," broken occasionally by a few tree limbs, roof peaks, and dike fragments.[13]

Fishermen in boats saved as many neighbors as they could. But no organized rescue effort materialized that horrible morning. Telephone and radio communications remained severed. When the first disaster reports reached newspaper offices at about 4:30 a.m., no one was there to read them.

Later in the morning, the water began to recede, allowing survivors to flee their flooded villages in search of higher ground. But soon, the tide began to rise again. More drowned in this second flood than in the first; others were crushed against the dikes. Houses that had hung on through the first flood collapsed in the second. People who'd been stranded in attics or on rooftops were swept away with their homes.[14]

Luijendijk was a four-year-old boy living with his family on top of a dike in Zeeland when the storm hit. Even at the highest elevation in the village, water flooded the ground floor. Luijendijk has vivid memories of the rising water, his parents' relief when it dropped, and their horror when it began to swell back up.

Around five o'clock Sunday afternoon, it grew dark again. Thousands of soaked survivors faced a second night—freezing, hungry, and thirsty—crowded together in attics or perched on roofs and dikes. As the scale of the disaster reached the outside world, Dutch soldiers and others began arriving to evacuate survivors.

In the official count, the storm killed 1,835 people in the Netherlands. Fifty thousand head of cattle also drowned. Three thousand homes were destroyed, along with three hundred farms. Another forty thousand houses and three thousand farms were damaged.[15]

The disaster "was a terrible shock," says Luijendijk, "because the Dutch felt at that time that we were very, very good at building dikes." As the floodwaters receded in 1953, Dutch consciousness turned toward one, unified ambition: "Never again."

Any water narrative—especially one critical of mega-hydraulics—would fall short without the rush of floodwaters and their deadly potential, incomplete as the Bible without Noah's Ark. Floods are so powerful a chapter in the human story that every civilization in history seems to have a deluge drama of its own.

Relayed more than four thousand years ago in the epic poem "Gilgamesh," Mesopotamian myth tells a flood story strikingly similar to Noah's. The gods are annoyed by humans "and their growing numbers and all the noise they make," so they brew up a flood to destroy humanity. But the wise and kind water god, Enki, figures out that no humans will mean no sacrifices and no one to work. So he tips off Utnapishtim and instructs him to build a boat and fill it with the seeds of all living things.[16]

In Greek mythology, Zeus becomes so disgusted with humankind that he unleashes a tremendous flood to wipe out almost everybody. Only ark-building Deucalion and his wife are saved. In Hindu lore, Brahma turns into a fish to warn his son Manu—the first man—of worldwide flood. Manu also builds a large boat and gathers seeds from all life. When everything else is wiped out, he makes an offering to the gods, who then produce a beautiful woman, with whom he parents a new human race.[17]

In Incan myth, the sun and storm deity, Viracocha, is so disappointed with his first creation—humans—that he destroys them in a flood. In the Mayan version, gods try various ways to make people, but none work out. After the third try, when the people are made of wood, the god Huracan splinters them in a huge rainstorm and flood. (The deity's name gives us *hurricane* and *orcan,* a word sometimes used to describe Europe's fierce windstorms.)[18]

The torrent tales from around the globe lead some scientists to speculate that one cataclysmic flood in ancient times might have spurred them all.[19] Others argue the end of the last ice age, about sixteen thousand years ago, brought rising seas so catastrophic that they created historic memory for the narratives.[20]

But the only incontrovertible answer is that humans have flood stories because we're so naturally drawn to places that flood, especially the world's deltas. The word *delta* comes from the ancient Greeks, who so named the mouth of the Nile for its resemblance to the fourth letter of their alphabet, the shape of a triangle. River mouths speak to great human convenience: passage to both hinterlands and sea, and rich alluvium that forms fertile agricultural lands.[21] And so some of our most productive population centers are also the most dangerously vulnerable to flood: the Sacramento–San Joaquin Delta; the Mississippi River Delta of the Gulf Coast; the famous deltas of the Nile, the Ganges, the Mekong, the Rhone, the Yangtze.

In the United States, flood is as much a threat as drought, if not more: 42 percent of Americans live in areas protected by levees.[22] It's not unusual for different parts of the country to suffer from both water plagues simultaneously. But despite our own painful flood history, we haven't caught the "Never again" spirit of the Dutch.

It's impossible to ponder the military effort and lives saved in 1953 without remembering the paralysis that marked the Hurricane Katrina tragedy in America's Gulf Coast more than a half century later. On Sunday, February 1, 1953, as freezing survivors endured the first full day of their mythlike flood, the Dutch government hastened more than 4,000 soldiers to the southwest. By nightfall, they were on the ground with supplies and sandbags.[23] By day three, more than 12,000 soldiers were moving families in a large-scale evacuation. In just a few days more, the Dutch had relocated 72,000 people from the southwest floodwaters. Before the one-week anniversary, the work of inspecting damage and restoring dikes had begun.[24]

In contrast to the Netherlands storm, Hurricane Katrina was no surprise to Americans. We watched its slow, urgently predicted approach for days on our computer and TV screens. Katrina hit south Florida as a category 1 hurricane on Thursday morning, August 25, 2005, giving the rest of the nation four days to watch it power up over the warm waters of the Gulf of Mexico and zero in on Louisiana and Mississippi.

The National Weather Service's National Hurricane Center predicted "a most powerful hurricane with unprecedented strength . . . . [M]ost of the area will be uninhabitable for weeks . . . perhaps longer."[25] But New Orleans mayor C. Ray Nagin waited until ten o'clock Sunday morning to evacuate the city built below sea level. That was too late for about 20 percent of residents, including the vulnerable elderly in their homes or nursing homes, and poor residents who had no cars or cash with which to flee.[26]

Katrina plowed into southeast Louisiana and the Mississippi Gulf Coast with 125-mile-an-hour winds on the morning of Monday, August 29. In New Orleans, the catastrophic storm surge broke through fifty-three levees and drowned 80 percent of the city. As shocked as Americans were by Katrina's force, we felt just as shocked that the hurricane paralyzed government at all levels.[27] The feds proved unable to come through with food and water for flood victims, much less evacuate the city, for a full four days after the storm struck.[28]

In the many comparisons made between the 1953 storm and Katrina, the most remarkable may be the death tolls. While the North Sea storm officially killed 1,835 people, people in the southwestern Netherlands like to make it 1,836, for a nameless baby born and drowned. Katrina killed 1,836 as well, if you accept *Wikipedia* and other unofficial sources that counted two additional victims in Ohio and one in Kentucky. The National Hurricane Center's official count is eerily close enough: 1,833.[29]

Few would argue that the Netherlands's quick response saved Dutch lives, while the U.S. government's immobility cost American lives. But the *why* is a matter of eternal debate. The spectrum of possible answers is as wide as the mouth of the Mississippi, covering everything from politics and bureaucracy to poverty and race. No single one of them can explain how it was that three days after Katrina's Gulf of Mexico landfall, "absolutely nothing was getting better in New Orleans and almost everything was getting worse," in the words of Tulane University historian Douglas Brinkley, who rode out the storm.[30]

Hands clasped in prayer before landfall turned to finger pointing quickly after. Mayor Nagin was among those to also claim the "vengeful-God theory" straight out of ancient mythology. He said in a public speech on Martin Luther King Jr. Day in 2006 that "surely, God is mad at America. He sent us hurricane after hurricane, and it has destroyed and put stress on this country."[31]

A more rational explanation as to why we couldn't get our act together: America's widespread lack of respect for water—our lack of a water ethic—means we don't take it seriously enough. Not when there's too much. Not when there's too little. Not when salmon go belly-up. Not even when people do.

Americans haven't taken water seriously since the era when we had to tote our own drinking water and protect our own families from floods. And we haven't said "Never again" for a very, very long time. In the wake of America's 1927 Mississippi flood; the '28 hurricane that killed 2,500 people south of Lake Okeechobee; and after Katrina, Congress admonished the U.S. Army Corps of Engineers to get to work building protective barriers. But the rest of us quit paying attention. We were distracted by the economic crises that happened to follow all three storms, apathetic to the natural element that shapes our lives more than any other.

The greatest flood disaster in modern Dutch history came to be known as the North Sea Flood of 1953. It also became *the* national cause, on which Dutch science, policy, education, and politics—and funding—would all fixate for the next four decades. Within two weeks after the disaster, the Dutch rallied around the goals of rebuilding the southwest and fortifying the nation's coastline with remarkable sense of purpose. Prime Minister Willem Drees proclaimed levee repair the highest priority in the land. He installed a scientific panel, the Delta Commission, to develop a plan that would ensure "such a disaster could not happen again."[32]

By the end of 1953, the breached and broken dikes were repaired. The polders were pumped out. And the Delta Commission had made its recommendations. Its massive Delta Plan called for barricading all the river estuaries of the southwest except those vital to trade.

Like a cast net cinching up islands instead of fish, it would shorten the Netherlands's coastline by 435 miles.[33]

The personal force behind the Delta Plan was a grim genius named Johan van Veen.[34] An expert in the movement of sand and waves, he was chief engineer at Rijkswaterstaat, the national public works agency in charge of both water and road infrastructure. Throughout the mid-1930s and '40s, van Veen had obsessed over the vulnerabilities of the southwestern dikes. He'd advocated extensive schemes to close off the region's rivers from the North Sea to prevent major floods. But the government's attention and resources were on World War II, then the work of rebuilding the country in the wake of the German blitzkrieg and occupation.

Van Veen felt like the proverbial prophet ignored in his own land. He began to write books and papers on polder drainage, dredging, and reclamation under the pseudonym Dr. Cassandra to take stands bolder than his bureaucrat position would allow. (Cassandra was the mythological Greek beauty Apollo bestowed with the gift of prophecy. When she refused to return his love, he turned his gift into a curse with the twist that no one would believe her dim predictions.) Van Veen had updated his book *Dredge, Drain, and Reclaim: The Art of a Nation* in 1952 with dire warnings about the inadequate dikes of Zeeland. When they came true, he suddenly had all the attention he ever wanted. He was named secretary of the Delta Commission. The Delta Plan would rely heavily on his work.[35]

Van Veen's strategy to clamp river mouths shut and shorten the coastline was appealing to the Dutch, already world famous for their hydraulic handiwork. American proponents of Everglades drainage and similar schemes often pointed in admiration to the "Dutch way." Dutch engineers had claimed a new chapter in water history in 1932, when they completed the Afsluitdijk, or Barrier Dam, which eliminated an enormous inland sea, the Zuiderzee, in the country's northwest. The Zuiderzee stemmed flooding and shaved 186 miles off the north-central coast. It turned the North Sea inlet into a huge freshwater lake, the Ijsselmeer. It drained hundreds of thousands of acres of former sea bottom that became farms, villages, and, in 1986, an entire new province—Flevoland.[36]

The Delta Plan called for a similarly dramatic change in Zeeland. It would dam the tidal channels of the southwest delta, where
the Rhine, Meuse, and Scheldt Rivers completed their journey to the
North Sea. And it would raise sea and river dikes nationwide to hold
back a tide sixteen feet above normal. That's six feet higher than the
record-breaking 1953 swell, constituting a fortress that promised to
reduce average inland flooding to once every ten thousand years and
flooding in inlets to once every four thousand years.[37]

It seemed like a safe bet.

The plan had great public support. In addition to flood protection, freshwater lakes would irrigate farms and create placid new
recreational areas. New coastal highways would stretch across the
tops of the barriers.

Parliament passed the Delta Act in 1958. Dutch hydraulic engineers got to work designing gargantuan dams for the four tidal inlets
where Zeeland's island fingertips turned into sea: the Veerse Gat,
the Eastern Scheldt, the Brouwershavnse Gat, and the Haringvliet.
The dams would shrink a winding, 435-mile collection of sea dikes
in the southwest to just fifteen miles of hulking caissons and other
barriers. Further inland, three more large dams would connect the
island fingers to the mainland, eliminating tidal currents and sepa-
rating freshwater from saltwater in the Volkerak, Grevelingen, and
Zandkreek channels.[38]

Rijkswaterstaat, the public works ministry, set out a logical order
for what came to be known as the Deltawerken, or Delta Works—
small projects to large, simple to complicated. In a fawning travel-
ogue on the project in 1958, the *New York Times* reported the plan
would be finished in twenty to twenty-five years at a cost of about
U.S.$600 million.[39]

Instead, the project took nearly four decades and added up to
roughly U.S.$6 billion.[40] In May 1997, the queen of the Netherlands
opened the final storm-surge barrier of the Delta Works. The Mae-
slant barrier protects the Port of Rotterdam with two gates, each the
size of the Eiffel Tower, which automatically swing closed on 680-ton
ball-and-socket joints when the tide swells nine feet above normal.

Beatrix, the princess who turned fifteen on the weekend of the

North Sea Flood, was now a graying queen. By then, the costly flooding solutions pushed by the gloomy Dr. Cassandra had gotten old, too.

Today in Zeeland, looming white wind turbines spin their steel-blade triads on the same horizon where pastoral wooden windmills churn from centuries past. The province is a portrait in miniature of the Netherlands's peculiar dichotomy of old and new, where thirteenth-century villages lie minutes from the most modern, busiest ports in Europe.[41]

It's the same for Zeeland's water defenses. At the outer coast, some of the most colossal barriers in the world stand rigid against the North Sea as they connect the former finger islands. In the province's interior, grass-covered dikes still stretch throughout the bucolic countryside, ramparts defending every imaginable asset.

Zeeland's hill-shaped dikes border the winding roads. They ring the neatly tended farms and villages. The dikes' lush green slopes are set off by a flock of white sheep here, a hopping brown rabbit there, a golden patch of wildflowers lit by the sun. Tidy brick homes add to the idyllic picture; sometimes only their red-roof peaks are visible from behind the dikes. Beyond the homes, crop rows of potatoes, onions, and sugar beets thrive in the soils reclaimed from the sea.

But not all is picturesque or productive. Closing almost every inlet in the province has brought a flood of negative repercussions to the region, some expected and some not. Zeeland's water and wildlife depended on the delta's unique blend of river and sea. The Delta Works transformed it into a number of separate, mostly stagnant bodies of water no longer influenced by tides. Marshlands are dying, and with them entire ecosystems. Many saltwater fish species have disappeared, and signature birds, such as the Kentish plover and the little tern, have moved away.

Pollution is building up behind the dams; more than five billion cubic feet of toxic sludge from the Rhine and the Meuse has settled in the Haringvliet lake.[42] Water quality is so poor in some lakes that they cannot be used for irrigation. They are unfit for drinking for livestock, much less humans. Water-sports enthusiasts who looked forward to the Delta Plan's recreational waters have also been foiled, in some places by the hulking barricades themselves, in others by rotting vegetation and other problems.

Major freshwater lakes like the Volkerak-Zoom now teem each year with blue-green algae. The poisonous bloom kills off fish and birds, brings swimming bans, and scares tourists off with putrid odors.[43]

But most ironic for the safety-minded Dutch, the intense barricading of Zeeland and other parts of the Netherlands has created a new flood threat in the age of climate change. Surprisingly, sea-level rise is not the most immediate climate-change worry in the Netherlands. River flooding is the pressing concern. The Dutch are experiencing wetter winters and more extreme summer showers. Those changes, along with deforestation and urbanization, mean much more river runoff than ever before.[44] Meanwhile, glacial rivers like the Rhine, which begins at the Rheinwaldhom Glacier in the Swiss Alps, will swell with more melted water in the future, when rainfall is also expected to increase.[45]

The shuttered estuaries of the Delta Works means there's no place for all the extra river water to go—no place but up and over dikes. In 1993 and 1995 and again in 1998, the Netherlands was surprised by mighty floods of the Rhine and Meuse Rivers. The 1995 flood forced 250,000 evacuations and caused U.S.$1 billion in economic damages to industry and agriculture. This was after the country had spent U.S.$6 billion and nearly four decades' work on the Delta Plan, meant to relegate serious flooding to the history books.

Today, the new dangers posed by river flooding, the pollution, the vanished fish and birds, and other problems have led to an extraordinary shift in the nation's water ethic, says longtime water engineer Arthur E. Mynett.

Mynett is head of research and development at Deltares, the Netherlands's independent research institute that advises governments and private industry around the world on water. After centuries of building the biggest hydraulic barriers on the planet, Mynett and his fellow Dutch engineers are taking a new approach.

In the past, they always viewed water as the enemy. Now, they're holding out an olive branch. "The lesson," says Mynett, "is that we should have paid more attention to what nature was telling us."

Nature had been shouting pretty loudly for some time. In 1961, the first Delta Works dam completed—the Veerse Gatdam—choked off an inlet called Veerse from the vast Eastern Scheldt estuary. The Veerse, a once favorite commercial fishing spot, turned into a stagnant, brackish lake best known for massive mats of stinking sea lettuce.[46] Another Delta Works dam, the Brouwers Dam, was completed in 1971 and within days killed off almost all sea life in a channel called Grevelingen. In two weeks, "the shore had become a large cemetery," with rotting plants and fish lying dead everywhere.[47]

About a decade into the dam building of the Delta Works, public and political will began to shift. The same changing consciousness was spreading across the United States with the dawn of the environmental movement. But the rancor and litigation that marked clashing opinion here gave way to a unique brand of compromise among the Dutch—one based on a shared belief in the vital public importance of water.

Water management is considered the oldest form of democracy in the Netherlands. The polder boards formed in the mid-1200s by farmers who had to work together to maintain dikes and drain land evolved over centuries into large, diverse groups of stakeholders. Polder boards became well known for their ability to reach consensus on water through community dialogue. Polder members, no matter which sector they came from or which political flag they waved, had to learn to work together on the common goal of keeping land dry.

This so-called polder method of community consensus became an indelible part of the Dutch psyche and political system. It was on display in the wake of the North Sea Flood, when the nation rallied to support the costly Delta Works to prevent future flood disasters.

The devastating impacts of the Veerse Gatdam, the Brouwers Dam, and other Delta Works sparked groups from fishermen to envi-

ronmentalists to speak out against the last, largest, and most complicated barrier planned, across the mouth of the Eastern Scheldt. The
Delta Plan called for a 5-mile barricade of artificial islands linked
with thick walls of concrete and steel. Local villagers who'd lost loved
ones in 1953 insisted that keeping to the original plan was a matter of
life and death. But environmental groups and mussel and oyster fishermen argued that the death of the entire Delta would be a tragedy
all its own. They wanted to keep the inlet wide open.[48]

The strong feelings and extreme differences of opinion made
middle ground hard to imagine. But in the polder tradition, Rijkswaterstaat in 1973 put together a committee to consider new options.
By the following spring, the panel had proposed an archetypal Dutch
compromise.[49] The inlet would be neither completely open nor completely closed. Instead, engineers designed an enormous bridge of
sixty-five concrete piers, between which hang sixty-two steel gates
that are open almost all the time but shutter in a dangerous high tide.
The compromise maintained three-fourths of the Eastern Scheldt's
tidal flow. It took eight years and cost much more than the original
design: the final price tag was $2.5 billion Euros.[50]

Today, the Eastern Scheldt storm-surge barrier is considered a
global engineering marvel; it's a tourist attraction akin to America's
Hoover Dam. Visitors who don't mind booming traffic noise, high
winds, and heights can walk underneath the highway that traverses
the barrier to look up close at the eighteen-thousand-ton piers and
colossal construction techniques: one ship specially made to build
the barrier, the *Mytilus,* carried sixty-foot-long vibration needles that
pummeled the seabed twenty-four hours a day to make it compact
enough to hold the weight of the mammoth structure.

The barrier is far from perfect. Some Dutch engineers consider
it "a magnificent mistake," though they say either the original dam
or the option of leaving Zeeland exposed would have been worse.[51]
Two decades after its completion, ecologists say the barrier has had
numerous "unexpected, undesirable" effects on the Eastern Scheldt,
including a surprising loss of intertidal flats, essential habitats for
local shellfish and shorebirds.[52]

Still, the general sense among water officials and the community is that the polder method led to the best option. Citizen input forced water managers to take a more holistic approach. Dutch engineers acknowledge it's a better approach. "We are used to involving many, many groups, because the polder method tells us we must work together, or we won't survive," says Deltares's Arthur E. Mynett. "Public opinion told us we must stop fighting the coast and build with nature. Over time, the engineers have changed their minds. They have learned more about nature. And they have learned much more about how the environment impacts safety."

Today, the Dutch are at work on a national effort called Room for the River that involves tearing down some dikes, flooding polders with compensation to farmers, and restoring wetlands—in general, giving peak river flow a place to go, rather than relying on ever-higher dikes. And in almost every major water body in the Delta, work is under way to expand estuaries and bring them back to life. In 2004, engineers removed two of the Veerse Gatdam's warehouse-size concrete caissons and replaced them with a sliding passageway that lets the tide flow between the Veerse and the Eastern Scheldt. Scientists see significant improvements in oxygen and nutrient levels, though vanished fish and shellfish have not yet returned.[53] Engineers also have built a sluice into the Brouwers Dam that lets seawater flow in and out. Similar plans are under way to increase tidal flows in the Haringvliet, the Volkerak-Zoom, and other areas.

But the Netherlands's crucial water lesson is not all about nature over infrastructure. That moral is well established, if often unheeded, in America and other parts of the world. What the Dutch have right is the water ethic—the shared, fundamental belief in water as a national priority that must be managed with the serious input of everyone who cares enough to want a say.

For a time, in the 1980s and '90s, the Dutch polder model of compromise became a global political fad, extended to national economic policy and other issues outside the realm of water. The *Wall Street Journal*, the *Financial Times*, and the *Economist* all devoted feature articles to the way Dutch labor unions and corporations worked hand-in-hand to help the country out of an economic crisis in the '80s. Former U.S. presidents Bill Clinton and George W. Bush were among many who gushed admiration for the polder model, also dubbed the Third Way or the Dutch Miracle.

What the business reporters and politicians failed to understand was that the polder model couldn't be typed in a textbook and transferred to other sectors, because it evolved to care for water. And water is different. As the early Greek philosopher Heraclitus noted 2,500 years ago, water is *literally* different: you can never, ever step into the same river twice. Even if you hop onto the precise same rock you were on just a moment before, the water will have changed.[54]

Water doesn't adhere to political boundaries, or even its own riverbanks. Water befuddles economists. It embarrasses engineers. It often surprises the scientists who study its movement, such as those who determined that the open Eastern Scheldt storm-surge barrier would ensure healthy tidal flats for Zeeland's shellfish and shorebirds.

Water is art as much as science. In the Netherlands, the city of Delft has become the nucleus of water research for the Dutch, home to UNESCO's only degree-granting program, along with the research institute Deltares and the Delft University of Technology. The thirteenth-century town, with its brick streets and its footbridges over canals, looks much the same today as it did in 1659, when its most famous resident, Johannes Vermeer, painted his enchanting water landscape *A View of Delft*.

Vermeer's idealized image captures an essential union: water and hope. In the foreground, heavy clouds are lifting over a broad river. In the distance, the sun is beginning to shine on village rooftops and steeples.

Water needs the Johannes Vermeers as much as the Johan van Veens—the artists as much as the engineers. It deserves the input of anglers and other ordinary people as much as politicians, large water users, and water managers. It benefits from the voices of the young, with new ideas and hopes, as much as from elders who lived through 1953 and other defining events. To see an entire nation come together this way on water—*that* is the Dutch miracle.

In twenty-first-century America, the language of *stakeholder engagement*, *consensus*, and *common ground* have become increasingly popular among water managers and engineers perceptive of the coming blue revolution. But in practice, the nation's water decisions are still top-down, our water trade-offs still fought over by lawyers billing by the hour rather than by communities drawn together in a shared ethic. Along North Carolina's Catawba River, the largest energy company in the nation had gotten poldering down to a science. But as the largest water user on the river, Duke Power was not exactly an objective convener.

CHAPTER 4

Powerful Thirst

Spreading out from the Catawba River just north of Charlotte, the largest lake in North Carolina is shaped like the state's signature long-leaf pine. Called Lake Norman, its many branches create 538 acres of shoreline and a surface as big as all of Charlotte-Mecklenburg County, which relies on the lake for its every water need.

In winter 2008, the branches of Lake Norman began to shrivel. Drought sunk the lake to the lowest levels since it was created fifty years ago by the last dam ever built on the Catawba River. The 32,475-acre reservoir, larger than the river's ten other constructed lakes combined, dropped to less than a foot above the minimum level required to run the McGuire Nuclear Energy Station, owned and operated by Duke Energy on the lake's south shore.[1]

Charlotte residents fretted during the drought about brown lawns and dried-up docks. But they should have worried about their ability to flip on lights and power up laptops. For though the name on their electric bill says "Duke Energy," the true source of their power is the Catawba River, which runs for 225 miles through North Carolina and South Carolina.

Though it is often left out of the public debate, energy production now requires more water than any other sector in America, including agriculture. In 2005, withdrawals for thermal power accounted for 41 percent of all freshwater sucked up in the United States, nearly all of it surface water used to cool power plants.[2] Thanks to conservation and efficiency, the nation's other water demands have flattened slightly despite population growth. But water demand for power grew 3 percent between 2000 and 2005.[3]

Charlotte-based Duke, founded more than a century ago to electrify the Carolina Piedmont region with Catawba River hydropower, is now the largest energy company in the nation. But Duke relies more than ever on the 225-mile-long river, which today powers thirteen hydroelectric facilities and cools three coal plants and two nuclear stations. The Catawba is stretched so thin, and Duke's customer base in the Carolinas growing so fast, that the company is pushing new plants to another river, the Broad River, which also flows through both Carolinas.

Duke Energy is constructing what CEO James E. Rogers calls "the last coal-fired plant I will ever build"[4] on the Broad, where it has also proposed two new nuclear reactors—and three reservoirs to feed them. Company officials fear that one, or even two reservoirs, won't be enough to keep the reactors running during inevitable future droughts.

That just-add-more-water approach to making energy has not changed in more than a hundred years. But it can't last. In the Carolinas and across the nation, a growing population is demanding more energy at the same time it is limiting the supply of water to generate that energy. The more electricity is needed, the more water supplies are depleted. The more water supplies are depleted, the more electricity is needed to concoct new water and bring it to people—with larger pumps, longer pipelines, or energy-intensive desalination.[5]

The Catawba is only a small, southern stretch in the thousands of miles of rivers that quietly carry this energy burden for America. But the story of Duke Power and the Catawba reveals how it came to be that energy has tied up so much of the nation's water supply—and why it seems to be that the sector is last to join the blue revolution.

Born in a modest farmhouse outside Durham, North Carolina, in 1856, James Buchanan Duke is remembered as the most powerful of the early U.S. tobacco barons, and for his philanthropy, which turned the small Methodist Trinity College into the Ivy League of the American South. He spent most of his working life in New York City, where he built the American Tobacco Company and related businesses until his family controlled four-fifths of the U.S. tobacco production lines.[6] Duke also brought North Carolina's fragrant, golden-leafed tobacco to the world. Before the U.S. Supreme Court ordered the firms dissolved under the Sherman Anti-Trust Act in 1911, Duke family companies controlled 100 percent of America's cigarette exports.[7]

But James Duke had another particular passion, and that was water.

"Especially dramatically moving water," writes biographer Robert F. Durden, professor emeritus of history at Duke University.[8]

In the 1890s, as Duke aggressively acquired firms and soon surpassed three billion cigarettes manufactured a year, in his private life he began to buy parcels of what became a 2,200-acre estate on New Jersey's Raritan River. The times, much like the present, were marked both by conspicuous consumption—it was the Gay Nineties—and economic depression, with widespread unemployment.

Duke hired engineers, landscape architects, stonemasons, and builders to turn his river property into a water wonderland. He also bought controlling interest in the local Raritan Water Power Company to ensure a steady supply to the estate, called Duke Farms.[9]

His construction crews built a chain of nine lakes over 75 acres. They mounded the excavated land into knolls and hills reminiscent of the Carolina Piedmont. At the top of the chain, a two-million-gallon reservoir sent water from the Raritan tumbling from one lake to another. To enjoy the water in action, Duke had it "flowing over boulder-made rapids, and small dams, tumbling over craggy cliffs, and rising skyward in jet streams, falling in multiple arrangements, overflowing bowls and basins."[10]

The stone dams, waterfalls, and well houses were designed artfully among what Duke estimated were two million planted trees and shrubs, including blue spruce, native hardwoods, thousands of rhododendrons, and many tens of thousands of evergreens he ordered from Europe. Duke spent so much time on the water and the trees that he never built the mansion he'd planned—except for its grand, European-inspired fountains. *American Home and Gardens* in 1914 described the thirty-five gushing water features among "the most beautiful in the world."[11]

But, just like the fountains at Versailles, there simply wasn't enough water to run them all. One July day in 1907, Duke turned his entire wonderland on at once to impress his new wife, Nanaline. The system sucked so much of the river that the intake pipe downstream at the Raritan Woolen Mill ran dry and the plant had to temporarily shut down. By 1910, Duke engineers had fixed the problem, with a remarkably modern recycling system that recirculated twenty million gallons of water through the estate every day.[12]

In 1911, Duke was so angered by the Supreme Court's decision to dissolve his companies that he abruptly gave up on both his mansion and the domestic tobacco industry. He spent an increasing amount of time in London running his British-American Tobacco Company and came close to settling there permanently.[13]

What brought Duke home again was water, the "dramatically moving" kind he loved best. At the turn of the twentieth century, electric power was just beginning to light up the United States. Intrigued, Duke made a substantial investment in hydropower along the Catawba River. The investment would become "the most creative economic endeavor of his life," writes Robert F. Durden, who argues that Duke's hydropower work also represents "the most positive, long-lasting, and far-reaching impact on his native region and its economic health." It certainly changed the Catawba River forever.

With a small hydropower plant at his Raritan River estate, James Duke already understood the power of water. Now, experiments at Niagara Falls and in other parts of the country were proving its potential to electrify entire regions. Duke was heavily invested in textile manufacturing plants in the Carolinas. A competitor's mill had tapped a river and was running with "the cheapest power in the nation."[14]

Duke became interested in the Catawba, named for the Native Americans who lived along its banks beginning in the 1500s. The river originates on the eastern slopes of the Blue Ridge Mountains, flows through Charlotte, changes names to the Wateree River in South Carolina, and eventually joins with the Congaree, which carries it on to the Atlantic Ocean.[15] The trusted general manager of the Duke textile operations reported to the family in 1899 that he was "making a special effort quietly to learn the status of the Catawba River Falls, which is unquestionably the biggest thing in the South." The rocky, four-mile stretch is known as the Great Falls of the Catawba River, near the town of Great Falls in South Carolina.[16]

James Duke and his brother, Benjamin, who ran the North Carolina side of the family empire, lost no time buying up land and water rights along the Catawba. Durden writes that Duke "believed in carefully looking ahead and acquiring water rights as early as possible, long before the public announcement of a project."[17] In 1901, they bought Great Falls for the astonishing bargain of $42,000. Downriver, New York City physician and South Carolina native W. Gill Wylie had just built the first hydro station on the river at India Hook Shoals near Rock Hill, South Carolina. In 1904, he built the first of the river's dams, creating Lake Wylie, which straddles the Carolinas state line. The doctor hired engineers to design his larger vision, a series of plants all along the Catawba linked with dams and reservoirs to capture the power of the entire river. But he needed capital, an estimated $8 million, and of course he needed Great Falls.[18]

Company lore has it that James Duke became a captive audience to Wylie and his grand scheme when his foot got inflamed and the doctor treated it. Duke began to seriously analyze Wylie's business and engineering plans. In spring 1905, the men incorporated the Southern Power Co. in Charlotte. They immediately went to work on a $1.6 million plant at Great Falls. Soon, power lines delivered electricity first to Charlotte, later to Gastonia, Shelby, and other towns and mills throughout the Piedmont.[19]

Duke was especially interested in using electricity to recruit textile mills. Many businessmen were skeptical or frightened of the technology moving in on their coal and steam systems. One mill owner told a Southern Power engineer, "You must be drunk or a damned fool if you think I will bring electricity into my mill to kill my people." Duke agreed to finance those mills that were willing to locate in the region. By 1911, Southern Power had linked four hydro plants, Catawba, Great Falls, Rocky Creek, and Ninety-Nine Islands, and had begun to connect its transmission lines to other companies throughout the Southeast. *Electrical World* magazine called the network "by far the most extensive interconnected transmission system in the world."[20]

While Southern Power and its subsidiaries developed the northern section of the Catawba, James Duke organized another company, Wateree Power, to build plants on the South Carolina side, where the Catawba turns into the Wateree. The companies dammed up more of the Catawba after back-to-back hurricanes in summer 1916 destroyed plants and the Lake Wylie Dam and washed millions of Duke dollars down the river.[21]

Duke and Wylie's hydropower transformed the Piedmont, and especially Charlotte, from an impoverished farming area in the wake of the Civil War into a booming industrial economy with New South clout.

In the larger region, hydropower helped the rainy and river-rich eastern half of the United States overtake Britain as the world's greatest economic power at the turn of the twentieth century.[22] Between 1907 and 1929, American homes with electricity grew tenfold, to 85 percent. By 1930, Americans consumed more electricity than anyone else on the planet combined. Engineers soon figured out how to make giant, manmade alternatives to the power of naturally falling water, and hydro infrastructure spread industrial development west. Hoover Dam, on the Colorado River, completed in 1936, became the largest hydroelectric facility in the world.[23]

Today, as prolonged droughts in the arid southwestern United States sink water levels in Lake Mead to the point of threatening Hoover Dam's intake pipes, it has become the largest symbol of the need to change our thinking about water and how much we use. Especially to make power.

◆   ◆   ◆

In 1927, a few years after the death of James Duke, his various power concerns merged into the southern energy behemoth now known as Duke Energy. The $13 billion, publicly traded utility (NYSE: DUK) has had more influence on the waters of the Catawba than any other force, natural or artificial, in modern times.

Duke's dams altered the physical shape and flow of the Catawba, from the fast-flowing, rocky river pictured on turn-of-the-century postcards to today's chain of eleven branching reservoirs with water levels controlled by Duke Power. But the company also transformed the human ecology of the waterway almost as profoundly as hydro-power changed the Piedmont's industrial economy. Today, the lakes are known for massive shoreline golf course communities and mini-mansions more than for hydro, coal, and nuclear plants. This, too, is Duke's legacy.

After the company built its more-than-mile-long Cowans Ford Dam and created Lake Norman in the 1960s, it was sitting on a lot of excess real estate. Duke—first the man, then the utility—had been buying up Catawba land since 1901, some of it for as little as $1 an acre.[24] In 1969, the company created a real estate subsidiary called Crescent Resources, transferring thousands of its surplus acres along the river. Crescent instantly became one of the largest private land-owners in the Carolinas.[25] It developed upscale communities around Duke's northernmost lake—Lake James, as well as Lake Norman and Lake Wylie, and later expanded into luxury resorts in areas such as Hilton Head, South Carolina, and commercial and residential de-velopments in half a dozen states.[26] In 1996, the company was valued at $2.1 billion when Duke sold half of it to Morgan Stanley's real estate investment arm.[27] In 2009, Crescent filed for Chapter 11 bank-ruptcy reorganization in the wake of the housing bust.

One summer afternoon, a retired Charlotte contractor named C. D. Collins and his wife, Judy, offered to give me a tour of Lake Wylie on their pontoon boat, the *Pinch Me*. Fifty years ago, C. D. bought a tiny, remote fishing cabin in one of the river's curving coves not far from where Judy's parents owned a cabin. The couple met there, but it took them five decades to marry.

Today, they live in Collins's cabin, now dwarfed by three ostentatious mini-mansions crowded onto the point, their treeless, grassy lawns unfurled like a carpet all the way to the shore. Development practices have pushed so much silt and debris into the river that it's no longer navigable in places Collins used to zoom through. The couple is distressed by the impacts of development and energy production on the Catawba and its lakes. But they don't heap all the blame on Duke Energy. "We need the power," Collins says. "But there's got to be a better way."

Collins motors us to a 1957 coal plant called the Allen Steam Station. Except for the plant's new pollution scrubber, it looks like a scene from a half century ago. A train slowly rolls by at the waterfront to deliver a load of gleaming black fuel. Inside, Allen sucks in 785 million gallons of water a day,[28] coal-fires it to temperatures up to 1,000 degrees Fahrenheit to turn it into highly pressurized steam, then pipes the steam into a giant turbine that spins magnets inside wire coils to produce power. After its work in the turbine, the steam is drawn into a condenser in the plant's basement, cooled off, and turned back into water.[29]

Duke and other thermal-power-plant operators say it's not fair to compare their large water withdrawals to those in other sectors of the economy, because most of the water they use is returned to its source rather than consumed. That is true; however, the increasing conflicts in the United States over water for energy involve the vast amounts power generation makes unavailable for people and aquatic ecosystems—especially during times of drought. The returned water is also sent back at higher temperatures, which means that a good deal of it evaporates immediately.[30] The warmer water that is returned to lakes, rivers, and oceans from power plants is also biologically different than the water sucked in. Its temperature can be deadly to fish and other aquatic creatures. The U.S. Environmental Protection Agency blamed hot discharge water from the Brayton Point coal plant on the border of Massachusetts and Rhode Island for contributing to an 87 percent reduction in fish in Mt. Hope Bay.[31] North Carolina environmental regulators have granted the Allen plant a variance to release warmer water than state administrative law allows—up to 102 degrees Fahrenheit in the summer.[32] This is in direct conflict with the code's requirement that effluent should "in no case" exceed 89.6 degrees Fahrenheit.[33]

C. D. Collins steers upriver five miles to a canal that locals call the "hot hole." This is where the Allen plant's spent water flows back to the lake. I stick my feet in. It feels bathtub warm. David Merryman, a former Duke Energy chemist who, as one of a nationwide network of waterway wardens, serves as Catawba's Riverkeeper, blames the warm outfalls for fish and shellfish kills that tend to hit this area and some of the other lakes this time of year. Other scientists are unsure what combination of summer temperatures, the energy plants' water withdrawals, and warm-water returns are to blame for fish kills.[34]

Of all the impacts of living on an energy-producing reservoir, the one that worries C. D. and Judy Collins most is coal ash, the waste left over after plants burn coal. They never fretted about it until 2008, when an eighty-four-acre pond of the stuff collapsed in eastern Tennessee, sending more than a billion gallons of arsenic- and mercury-laden sludge into the Emory River and a nearby neighborhood. The spill, from the Tennessee Valley Authority's Kingston plant, damaged forty-two homes and created mounds of gray toxic waste locals called ashbergs.[35] Collins shows me the tall ash pile adjacent to the Allen plant. It will end up in the large ash pond Duke stores here at Lake Wylie. The company has four ash ponds on the Catawba, all on reservoirs used for drinking water.

The gray, pointy top of the ash pile juts up over the poplar trees at the riverside. It brings to mind the silvery, pointy top of the new Duke Energy Center in downtown Charlotte, stretching above the surrounding buildings. The week I visited Charlotte, Duke employees were just starting to move into the towering, ultraefficient headquarters downtown. The skyscraper had been under construction as the Wachovia Corporate Center when Wachovia was gobbled up by Wells Fargo.[36] With Charlotte banking giants Wachovia sold and Bank of America retrenching, Duke has become the most influential corporate player in town.[37] This is part of the reason that, with the exception of protests over its forthcoming Cliffside coal plant on the Broad River, few people fuss about Duke Energy in its hometown—a city that owes much to James Duke and his hydropower.

Duke is also one of the most generous corporate donors at the statehouse in Raleigh, where its political action committee is one of the top three in North Carolina sponsored by a single company, funneling $278,000 in 2008 statewide elections.[38] The fact that Duke could secure state regulatory approval for the coal plant in 2010, when similar proposals around the country were being scuttled over carbon concerns, is testament to its influence in the Tar Heel State.

Duke's gray ash pile stands for the dirty power generation of the past. The company is the third-largest corporate emitter of CO_2 in the nation, with 62 percent of its electricity coming from coal-fired plants. The corporate headquarters, awarded silver Leadership in Energy and Environmental Design (LEED) certification from the U.S. Green Building Council, symbolizes hope for clean energy in the future. Duke CEO James E. Rogers, nicknamed "the green coal baron" by the *New York Times,* has pledged to "decarbonize" Duke Energy by 2050.[39]

But long before he arrives at that carbon-constrained destination, Rogers and his fellow power brokers will have to face the limits of America's water supply.

Rogers touts nuclear energy as "tailor-made for climate change" for its lack of carbon emissions.[40] But this is another shade of green that ignores the blue. Coal and waste-incineration plants demand about thirty-six gallons of water per kilowatt-hour; natural gas plants, around fourteen gallons. The industry averages twenty-five gallons of water per kilowatt-hour. But nuclear facilities drink a much taller serving of water than any other type of power plant, demanding about forty-three gallons of water for every kilowatt-hour they generate.[41]

Here is what that means to American families: the average household burns about 30 kilowatt-hours of electricity a day.[42] That's 750 gallons of water a day per family, just to run the AC and keep the lights on. (And we thought 150 gallons of water a person was a lot. So-called virtual water calculators, which include water used not only for electricity but also for our cars, as well for the pounds of beef and veggies and grains consumed, put the per capita number closer to a thousand gallons of water a day for the average meat-eating American.)

No one paid much attention to the thirst of power plants until the early twenty-first century, when their demand for water began to clash with that of growing urban populations. Since then, water-scarcity worries have halted or held up new thermal plants across the country. In 2002, Tennessee's governor imposed a moratorium on new merchant power plants because of cooling constraints. Georgia Power lost a bid to draw water from the Chattahoochee River for cooling because of flow concerns. Arizona officials rejected at least two plants because of the potential stress to a local aquifer. Idaho opposed two natural gas plants, also because of impacts to an aquifer.[43]

Opponents of Duke Power's proposed nuclear reactors on the Broad River in South Carolina also are zeroing in on the facility's water use, especially during future droughts. In summer 2008, the Tennessee Valley Authority had to shut down one of three reactors at its Browns Ferry plant in Alabama because of low water levels.[44] In summer 2010, the plant—the TVA's largest nuclear facility—was again forced to operate at partial capacity. The slowdown cost the TVA $50 million it expected to pass on to customers.[45]

But nuclear energy isn't the only low-carbon power source with big water needs. At this point, every single alternative fuel source being considered for large-scale power generation is projected to further hike freshwater demand.[46] The nation's current favored ethanol source is particularly thirsty. As corn-based ethanol production doubled between 2005 and 2008, related water use has more than tripled.[47]

Large-scale solar plants are no exception. The most well-known solar technologies, the photovoltaic panels you see on rooftops, use almost no water. But photovoltaic isn't yet cost or energy efficient on a large scale. That's why most plants under construction rely on a technology called concentrating solar power. CSP plants collect sunlight with solar panels and use the heat to create steam just like traditional power plants do. To make the steam and cool the system, CSP facilities can demand as much water as nuclear or coal plants. And the most attractive sites for the operations—wide-open deserts, namely—also happen to be the hottest and most water-scarce places in the United States.[48]

In 2010, California energy regulators made Genesis Solar, a subsidiary of Florida Power & Light, change the design of its 250-megawatt CSP plant before it could break ground. Original plans called for pumping 1,600 acre-feet of groundwater a year from the site—in the middle of the Sonoran Desert. Genesis reduced that by a factor of eight by switching to an air-cooled system. But solar-energy companies rushing to build the plants on federal and state lands before financial incentives from the 2009 federal stimulus bill expire have been protesting the air-cooling alternative because it's more expensive.[49]

Wind power appears to be the water-friendliest form of alternative energy. Like photovoltaic panels, wind also uses a tiny amount of water—just enough to wash the blades off in arid climates where rainfall doesn't keep them clean.[50] But Duke and other companies devote an equally tiny sliver of their energy portfolios to wind, which provides less than 2 percent of power nationwide.[51] Duke often touts its ramped-up investment in wind farms, yet the turbines have been slow to turn the company's net U.S. megawatt-hour generation. In 2009, it remained 62 percent coal, 5 percent natural gas/oil, 30 percent nuclear, 2 percent hydro, and only 1 percent wind.[52]

Water hasn't become an urgent enough element of the energy debate to influence utility portfolios—at least not yet. Investment is lacking to ramp up from laboratory prototypes to utility-scale reality. It's still cheaper to keep mining coal. Inventor Saul Griffith, a MacArthur "genius grant" winner and cofounder of the San Francisco–based wind startup Makani Power, has spent years and millions invested by Google to develop a promising technology to capture wind at high altitudes, thousands of feet above traditional turbines. The experience taught him that "no obvious financial mechanism exists to take a company like Makani from prototype to industrial implementation."

In the meantime, Griffith, who earned his engineering doctorate from the Massachusetts Institute of Technology, has come to believe the most urgent environmental need "is not for some miraculous-seeming scientific breakthrough but for a vast, unprecedented transformation of human behavior."[53]

In other words, we all could use a lot less energy, and a lot less water. Each resource is integral to the other. Just as we've never paid much attention to how much water it takes to make energy, we've ignored the amount of energy it takes to pump and pipe water. Turns out, moving water around is one of the most energy-intensive things we do as a society. Take California's State Water Project, the largest single user of energy in the Golden State. To deliver water from the Delta to Southern California, the project pumps water 2,000 feet up and over the Tehachapi Mountains—the highest lift of any water system in the world. The energy it takes to transfer that water to residential customers in Southern California is equal to one-third of total average household electric use in the region.[54]

If we can figure out how to move water over mountains, surely we can figure out how to use less of it.

Exactly one hundred years after the U.S. Supreme Court broke up James Duke's cigarette empire, the utility that carries his name found itself at the center of another high-court drama. The battle was over water; the combatants, North Carolina and South Carolina. But this time, the company entered the fray by choice.

In 1991, North Carolina's legislature passed a law that said water could be moved within the state, from one river basin to another, to meet the needs of growing communities. In the middle of a severe drought in 2002, Charlotte-Mecklenburg Utilities took advantage of the law to transfer thirty-three million gallons a day from the Catawba to the Rocky River Basin in the city's northern suburbs. Downstream in South Carolina, Catawba River levels ran so low that the only thing flowing in major tributaries was discharge from wastewater-treatment plants.[55]

In 2007, two suburbs, Concord and Kannapolis, landed a permit to pull up to ten million gallons of water a day from the Catawba and return the treated wastewater to the closer Rocky River Basin. Those were the last straws for South Carolina, which relies on the Catawba to supply eight counties, along with irrigation, industrial, mining, and other water needs.[56]

States that share water resources and disagree about how to divvy them up generally solve their disputes in one of three ways: States can come up with their own water-sharing agreement and enter into a compact. Congress, with its authority over interstate commerce, can approve a division of water. Or states can put their fate in the hands of the U.S. Supreme Court, which has "original jurisdiction" in such disputes.[57] Saying his state had struck out on number one, South Carolina attorney general Henry McMaster went for number three.

In June 2007, as drought again choked the Catawba's lakes and stream beds, McMaster went to the Supreme Court with the claim that North Carolina had violated the U.S. Constitution by taking more than its fair share of the river. Duke Energy, which has controlled the Catawba for more than a century, was not about to stand by and let the river be divided without its input. Duke owns almost all the land under the reservoirs that it made and has officially managed the river since 1958 through the Federal Energy Regulatory Commission (FERC) license that allows it to operate its eleven reservoirs and thirteen hydroelectric plants.

The company has been working toward its new, 50-year FERC license since 2003. It convened eighty-five local, regional, state, and federal parties with interests in the Catawba for nearly a decade to develop a long-term management plan for the river, including extensive protocols for drought. The 62,000-page document covers everything from fish management to how much water flows through dams to public access to beaches. One point that won whitewater enthusiasts over, for example, was scheduled releases of water over Great Falls, the once-rushing, 2-mile stretch of canyon in South Carolina that had been dried up by Duke's oldest dams.[58] In the end, seventy of the eighty-five participants signed off on the plan. David Merryman with the Catawba Riverkeeper Foundation, one of the organizations that did not, says Duke wields so much power that people lose sight of the fact that its primary responsibilities as a corporation are to shareholders and the bottom line rather than the Catawba. Despite all its consensus building, Merryman says, the company still demands too much water to make power, and still pays too little attention to the quality of water in its reservoirs.

Merryman hoped to see an interstate compact between the Carolinas that equitably shares the river, makes water quality a top priority, and considers Duke a major stakeholder of the river—but not its king. Instead, Duke got the royal treatment. First, Duke, along with the City of Charlotte, filed to become official interveners in the case, with Duke's lawyer arguing that the utility is more than a "mere" user of the river. "There is no one else like Duke on the Catawba," he told the justices.[59] The justices approved Duke's motion—and denied Charlotte's—over the objections of attorneys with the U.S. Department of Justice, who argued that a private company, particularly "the largest consumer of water on the Catawba River," should not be entitled to intervene in an original jurisdiction case between two states.[60]

Later in 2010, the attorneys general of North Carolina and South Carolina announced they had reached a settlement in the dispute based on Duke Energy's management plan and low-flow protocols for the Catawba.

One afternoon, under a brilliant, Carolina-blue sky, not far from Duke's new corporate headquarters in downtown Charlotte, I had lunch with Steven Jester, the company's vice president for hydro strategy, licensing, and lakes. Jester has handsome silver locks, a gray suit, silver eyeglasses, and a jeweler's precision with language: "There's no one who better understands this river and its reservoirs," he says. "Our understanding spans one hundred years, droughts and floods, and now, our understanding is shaped by people, industry, and governments who've thought about what's best for this river basin for fifty years into the future. We gave all those stakeholders a voice. We included science, emotions, worry about grandchildren, worry about the environment, all in one document. In my entire life, I've never witnessed a better piece of regional thinking.

"You have one state suing another state, and we represent both," Jester adds. The best proof that Duke can sustainably manage the Catawba, he posits, is the region's emergence from the record drought of 2007–2008 with no loss of either water or power. Jester keeps using the word *responsibility*: Duke has an enormous responsibility to the river. Part of Duke's responsibility is to show others their responsibility—to help other water users see that small changes can save a lot of water. But it takes him most of our lunchtime to answer my primary question: what about Duke Energy? Does he agree that an ethic for water use must apply to everyone—not just us citizens taking care not to overwater our lawns but to the nation's utilities as well?

Duke's low-flow protocols for the Catawba lay out in detail how all the river's *other* dependents will reduce water use at various drought triggers; the corporation, though, has sole discretion over its use during such emergencies. The Catawba-Wateree Water Management Group, a nonprofit organization made up of Duke and seventeen public water system owners along the Catawba, is funding programs to help local utilities manage demand and find smart irrigation technologies to "help lakeside residents better manage their lawn-watering systems," according to Duke There was no similar urgency to curtail demand for power-related water use.[61]

Shouldn't Duke be trying to figure out how to use a lot less water, too? Jester finally says that while his PR guy who is sitting with us may not like it, he concurs: "We have no less responsibility to reduce our reliance and use of water in a mindful way," he says, "and to reduce our water footprint."

Before I left Charlotte, I needed to make one last stop. I knew I'd arrived when I saw the large spraying fountain James Duke built in the front yard of his mansion in the Myers Park neighborhood. This Colonial summer home was the base for Duke's hydropower interests on the Catawba, the place where he could introduce his beloved only child, Doris Duke, to her Southern heritage.[62] In 1919, Duke famously piped the Catawba twelve miles to Myers Park, at the time a streetcar suburb, to create four large water features. The most famous, the Wonder Fountain, shot river water 150 feet into the air from a round pool and drew visitors from Charlotte and beyond.

Today, the only water features left from James Duke's time are a tall front yard fountain and a small lion's head that trickles water from a garden wall. The Duke Mansion itself was preserved by a nonprofit organization, but its sprawling fourteen-acre grounds and Wonder Fountain were urbanized long ago. Modern Charlotte had bigger ambitions. Modern American does, too. But its endless demands for energy and water may prove humbling.

The nation's energy and water problems are remarkably similar. So are the solutions: focusing on the demand side rather than constantly growing the supply side will help save the nation's water resources and billions of dollars. At the very least, we should put the water and energy conversations together. What good will it do to build an army of biofuel plants if there's not enough water to run them—or enough to irrigate the crops that fuel them?

CHAPTER 5

Taproot of the Crisis

Tucked between the merging metros of Tampa and Orlando, the community of Plant City, Florida, likes to call itself the winter strawberry capital of the world. A rare Florida freeze threatened that title in January 2010, with plunging temperatures that dusted nearby Walt Disney World with snow and hung palm fronds with icicles.

To protect their fruit, strawberry growers, along with citrus farmers in the region, went on a groundwater-pumping binge. If farmers can keep a steady flow of water on their fruit during freezing winter nights, they have a chance—and it's just a chance—of saving it. As groundwater at 70 degrees Fahrenheit meets freezing air and transforms to ice, it releases heat. Oranges, berries and other fruits encased in a layer of ice remain a survivable 32 degrees, even as the air dips much lower.[1]

How well the efforts worked to save the fruit is a matter of debate; Florida's farmers lost about 30 percent of their crops in the freeze.[2] But what happened to the Floridan Aquifer was pretty obvious. The cavernous limestone aquifer underlies almost all of Florida, as well as southern Alabama, southeastern Georgia, and lower South Carolina. It's holey in the way we imagine moon rocks, and prone to surface collapses called sinkholes. In nature, sinkholes form gradually over years, becoming lakes and other depressions in the land. But geologists say that human activity—specifically dredging, building reservoirs, diverting surface water, and pumping groundwater—speeds up the process, "resulting in the abrupt formation of collapse-type sinkholes, some of which are spectacular."[3]

The word brings to mind the gaping sinkhole that swallowed a nearby Porsche dealership in 1981.[4] But in winter 2010, central Florida's farmers made some spectacular holes as well. To protect their ripening fruit, they ran hundreds of industrial pumps nonstop for eleven nights in a row. The massive water withdrawal dropped the level of the aquifer sixty feet in a week and a half. One hundred and forty sinkholes opened up in communities surrounding the farms.[5] Seven hundred and fifty residential wells dried up. An underground chasm closed Plant City's Trapnell Elementary School, which remained shuttered for three months while engineers plugged the ground with concrete grout to make it safe for students to return. In the interim, the kids attended a school called Strawberry Crest.[6]

One sinkhole took a bite out of Interstate 4, snarling traffic on the arterial highway between Tampa and Orlando for several days.[7] Sinks yawned open under homes and sheds, yards and driveways. "No one can guess whose house or street might suddenly cave in," the local paper reported.[8]

Residents whose homes collapsed into sinkholes were the lucky ones; their insurance companies ponied up replacement value and helped them move out. Those whose homes merely shifted and sprung cracks got the same grout injection as Trapnell. Even with no obvious sinkhole, they're trapped—unable to sell homes in neighborhoods once known for their proximity to pastoral berry fields but now derided as "sinkhole subdivisions."[9]

Farmers and water managers called it an unprecedented event they never could have predicted. But it was not the first time freeze pumping had set off a scourge of sinks. A three-day freeze in 1985 opened up twenty-seven sinkholes in the same area; a six-day chill in 1977 opened up twenty-two.[10]

In the past, the sinks and dried-up wells affected mostly the farmers themselves, and sympathetic rural neighbors who understood the event as one of country living's trade-offs. By 2010, however, so many subdivisions, schools, and streets had been planted on former agricultural lands east of Tampa that Plant City was now suburbia for the nineteenth-largest metro area in the nation. The pumping disrupted thousands of families and required millions of dollars in repairs. Newcomers didn't know to shut off wells when farmers ramped up theirs, and when the aquifer plummeted, backyard-well motors burned out. Residents showed up angry at public meetings organized by the Southwest Florida Water Management District, some of them waving thousand-dollar repair bills.[11]

"Isn't it hypocritical . . . to allow farmers to pump this water when they plant, and during frost/freeze events, but then homeowners are put on water restrictions?" asked Plant City resident Bruce Allen. "You don't see any inconsistency in that?"[12]

"Who would want to buy a home in the Plant City area now?" asked homeowner Bill Reed, who spoke of tumbling market values and skyrocketing insurance costs. "The homeowners may contribute more to the economy than the strawberry farmers, but nobody seems to care."[13]

Indeed, the largest chasm cracked open that winter was the one between farmers and suburban Floridians. Such unfortunate fractures over water were spreading across the nation, pitting Americans against the farmers who feed them.

Farmers, like energy providers, once had a bountiful supply of the nation's water to themselves. They got used to using a lot of it. If you don't count the tepid water that power plants return to their source, agriculture taps three-fourths of all the water used each day in the United States. This makes agriculture the deepest root of America's water crisis—and the one with the most potential to solve it.

Unlike water for power, most irrigation water is consumed, meaning it doesn't necessarily make its way back to the stream or aquifer where it came from. Some runs off into ditches and canals, flowing eventually into rivers and out to sea. That soaked up by plants is ultimately released as evapotranspiration and sent back into the atmosphere. In turn, atmospheric moisture forms clouds, which create precipitation. But the rain could fall over the ocean, or in an already wet region.[14]

New technologies have farmers pulling up a little less each year to irrigate more total crop acreage. Sprinkler and microirrigation systems now account for a little more than half of America's sixty million irrigated acres.[15] Yet that means the other half are still quenched as if we had an endless supply of water. Hydrologists say the transition isn't happening nearly fast enough to save the nation's aquifers.

One of the largest aquifers in the world, the High Plains Aquifer, which stretches beneath eight states from the Great Plains to the Southwest, is undergoing the most serious and best-known groundwater depletion in the country. Irrigation systems for wheat, corn, and other crops pump High Plains fossil water from hundreds of feet underground at between 800 and 1,200 gallons a minute. Most of that is never returned, and there is no means of replenishment; the aquifer's glacial source melted some ten thousand years ago.[16]

The High Plains Aquifer once held more water than would flow through the Colorado River in two centuries.[17] Industrial irrigation managed to deplete a third of that in a mere thirty years, between 1960 and 1990.[18] In California, farmers had depleted their groundwater earlier, leading to the north-south river transfers of the Central Valley Project and the State Water Project. Groundwater pumping in the San Joaquin Valley between 1925 and 1977 caused one of the single-largest human alterations of surface topography anywhere on Earth: near Mendota, California, in those years, the very ground sunk twenty-eight feet.[19]

The decimation of aquifers in the High Plains and in California is well known, often cast as an unfortunate price paid for the bounty of the nation's breadbasket and its fruit bowl—two of the most productive agricultural regions in the world. But groundwater is vanishing in every region of the country—even the wet East.

Across the East, farmers drained wetlands for agriculture, then turned around to irrigate the reclaimed land for crops. Rice farming in the Arkansas Delta has dropped the Mississippi River Alluvial Aquifer ninety feet in a century.[20] Arkansas farmers have known since the early 1930s that they would eventually drain the Alluvial. Now that it's happened—the aquifer is expected to be depleted for commercial use by 2015—the region is shifting to a major diversion of the White River to flood rice fields.[21] Trepidation over that plan has been considerable ever since it was proposed sixty years ago, even among the farmers who will benefit from it. Environmentalists are concerned about the nearby White River and Cache River Wildlife Refuges, where wetlands and bottomland forests have dried up along with the aquifer. Hunters and related industries worry, too, about the impacts on wetland habitats crucial to the region's lucrative duck-hunting trade.[22]

Others oppose the White River diversion on economic grounds, disapproving of a $1,525-an-acre irrigation benefit to an already heavily subsidized industry.[23]

In Northern California, bright green sprigs of young rice plants shoot up in vast, flooded fields that stretch for miles along the highways, making one of the most water-stressed parts of the nation look like a Louisiana swamp. Arkansas grows more rice than any other state, but California boasts the highest yields, in part because growers keep their fields submerged. The fields lie four to six inches under water for most of the season to achieve the maximum yield on more than 500,000 acres statewide. Despite this practice, rice farmers estimate they are doubling crop yields since the 1960s while using about 40 percent less water. The savings are attributed to modern technologies that laser-level fields and more carefully control flow.[24]

During intense debates over water allocation in California's last drought, environmentalists decried the "virtual water" exports in rice, one of the most water-intensive crops in the West, given scarce supplies.[25]

Professor Tony Allan of King's College in London was awarded the Stockholm Water Prize in 2008 for his concept of virtual water— a measure of how water is embedded in the production and trade of food and consumer products and exported by countries. With the matrix of virtual water, Allan has helped nations see how they ship water around the globe in everything from short-grain rice to iPods. The United States, according to virtual-water calculations, is the world's largest net exporter of water, sending out of the country about a third of the water it uses to grow agricultural crops and make consumer goods. Much of that is in grains, exported either directly or via meat.[26]

The United States exports about half its rice crop, most to Latin America.[27] But farmers are simply doing what makes economic sense for them. Federal policies make it profitable to grow thirsty crops in water-stressed places, the Sacramento–San Joaquin and Arkansas Deltas being only two of them. Some of the most generous U.S. subsidies buoy the most water-intensive crops, especially rice, wheat, corn, soybeans, sugar, and cotton.[28] Government payments to the rice sector are particularly large compared to those for most other crops, averaging nearly 40 percent of rice farmers' gross receipts between 2002 and 2006.[29]

Federal water schemes, from the Central Valley Project in California to the Central and Southern Florida Project, are agricultural subsidies, too, just like farm credit, export promotions, and university extension services. American irrigation subsidies are some of the largest in the world, amounting to $4.4 billion a year in the western United States alone.[30] They date to the Reclamation Act of 1902, which encouraged families to settle and farm the country's arid and semiarid regions. But today's industrial irrigation is not what boosters like William Smythe, editor and publisher of *Irrigation Age* in the late 1800s, had in mind. Smythe believed that "the miracle of irrigation" would further the cause of democracy, and that the West would "become the egalitarian domain of small, prosperous farmers," fulfilling the Jeffersonian ideal of the independent yeoman.[31] It led to just the opposite. Over time, the number of acres on which farmers could qualify for subsidized water increased sixfold, from 160 acres to 960, helping lead to today's mega-farms. During the twentieth century, the number of farms in America fell by 65 percent—about the same percentage by which farms grew in size.[32]

Has the nation's water crisis become severe enough that we should rethink subsidies where industrial irrigation is doing irreparable harm? What about trade policies? Sugarcane has been able to flourish in the Everglades thanks to the flood-control project, tariff and import policies such as the Cuban sugar embargo, and subsidies and price controls that keep sugar expensive for Americans.[33] Should saving America's freshwater become a key consideration in such foreign trade policies?

At the very least, we could shift the nature of subsidies to stave off more water losses. Many small and midsize farmers can't convert to precision irrigation and other water-saving technologies, because their margins are so small. Helping farmers use less is often a wiser investment than building new supply projects that goad them to use more.

In the twenty-first century, local, state, and federal governments have upped incentives to help farmers pay for new technologies that slash water use. After the sinkhole scourge, the Southwest Florida Water Management District paid three-fourths the cost for any upgrade that would cut a farm's pumping in half. Farmers lined up to install tailwater-recovery ponds, which collect excess irrigation and rainwater for reuse, soil-moisture probes and weather stations to prevent overwatering, and other technologies.

But nationwide, funding for these programs is a drop in the bucket compared with traditional agricultural and irrigation subsidies. And one sector that is a particular drain on water is getting a particular boost from the government.

In 1925, Henry Ford told the *New York Times* that ethanol would be "the fuel of the future." His Model T was designed to run on gasoline, ethanol, or both. But ethanol would be the best bet for America long term, he believed: "There is fuel in every bit of vegetable matter that can be fermented. There's enough alcohol in one year's yield of an acre of potatoes to drive the machinery necessary to cultivate the fields for a hundred years."[34]

The point was crucial to Ford because Midwestern family farms like the one he grew up on in Michigan were facing an economic crisis that would soon worsen in the Great Depression. He promoted ethanol as a way to boost markets for American corn. Black-and-white photographs from the 1930s show Nebraskans fueling their Fords at corn-ethanol blend stations, juicy ears of maize painted on the tall fuel pumps. Thomas Edison and Alexander Graham Bell were among those who joined Ford in calling for homegrown fuel. But ethanol ended up on the historic road not taken after some dramatic twists and turns driven in part by cheaper petroleum prices. In any case, it did not turn out to be the panacea Ford imagined.[35]

Nor is it quite the elixir hoped to cure the nation's current dependence on petroleum—at least not when made from corn. When oil prices spiked in 2007, along with violence and uncertainty in the Middle East, Congress overhauled U.S. energy policy with the Energy Independence and Security Act. The original aim was to cut petroleum subsidies to encourage private investment in alternative fuels. But the well of government largesse proved impossible to cap: Congress illogically kept the petroleum subsidies and created huge new ones for biofuels to help reduce our oil dependence. Ultimately, Congress settled on a strategy to improve fuel efficiency in our cars and require a higher percentage of biofuels in our tanks. The act calls for a nearly fivefold increase in U.S. ethanol production, to 117 billion liters—that's almost 31 billion gallons—by 2022. By 2015, nearly half of that is supposed to come from corn ethanol.

The ramp-up has serious unintended consequences for America's freshwater. Demand for corn has pushed crops beyond relatively rainy states such as Kentucky, Ohio, and Iowa, where it grows with little to no irrigation. Now, the ethanol craze has farmers planting more corn in states such as California, Colorado, and Nebraska—where it needs a lot of water, and where water resources are some of the most threatened in the country.

Scientists always knew corn ethanol would be a thirsty proposition. They estimated that between 263 and 784 liters of water would be required to grow and convert corn for each liter of fuel. But in the driest western states, researchers have found the water usage needs to be much higher than they projected, as much as 2,138 liters of water for one liter of ethanol.[36]

The drain on aquifers is only part of the problem. Of the agricultural water that does return to nature, roughly 30 percent is contaminated with nutrients, soil particles, pesticides, minerals, and salts picked up on the farm.[37] Midwestern cornfields send large amounts of fertilizer into streams that meet up with the Mississippi as it flows to the Gulf of Mexico. As they make their way into the Gulf, the nutrients feed giant algae blooms that suck up oxygen as they decompose, wiping out sea life. The result is Gulf hypoxia, occurring in a widening dead zone that at times is as large as Massachusetts.[38]

All of this makes biofuels little more sustainable than petroleum—"at least not in the way we practice row-crop agriculture to produce the feedstocks for bioethanol and biodiesel in the United States today," says Jerald Schnoor, an environmental-engineering professor at the University of Iowa.[39]

Nearly thirty years ago, Schnoor was one of the first scientists to model the impacts of acid rain on aquatic ecosystems—and the solutions that helped clean up the nation's watersheds. He's convinced that the models for sustainable biofuels are out there, too: they include municipal and yard wastes, wheat straw and other nonedible parts of grain crops, woody trees like poplars or willows, and perennials such as sweet sorghum and switchgrass. Perennials have long roots that hold soils in place and tap deep sources of water—meaning they require little to no irrigation. They are more resilient than the annuals we rely on for agricultural crops. Switchgrass was once one of the most ubiquitous prairie plants on the Great Plains. Schnoor envisions a day when it dominates the prairies once more, creating fuels as it enhances bird habitat, improves water quality, and captures carbon in the soils.[40]

A water ethic for agriculture means this sort of holistic thinking—about where to grow which crops, their water demands, their impact on soils, their fit with local ecosystems. At least that's how Aldo Leopold envisioned it.

"There are two spiritual dangers in not owning a farm," Leopold wrote in *A Sand County Almanac,* which recounts many of his own farming experiences at his Wisconsin River property. "One is the danger of supposing that breakfast comes from the grocery, and the other that heat comes from the furnace."[41]

Leopold had both great affinity for farmers and great concerns about the agricultural practices of his time. Just as he drafted America's ecological conscience, Leopold articulated the wisdom of sustainable agriculture before its time.[42] Then and now, agriculture missed the "complex web of living relationships" that Leopold considered key to the land ethic, says farmer-philosopher Fred Kirschenmann. Leopold's web included not only water but also soil, climate, biodiversity, husbandry, and much else. "Yet we still manage farms as if all of their parts, including water, are separate entities," Kirschenmann says.[43]

A distinguished fellow at Iowa State University's Leopold Center for Sustainable Agriculture, Kirschenmann converted his family's North Dakota farm to organic in the 1970s. It was a natural outgrowth of his father's teaching. His parents began their life together farming in 1930, during the Dust Bowl. They understood that the devastation was not solely about the lack of water but also about the way the land had been used. Rain scarcity was the immediate cause, but farming methods had devastated the soil. "As a result, my father became a radical conservationist, and from the time I was five years old, I can remember him admonishing me to 'take care of the land,'" Kirschenmann says. "As far as he was concerned, that was the most important moral duty imposed on any farmer—not only for the sake of the land but also for the economic survival of the farmer."[44]

That moral duty was the same articulated by Leopold in his call for "extension of the social conscience from people to land." It was no coincidence that Leopold's land ethic also emerged in the wake of the agricultural disaster of the Dust Bowl. Yet he predicted that agriculture would have the toughest time embracing the ethic, given the lack of economic value attached to ecosystems and because "scientific agriculture was actively developed before ecology was born."[45]

Kirschenmann says his farm's conversion took a lot of tweaking, still ongoing. But in the first decade, he hit on a crop rotation that controlled weeds, recycled nutrients, reduced disease, and, perhaps most important, improved the soils. In 1988, when North Dakota was hit with one of the worst droughts in its history, Kirschenmann's land absorbed and retained enough moisture to sustain his crops. His fields produced a decent harvest, while conventional fields around him dried up and yielded nothing.[46]

Despite those results, he doesn't consider his farm resilient enough for a future with less water, higher fuel costs, and the rising numbers of extreme weather events that climate scientists predict for the Midwest. In the short term, Kirschenmann is increasing the perennial grasses and legumes in his crop rotations. Someday, he hopes to be able to convert annual grains to perennials—the dream of an increasing number of farmers and scientists who are worried about the impacts of agriculture on water, land, and energy resources.

Writing in the journal *Science* in 2010, soil scientists from Washington State University and the Land Institute of Kansas said a transition from annuals to perennial grains—that is, grains that regrow each year, rather than having to be replanted—"would be one of the largest innovations in the 10,000-year history of agriculture." Perennial grains—which at this point exist only in experimental strains—have longer growing seasons than annual crops and deeper roots that reduce erosion and build up soils. They require far less fertilizer and herbicides. Reaching 10 to 12 feet below the surface, their roots can better tap into water as they create paths for rainfall to recharge aquifers. Annual grains can lose five times the water of perennial crops and thirty-five times the nitrate—a valuable plant nutrient that pollutes drinking water when it flows off fields. The authors said it could take as long as twenty years before the experimental perennial grains are ready for prime time. However, breakthroughs could come sooner with more research and investment into their breeding.[47]

Also still in the laboratory are the technologies that could break down cellulose in switchgrass and other perennials to turn them into starch and sugar for fermentation into biofuels. That makes the nation's research funding and its universities key accelerators for the blue revolution. Unfortunately, some agricultural research is putting on the brakes instead.

One Nation, Under Sod

When you talk to farmers about water policy, they like to make two points: One, we need to eat. Two, keeping food supply in the United States is a matter of national security; it's not a good idea to become overreliant on the rest of the globe for food, any more than we should depend on other nations for oil. Both points are true. But here is another truth: farmers in Florida passed a poignant milestone in 2000. As of that year, oranges were no longer Florida's top crop. The number-one crop in the Sunshine State for the past decade has been landscape materials, primarily sod and shrubbery.[48] The state's license plates, instead of that iconic image of two plump oranges, should sport a square of green turfgrass.

Sod and shrubs are not food, of course. Nor are they matters of national security. But they are thirsty commodities that go on to require a lifetime of irrigation. Sod is a high-value crop, with about 400,000 acres in production over all fifty states and an annual value of more than $3 billion.[49] Growers harvest it with a mechanical slicer that cuts thatched 16" × 24" rectangles, or 24" × 60" rolls of grass, from the earth, along with a layer of soil. They pile it onto pallets and truck the heavy heaps to Home Depot and Lowe's, where it's sold to patch and expand America's 63,240 square miles of grass. Thirsty cotton may be the fabric of our lives, but sod is the fabric of our landscapes, from highway medians to mini-estates.

Part of the $80 billion U.S. landscaping industry, the sod profession touts a product as green as it looks.[50] Turfgrass helps reduce soil erosion. It captures stormwater runoff. It helps recharge aquifers. It absorbs carbon. The industry uses research results from remote-sensing expert Cristina Milesi at California State University, Monterey Bay to show that America's turfgrass could store thirty-six billion pounds of carbon a year. But Milesi says emissions from lawn mowers sputtering to and fro across the nation's grass, along with energy to pump water for irrigation, make the overall benefit small.[51]

If virtual-water calculations considered future demand as well as the water it takes to make commodities, sod's footprint would grow to the nineteen trillion gallons of water a year Milesi calculates. That's more than three times the irrigation demands of all the corn in the country.[52]

No doubt, turfgrass has its place in American culture: it feels good on bare feet; it's just right for kicking a ball; it smells good when you cut it. All those things are worth some of our water supply. But surely not 19 trillion gallons. Around the nation, some cities and real estate developers are reenvisioning green-carpeted landscapes and replacing sod with beautiful native grasses. They are leaving or restoring large swaths of urban space to forest and wetlands, eliminating irrigation and speeding groundwater recharge. Yet some leaders trying to steer their communities onto an ethical water path have found themselves up against an unlikely barrier: their own public research universities.

In 1862, the federal Morrill Act established land-grant universities to bring advanced practical research to Americans who didn't have access to higher education. Over time, Congress also asked these colleges to build networks of experiment stations and sent extension agents into rural areas to bring research to farmers. In recent years, university extension has turned its attention to the environmental challenges facing communities, from climate change to pressures on freshwater.

But research funding and personnel directed to the new path remain only a fraction of that devoted to the old. And in some instances, agricultural researchers have worked against local communities trying to change their water fortunes. In 2005, researchers at the Texas Cooperative Extension arm of Texas A&M University, working with the Turf Grass Producers of Texas, disputed San Antonio's decision to ban some grasses, including the widely used St. Augustine variety. At the University of Florida in recent years, researchers with the Institute of Food and Agricultural Sciences, which is partially funded by the turf industry, have recommended an *increase* in suggested fertilizer-application guidelines at the same time local governments around the state have been trying to enact ordinances to *reduce* nitrogen runoff into local waterways.[53]

Meanwhile at the University of California at Davis, agricultural economist Steven Blank calls "golf courses, nurseries, and turf farms" the only truly sustainable sector in American agriculture—because it will supply the greenery for city living and playing in our increasingly urban future.[54]

The nation's tapped-out aquifers and shrinking rivers are part of Blank's argument that most farming in America will come to its natural end. In his book *The End of Agriculture in the American Portfolio*, he predicts a time when the United States will import nearly all its food from other countries. Costs for land and labor, he writes, will become too high for American farmers to compete with their global counterparts. Depletion of the High Plains Aquifer and others will give farmers in key regions "no choice but to leave agriculture."[55]

Blank says we shouldn't lament his ultraurban vision of the future, grudgingly shared by a growing number of people in conventional agriculture, in which rural areas with open spaces will be transformed into residential developments for an increasingly affluent population. Communities of interest will replace physical communities, as telecommuters work thousands of miles from their offices.[56]

Of course, just like the dire visions of a parched American future in which we've overdrawn every aquifer and river in the land, it doesn't *have* to be this way. And by the looks of our newfound love for local farms and food, it won't be.

Inside the city limits of Milwaukee, farmer and MacArthur Fellowship winner Will Allen grows food for thousands of urbanites on two acres at his nonprofit farm, Growing Power. Six greenhouses grow twelve thousand pots of herbs, salad mix, beet greens, arugula, mustards, and sprouts. Interspersed among the plants are hydroponic systems growing tilapia, perch, and a variety of salad greens along with bins of wriggler worms—the key to the farm's rich soil. The small plot also houses chickens, goats, ducks, rabbits, and bees. The whole system demands less water than either irrigated agriculture or the urban-scapes the farm replaced, because its water needs are met via rainwater catchment and recycling systems that keep water flowing in a loop in which fish ponds fertilize plants and plants clean up fish ponds.

Allen is among a new breed of American farmers who embody Thomas Jefferson's vision of the yeoman spanning rural and urban life, growing food to enrich local communities and keep the nation self-sufficient. In 2010, private entrepreneurs began to launch commercial rollouts for Allen's aquaculture/agriculture model in other parts of the country.

While Allen turns abandoned factories into fish farms, farmer turned land planner Matthew "Quint" Redmond, in Golden, Colorado, is taking on both industrial irrigation and the lawn. Redmond wants to replace stretches of sod with community farms that use less water as they feed local residents and supply restaurants. Where golf courses border subdivisions, Redmond sees borders of herbs and gourmet lettuce; sand traps become kale traps. Where parking lots surround office buildings, Redmond envisions vegetable-crop lots. Workers on break from their cubicles can pull weeds or just enjoy the scenery. "When you do it really well, agriculture is stunningly beautiful," says Redmond. "That's why property values in Sonoma are so high."[57]

One of Redmond's companies, TSR Agristruction, is part landscape-design firm, part community farm. Homeowners and landowners hire Redmond to build gardens or farms, for personal use or to join his community-agriculture program, which harvests the produce year-round for sale to local restaurants. Redmond uses geographic-information-system technologies to analyze demand for produce by census track. He figures out how many calories each track would consume, and how many plants are needed to grow those calories. He waters with satellite-controlled computer systems that monitor moisture and drip-irrigate in forty-eight zones. In the first couple of years, the company has turned a profit and repaid landowners between $3,000 and $4,000 per acre per year. But the owners seem happiest with the beautification of their land, and with the fact that they no longer have landscape-maintenance costs.

Longer term, Redmond wants to develop former industrial croplands into agricultural-urban communities, a concept he calls Agriburbia. His first project, proposed for Milliken, Colorado, aims to replace 520 acres of flood-irrigated cropland with a community that weaves farming and urban life together rather than setting them up for collision. About 150 acres are slated for civic farmland, another 100 for privately owned crops. The original farm earned about $350,000 in annual revenue, Redmond says, and he estimates that

the Agriburbia design will net agricultural revenues in excess of
$1 million—with a third of the annual water use, thanks to recycled
water and efficient irrigation.

Fred Kirschenmann, at the Leopold Center for Sustainable Agriculture, says urban and suburban agriculture is poised to spread
quickly across the nation as Americans look for new ways to avoid
the steep water, energy, and pollution costs of industrial agriculture.
"Small-scale farmers have found ways to produce incredible amounts
of food on limited acreage for local populations," he says.[58]

He's been working with Columbia University's Urban Design Lab
to analyze how much food might be grown within a 200-mile radius
of New York City. Even the most optimistic locavore enthusiasts have
assumed metro areas that large could never home-grow enough food
for populations in the millions. The analysis found otherwise. When
you include all the sod, seven million acres are available for farming
around the city. "I'm increasingly thinking that urban agriculture is
really going to surprise us," Kirschenmann says.

One hundred years ago, visionaries like William Smythe were
saying the same about the potential for small farmers to feed their
local communities and further the cause of democracy. Industrial
agriculture usurped those ideas, taking advantage of Americans' love
for farmers to steer irrigation benefits in a much different direction.
Then and now, rhetoric over water and farms does not exactly match
the reality.

In spring 2009, the plight of farm workers in California's Central
Valley suddenly became as widely known as it had been during the
Dust Bowl seventy years before—at least for an Internet moment.
In 1939, the public had devoured two books, one nonfiction and one
fiction, exposing the wretched existence of migrant farm workers
in the place many Americans considered a cornucopia of goodness.
The agrarian mythology surrounding the fertile Central Valley gave
way to the reality of industrial agriculture as *Factories in the Field*,
by lawyer turned labor activist Carey McWilliams, and *The Grapes
of Wrath*, by John Steinbeck, rose on best-seller lists. To try to clean

up their tarnished image, growers commissioned narratives of their own—with titles like *Plums of Plenty* and *Grapes of Gladness*. But popular sentiment lay with the plight of the farm workers, especially Steinbeck's Joad family members and their sorrowful search for the American dream.[59]

Indeed, the dream denied tends to arouse American outrage. And on a dry April day during his final term, California governor Arnold Schwarzenegger tapped into the narrative to inspire some national outrage over water. Standing in front of the half-empty San Luis Reservoir, built in 1962 to store water for the feds' Central Valley Project, he painted a Dust Bowl–grim picture of Central Valley's storied farming economy. He spoke of lost jobs and suffering farm families. And he blamed it on water. "Farmers are leaving their land unused because they can't count on water," Schwarzenegger bellowed. "Farm workers are losing their jobs because crops are not being planted.

"In towns across our Central Valley, our unemployment is sky-rocketing," he added. "[California's] unemployment rate now is 11.2 percent, and this is absolutely unacceptable."[60]

Schwarzenegger's speech topped off a four-day March for Water along the dusty highways of the Central Valley organized by the California Latino Water Coalition. As California suffered in its third year of drought (and as the residents of Granite Bay kept topping off their grottoes), federal water managers had slowed the pumps that send water south to farmers through the Central Valley Project in an effort to protect migrating salmon and other fish in the Sacramento–San Joaquin Delta.

The March for Water brought hundreds of farm workers, farmers, and local elected officials together to protest the water cutbacks and to call for easing environmental protections for threatened species such as the Delta smelt.[61]

As the crowd chanted, "We need water, we need water," Schwarzenegger seemed to be channeling McWilliams and Steinbeck. He twice invoked the name of labor leader César Chávez as he used the plight of farm workers to highlight the importance of water for agriculture:

César Chávez knew the power of a good march—he led by example and he never stopped trying until he found a way. And this is exactly what we are going to do. We never will stop until we find a way, find a way together here, because this is the right thing to do, because we need water, we need water, we need water, we need water.[62]

But the governor's remarks were problematic. For one, the union founded by Chávez, the United Farm Workers of America, did not participate in or support the march. "In reality, this is not a farm worker march," said Arturo Rodriguez, president of the 27,000-member organization. "This is a farmer march orchestrated and financed by growers."[63] Moreover, the *New York Times* reported that "many of the protesters were paid by their employers to march in lieu of harvesting crops."[64]

Helping the Latino Water Coalition with its grassroots action was Burson-Marsteller, the global public relations giant known for its ability to generate news coverage. It also has a knack for spinning corporate interests in the voices of everyday people. Burson-Marsteller organized the purported citizens group National Smokers Alliance in the early 1990s to protest antismoking laws—on behalf of the Phillip Morris tobacco company.[65]

As it turns out, the jobs and unemployment crises Schwarzenegger talked about had little to do with water—or even with agriculture, according to state economic data. In spring 2009, the state was ground zero for the national recession. The major cause of California's downturn was a two-thirds decline in construction activity, which led to a loss of almost 400,000 construction jobs and another 200,000 jobs in finance and real estate, says Stephen Levy, director and senior economist at the Center for Continuing Study of the California Economy, in Palo Alto. During the drought and water crisis that coincided with the recession, "we didn't see real disruptions in agricultural exports or production or the job side," Levy says. "Nothing like you see when you go from building 200,000 homes to building 40,000 homes."[66]

No doubt, workers were hurting in the Central Valley. The unemployment rate in Merced County, where Schwarzenegger spoke, was

22 percent that spring.[67] But local and state economists alike blamed the moribund housing market and high foreclosure rates rather than agricultural job losses. In fact, Merced County ended the year pulling in the third-highest agricultural revenues in its history despite water rationing. If not for low milk prices, it might have been the highest.[68]

Not unlike Burson-Marsteller's smokers' rights campaign of a decade before, which attempted to crush the indoor smoking bans being launched in California, the workers' rights rhetoric was more about money and politics than about farms and farm workers. Schwarzenegger and the Latino Water Coalition were championing the $11 billion water bond—the one that promised to restore the Sacramento–San Joaquin Delta and ensure reliable supply for all of California's water users. It needed two-thirds approval of the state assembly to be placed on a statewide ballot. The state's agricultural lobby was "desperate" to see it pass.[69]

Burson-Marsteller landed impressive media saturation of the farm worker story, by outlets from 60 Minutes to Sean Hannity. And Schwarzenegger did muscle the water bond through the state assembly. Political compromise that it was, the bill contained its share of pork. Assemblyman Chuck DeVore, a Republican from Irvine, recalled the sausage making of one particularly torturous all-night session as supporters tried to line up votes. Leaders "added about $100 million an hour as we played Let's Make a Deal," he says.[70]

But a few months before it was to appear on the November 2010 ballot, Schwarzenegger and other supporters decided to delay the $11 billion question until 2012, "to avoid jeopardizing its passage." They worried that California's financial crisis—a $20 billion hole in the state budget—would make it a tough sell to voters.[71]

Schwarzenegger deserves a lot of credit for his administration's intense focus on water during his second term, and for his determination to fix the Delta. But the man dubbed Governor Green for helping rewrite America's energy screenplay was taking his cues from industrial irrigators when it came to water for agriculture. His invoking of César Chávez must have had the labor leader rolling in his grave at the nearby United Farm Workers headquarters in Keene.

While Schwarzenegger was the one who wanted to leave office

with a water legacy, Florida governor Charlie Crist was the one who may have done so. In his last term, Crist orchestrated a buyout of former Everglades marshland south of Lake Okeechobee, owned and farmed for decades by the U.S. Sugar Corporation. Florida's economic crisis shrunk the original deal, but in 2010, the South Florida Water Management District completed the purchase of forty-two square miles of sugar property for $200 million, with an option to buy five times more land if the economy turns.[72] The land buy did not make everyone happy. U.S. Sugar's main competitors in the Glades, the Fanjul family of Florida Crystals Corporation, were furious— and they got Florida's growing Tea Party boiling, too. It also may have helped Crist lose the first election of his career, his bid for U.S. Senate in 2010. But it was the right decision for the Everglades. Buying up farmlands in those parts of the nation where water can no longer survive agricultural practices will be far cheaper in the long run than the consequences of not doing so.

The blue revolution does not turn away from agriculture; it is a water ethic for agriculture. Farming and water have a lot in common. We have an emotional attachment to each. We are physically and aesthetically drawn to farms, as we are to water. We value both of them in ways that defy economics. We appreciate the regional imprint of peach orchards off Interstate 75 in Georgia and cornfields off Interstate 80 in Nebraska. We relax at the break of green from rice plants peeking out of their paddies on the drive to the Sacramento International Airport. Floridians who moved to Plant City did so in part to live among the bucolic green swaths of strawberry farms that ended up causing them so much trouble.

These intangibles are all the more reason to heed Aldo Leopold's warning that agriculture not be governed "wholly by economic self-interest."[73] Though California is the largest agricultural state in the nation, agriculture is no longer king in California. Technology and trade, tourism and entertainment are now kings. The farming sector accounts for only 4 percent of gross state product by even the most generous calculations. If you look at statewide employment, agriculture's impact is even smaller.[74]

There's no comparing the revenue and growth potential of rice paddies to iPads. Still, most of us would probably agree that rice is more important in the larger scope of life. No one wants to see the end of agriculture in the American portfolio, as the subtitle of Steven Blank's book puts it. With political will, we could reduce subsidies to those agricultural operations that flout the water ethic, and support those farmers who embrace it. We could invest in sustainable agricultural research and practices in rural America while we build urban farming into metro areas—reminding us all not only where food comes from but where water comes from, too.

As the March for Water made clear, however, heading down this new, blue path will require getting around—or winning over—a pretty big obstacle: the politically powerful sectors of the American economy that make their living off the old.

CHAPTER 6

The Water-Industrial Complex

Americans faced a bleak holiday season in 2008. Over the previous year, the worst financial crisis since the Great Depression collapsed the value of their homes and toppled their most trusted financial institutions. The stock market had crashed. Retirement savings had vaporized. By December, 1.9 million Americans had lost their jobs. Polls that month registered the largest decline in consumer confidence since researchers began taking the measurement in the 1950s.[1] Even those families with steady incomes clamped down on Christmas spending.

The deepening economic crisis had cast a shadow over the historic election of Barack Obama as forty-fourth president of the United States. But many Americans remained hopeful about Obama's call for change in the tone and direction of the country.[2] That December, Obama and congressional leaders were already working on the president-elect's foremost goal, an economic-recovery plan. The crux was government stimulus: a federal investment of hundreds of billions of dollars to both jump-start the economy and steer the country onto a more sustainable course.

Democrats and Republicans alike had for decades embraced economist John Maynard Keynes's post-Depression stimulus theory: when fear makes consumers and investors excessively cautious, government should step in to boost confidence, and public spending will keep factories humming until the "animal spirits" of people and investors return.[3] Outgoing president George W. Bush deployed his brand a year earlier, with a $1,200 check for many American families. But Obama wanted a stimulus plan that would at once jolt the economy and transform it. For one, targeted spending could help green America. The idea was to make the United States much more efficient and move the power grid toward clean energy, creating thousands of green-collar jobs to put Americans back to work. The plan would spark private investment in clean power with subsidies for solar arrays, wind farms, and biofuels. It would funnel billions of dollars in grants to state and local governments for renewable-energy, mass-transit, and other green economic-development projects. They could hire workers to weatherize hundreds of thousands of homes, to install smart meters to monitor and reduce residential energy use.[4]

Obama's stimulus plan held out the promise of both more jobs and less carbon. It was a unifying intention in the wake of a bitter election that pitted economy against environment with cries of "Drill, baby, drill!" reverberating at the Republican National Convention.[5] But there were a couple problems with the president-elect's eco-friendly plan: it ignored the number-one environmental concern of most Americans—and one of the best possible solutions for reducing the nation's energy demand.

The winter that President Obama and his family moved into the White House, the Gallup organization released its annual poll on the environment. The 2009 results showed that for the first time, Americans' top four environmental concerns were all related to water—from water pollution to freshwater supply. More respondents in the 2009 poll were "worried a great deal" about the availability of freshwater for household use than in any previous year.[6]

In fact, concern about whether freshwater would continue to flow out of U.S. taps was greater than worries about climate change.[7] California was grappling with the worst drought in modern history. Raleigh and Atlanta, both named by the Urban Land Institute as top retirement cities for aging baby boomers, had come within weeks of depleting their sole drinking-water reservoirs. Las Vegas—retirement hot-spot No. 5—faced running dry within six years, Patricia Mulroy, chief of the Southern Nevada Water Authority, told lawmakers that year.

But debate in Congress over the bill that became known as the American Recovery and Investment Act revealed how oblivious the nation's elected officials were to their constituents' most pressing environmental concern—and to the impact of water use on the energy grid. The enormous amount of U.S. power generation—upward of 10 percent of the total—spent pumping water, treating it, moving it around the nation, and treating it some more, means that investment in a blue revolution could have as much of an immediate impact on carbon emissions as any one new alternative energy source.

Yet, as Congress crafted the stimulus bill with an eye toward sustainability, it gave water barely a blink. Senators and representatives added to the bill until it was 1,100 pages long and $787 billion fat. They directed about $6 billion of that to water and wastewater projects—less than 1 percent.[8] (Six billion dollars is a lot, but it's a fraction of America's annual water and wastewater spending, which totaled about $45 billion in 2008.)[9]

In the end, water got far less stimulus funding than virtually all other public works needs. Given the green shade of the bill, you'd think that some of the $6 billion would go to programs for water efficiency, wetlands restoration, and green roofs—investments that would steer America toward the blue revolution, saving *trillions* of gallons of water and creating tens of thousands of jobs. But that was not exactly how it worked out.

During the 2008 holidays, as congressional staffers worked on the stimulus bill, Mary Ann Dickinson and her staff at the Alliance for Water Efficiency put in long hours over the usually dead week between Christmas and New Year's Day.[10] Dickinson helped launch the Chicago-based nonprofit organization in 2007 after running successful utility-conservation programs in Connecticut and California. She is one of the few voices in the utility industry willing to say that the country's approach to water is all wrong.

The conventional wisdom maintains that we can fix our water problems with more reservoirs and river pipelines, more diversions and desalination plants. But for Dickinson, these are last resorts—meaning, we should resort to them only after an obvious step: stop wasting a drop of the water we already have. In the world of the water-industrial complex, this precept is tantamount to accusing the emperor of having no clothes. But Dickinson's data is clear: efficiency can often net as much water as many infrastructure projects. And it saves a significant amount of money. Water efficiency costs between $450 and $1,600 for every million gallons it saves. Every other new water source costs a lot more. For example, desalination costs about $15,000 for the same million gallons.[11]

But hardly anyone is willing to admit Dickinson's right, because of all the *other* reasons we favor edifices over efficiency: politicians want to bring home visible new projects. Engineering firms want to land them. Communities want the jobs they bring. And utilities want to sell more water. Check out any multimillion-dollar water project in the nation, and behind it you will find a powerful set of backers whose profits are directly proportional to its size.

So it went with the stimulus spigot. Utilities, engineering firms, and water managers created a cacophony for infrastructure funding. Dickinson's was a relatively lonely voice for efficiency, despite powerful evidence that it's the wisest first-choice investment. An Alliance study found that a $10 billion infusion in efficiency projects would create 150,000 to 222,000 jobs and save between six and a half trillion and ten trillion gallons of water.[12] Dickinson talked up full-house retrofits, citywide leak-detection programs, and other ideas that could bring jobs to communities and capture the same water at less cost than new plants. The Alliance sent a letter to the president in late December detailing the thousands of jobs, billions of dollars, and trillions of gallons of water the United States would save with a national plumbing-retrofit program.

The arguments were similar to those advocates were making for energy efficiency. Still, congressional staffers kept responding to Dickinson with the annoying new buzzword flying around Capitol Hill, the soon-to-be-clichéd "shovel ready." President Obama used the term, which refers to thousands of projects nationwide with planning complete and permitting approved, but no funding, as one of his favorite selling points for the stimulus package. He wanted projects that would bring jobs right away. Staffers told Dickinson to come back with shovel-ready deals. It was a head-scratching task; by their nature, efficiency projects would require no dirt dug. Nevertheless, Dickinson and her staff spent the final week of 2008 on phone, fax, and e-mail, begging for ready-to-go efficiency projects at water utilities across the country.

By January 1, they had collected 575 of them worth about $2 billion. The nonprofit organization American Rivers worked similarly to collect wetland restoration and green-roof proposals, calculating their potential for reducing water pollution as well as jobs created.

By the time Congress passed the bill on February 11, 2009, lawmakers had agreed that 20 percent of the $6 billion in water funding should flow to green projects. Dickinson and her colleagues felt they'd made real progress. But then, it came time to spend the money.

Some was already spoken for despite the president's assurances that the stimulus bill was pork free. As a Republican taking heat from the Tea Party for supporting the previous year's bank bailout, U.S. senator Bob Bennett of Utah opposed the stimulus bill. But as the literal heir to Utah's largest federal water scheme—his father, onetime U.S. senator Wallace Bennett, fought to win passage and initial appropriations for the Central Utah Project in the 1950s—he was eager to land stimulus money to complete the six-decade-long pet project. Bennett managed to get a $50 million line item into the bill for the Central Utah Project—$41 million for a major infrastructure piece and the rest for environmental-mitigation efforts.[13] Then, he voted *against* the bill, declaring, "The only thing this bill will stimulate is the national debt."[14] Then, after it passed, he took credit back in Utah for bringing his state "projects that would create jobs."[15]

In other cases, sheer bureaucratic inertia funneled the water funds to old-style infrastructure projects. The water money was doled out in what are known as State Revolving Funds, pots of cash that finance each state's drinking-water and clean-water infrastructure improvements. In deciding how to spend the money, state regulators gave priority to large, supply-side projects requested by utilities, which has always been their role. When I asked a couple of these regulators why they didn't use the windfall to fund more of the progressive, demand-side proposals seeking funding in their states, they told me that would take too long. The only way to get the money out fast, they said, was to funnel it to utility projects, for which they already had a funding process in place. The result was that most of Dickinson's 575 proposals were shut out. "Almost all of the money went to infrastructure," Dickinson says. "Out of $787 billion of stimulus money, maybe a few million went to water conservation or efficiency.

"Where did we in the last twenty years get so left behind?" she asks. "How has energy efficiency progressed forward as a cause, as a source of billions of dollars in funding, and we haven't been able to do this with water?"

Each year, the American Society of Civil Engineers puts out its highly publicized Report Card for American Infrastructure to expose the nation's crumbling, woefully underfunded waterworks, roads, and bridges. America's water-infrastructure needs are usually given the lowest grade—a dismal D minus in the 2009 report. Water and wastewater also carry the highest price tag to fix: total investment needs of $255 billion.[16]

What the report never points out is that our water-management approach itself is part of the problem. In addition to new projects, utilities want billions of dollars to rebuild the nation's aging water lines, sewer mains, and treatment plants, many built more than a hundred years ago. True, these systems are leaking, collapsing, and overflowing. But often missing from the debate is the idea that rather than prop up failing systems, we should invest in *new* ways of living with water. Economist Valerie Nelson, director of the Massachusetts-based Coalition for Alternative Wastewater Treatment, says our waterworks have reached the classic run-to-failure moment, when it becomes more efficient to invest in something new than to repair the old. It's like the tipping point at which it's not worth replacing the transmission in your clunker. Instead, you save every last dime for a new car, maybe even a hybrid.[17]

In the mid-1880s, the country began building pipes that carry clean water into cities, another set to carry wastewater out, and yet another to rid cities of stormwater. Sticking to this big-pipe approach is like holding on to your grandparents' Buick Roadmaster from the 1950s—and paying large repair bills to keep it running for thirteen-mile-a-gallon commutes in the modern city. "The traditional, linear 'take, make, waste' approach to managing water increasingly is proving unsustainable," says Glen T. Daigger, president of the International Water Association. He is also senior vice president and chief technology officer at CH2M Hill, the Colorado-based company that is consistently one of the top water-engineering firms in the nation—where he has worked for more than three decades. Climate change and growing global population now have him calling on his own colleagues to change their mega-project approach.[18]

The old path—finding a pristine new source of water, conveying it with pumps, using it once, cleaning it up, then flushing it away—has led us to insufficient water supplies, unsustainable consumption of energy to move water around and chemicals to treat it, dispersion of nutrients, particularly phosphorus, into our waters, and financially unstable utilities, Daigger argues.

But moving his colleagues from their concrete-pipes position has been difficult. Part of the reason is that America's failing water systems have taken water managers by surprise. The National Academy of Engineering, in Washington, D.C., recently recognized modern water and wastewater systems as one of the greatest achievements of the twentieth century. Those 1800s systems saved lives by reducing exposure to pathogens and preventing flooding. "Given the outstanding success," Daigger says, "why should we change?"[19]

Aside from the energy demands of water, the answer is population pressure. The U.S. population is expected to climb 50 percent, from the current figure of 310 million to about 450 million, by 2050.[20] Essentially all of that increase is projected for urban areas. That fact makes cities sitting targets for increasing water scarcity and flood losses if they don't change. It gives them an unprecedented chance to remake their water fortunes if they do.

Some of the country's most progressive engineers and local governments are leading the blue revolution, and waving for the rest to follow. An early shift in mind-set came with New York City's decision to acquire tens of thousands of acres of watershed land surrounding its Catskills drinking-water reservoirs, creating a natural water-treatment system that saved $6 billion in capital and maintenance costs for concrete conveyances. Boston saved hundreds of millions of dollars when it closed the door on a plan to pipe the Connecticut River for water supply and opened one on an efficiency program that has cut water use 43 percent since 1980. Indianapolis saved more than $300 million in sewage costs creating a system of wetlands, trees, and downspout disconnections to filter stormwater.

Next-generation technologies and designs have made bigger leaps. New subdivisions are being built with little or no imported water. New York City's Battery Park City has several new high-rises that treat stormwater runoff and wastewater and recycle it back into landscaping, cooling towers, and toilets. Officials in New York City, San Antonio, and a few other cities are offering incentives for these approaches because, says the Coalition for Alternative Wastewater Treatment's Valerie Nelson, "they understand that each gallon of freshwater they don't need to pipe in, and each gallon of wastewater and stormwater they don't have to pipe out, reduces pressure on the city's aging underground water and sewer systems."[21]

In every case, the new, blue path has been much cheaper. This is another reason it's so difficult for the water-industrial complex to change course. The linear path has been lucrative for the utilities that sell the water, and the firms that design and build multimillion-dollar water projects. The financials are starting to change for utilities in water-scarce cities that see how every drop they save helps defer a much more expensive option—say, a desalination plant—in the future.

But at least for now, the firms that advise us on how to design our communities' water projects—often the same firms that end up with the contract to build them—have a financial interest in the old path. The allusion to the military-industrial complex is not random. Over the past two decades, the water-supply industry has been transformed from locally owned firms to global conglomerates with billion-dollar revenues. Such consolidation is contrary to the highly local, decentralized solutions of the future. Water development has grown nearly as large and high-stakes as private defense contracting.

A wave of acquisitions in the 1990s and early 2000s means the two industries are increasingly one and the same: three of the top twenty water-engineering concerns in the United States are part of global conglomerates that also make the list of top twenty private defense contractors in Iraq and Afghanistan: Parsons Corporation, with $579 million in federal defense contracts; Tetra Tech, with $362 million; and AECOM, with $294 million.[22]

Water is increasingly attractive to powerhouse contracting firms because it is lucrative not only when times are good but also when they are bad. During the global economic recession that began in 2007, water was one of the few engineering sectors to continue soaking up profits. Engineering firms in general suffered a year of pain in 2009 and one of uncertainty in 2010, according to the industry journal *Engineering News-Record*. Revenue for the top 500 design firms in the nation fell 11.7 percent to $80.02 billion in 2009, down from $90.85 billion in 2008.[23] But the water experts bucked the trend—particularly, the sector devoted to building new supply projects. An *ENR* market analysis found that revenue in water-supply design, construction, and management markets rose an astounding 17 percent between 2008 and 2009, amid the worst of the U.S. economic collapse.[24] Industry CEOs could thank the water crisis in the western United States and the nationwide drought.[25]

Through lobbying, involvement on boards and task forces, and campaign contributions, principals work to keep the money flowing to water projects at local, state, and federal levels. That's not a bad thing. The problem is that industry economic drivers favor the large, supply-side projects that helped lead to our water stress in the first place.

The American public routinely expresses anger at the influence of self-interested players in the nation's most important affairs: energy and automobile companies on climate policy, insurers on health care reform, defense contractors on military spending. Water engineers, by contrast, come across as brainy hydraulic heroes, in the room to help bring water to people or save them from floods. That is true for many of them as individuals. But engineering firms influence government policy and spending to maximize their profits just like other big business in America.

My writing about water over the years has allowed me to meet many longtime water engineers in the private sector and in government who fall into the hydraulic-hero category. Some of these sources and friends minimize their profession's role in influencing water management, arguing that federal water policy, agricultural irrigation and subsidies, and runaway sprawl led to the overwhelming drain on the country's water supply. Those points are right, but they are looking to the past. Many books have called out the "Lords of Yesterday," the term coined by author Charles F. Wilkinson, whose highly praised 1997 *Crossing the Next Meridian: Land, Water, and the Future of the West* attacks the five historic "lords" that prevent water sustainability in the West.

Wilkinson's top five are the Hardrock Mining Law of 1872, which dedicates more than half of all public lands to mining as the preferred use; public rangeland practices that devastate western ranges and rivers; forest policy that continues to push logging as the dominant use of our national forests; the mega-dams and other water-development practices that destroyed rivers in the name of "cheap" hydropower; and finally, the prior-appropriation doctrine, which allows the larger water users who got there first to extract as much water as they want at no charge, so long as it is put to a "beneficial" use, such as farming, mining, or hydropower.[26]

Those lords have not been toppled. But as population growth exacerbates pressure to move more water to urban areas, it is time to also open our eyes to the entrenched interests standing in the way of water sustainability in metropolitan regions across the nation, from West to East. Last century, federal taxpayers footed the bill for the country's current hydraulic empire, which, in historian Donald Worster's words, turned rivers into "abstracted water, rigidly separated from the earth and firmly directed to raise food, fill pipes, and make money."[27] In the twenty-first century, we can avoid that mistake, broadening the very concept of infrastructure to include nature— "healthy rivers, small streams, wetlands, and floodplains that are often more reliable and cost effective at providing clean drinking water and natural flood protection," says Katherine Baer, senior director for the clean-water program at American Rivers.[28]

That means paying attention to the ecological limits and stability of water in our local communities and states. Traditionally, we've taken notice only during a major drought or the rare boil-water alert. But who takes a few hours off work in the middle of the day to attend water meetings, filled with the mind-numbing business of water contracts, general-obligation bonds, and State Revolving Funds? When citizens do show up, they are not often appreciated. The public-comments portion of water meetings is often scheduled last. The Texas Water Development Board usually has somewhere between twenty-five and fifty agenda items for its monthly meetings. Public comment comes next to last.[29] The board of the South Florida Water Management District, based in West Palm Beach, goes to the trouble of taking its meetings on the road, ostensibly to make it easier for the public in far-flung counties to attend. During a rare board meeting at a St. Lucie County library in May 2010, dozens of local citizens arrived in the morning to complain about discharges of polluted freshwater from Lake Okeechobee into the St. Lucie River Estuary. Despite their frustrated pleas, board members made them wait through 6 hours of other business. By the time citizens were allowed to speak at 4 p.m., most of them were gone.[30]

Global water firms, on the other hand, are heard loud and clear when community, state, and federal water policies get made. They are not only *at* the decision-making table but setting it, which can create conflicts real and perceived. In Massachusetts, private engineering firms are helping state, county, and local officials plan for new wastewater systems to help stop the flow of nitrogen and phosphorus that is fueling algae growth in the freshwater and coastal estuaries of Cape Cod. In 2010, taxpayer-watchdog groups filed a formal complaint with the state Division of Professional Licensure after a professional engineer's report claimed that a more costly central sewage project was far cheaper than a decentralized neighborhood option called cluster systems. Claims of bias for big-pipe projects in the region have led U.S. representative Matthew Patrick of Falmouth, Massachusetts, to propose legislation that would prohibit engineering firms that consult on behalf of communities to design and construct the projects they recommended.[31]

From coast to coast, private engineering firms not only plan, design, and build water projects, they also increasingly run them. Their unique role and reputations would seem professional incentive enough to rise above politics. Instead, they are key players in local, state, and national races. Just like energy companies, agricultural interests, and other water users, global water firms and their employees are major donors at every level; some firms pressure their engineers to donate. Federal elections records show that every one of America's top twenty water-engineering firms, through employees or political action committees or both, gave thousands of dollars to congressional candidates in the last federal election cycle. Industry icon Ralph Peterson, the CH2M Hill chairman who built the firm into a $6.5 billion, 25,000-employee industry force, personally gave nearly $100,000 in federal campaign contributions between 1994 and his death in 2009.[32] Most of the top twenty firms also had registered PACs to collect money from employees and target donations to key members of Congress and state lawmakers who control infrastructure pocketbooks.[33]

At the state level, the top water-engineering firms have dropped the largest campaign contributions in recent years on big-infrastructure spender California. Their dollars have helped convince Californians to authorize multibillion-dollar water bonds that fund the projects for which the firms compete. In 2002, for example, Kansas City–based Black & Veatch spent $50,000 on the campaign urging voters to support Proposition 50, which authorized $3.44 billion in bonds for various water projects.[34] Those projects included funding for the restoration of California's ailing Salton Sea; Black & Veatch has long worked to convince California to adopt its $1 billion solution for restoring the Salton.[35] Parsons Corporation spent $25,000 on the same campaign for Proposition 50, which included $10 million for a project it managed on behalf of the All-American Canal.[36] CH2M Hill's California PAC gave $342,207 in 2006 alone, including a $50,000 chunk to help pass that year's Proposition 84, which authorized $5.4 billion in water bonds.[37] CH2M Hill officials worked to make sure Proposition 84 funding would cover the long-term management plan for the Sacramento–San Joaquin Delta; later, the company was awarded a $9.5 million contract to develop the plan.[38]

AECOM, headquartered in Glen Allen, Virginia, also has a keen interest in statewide races on the West Coast. Its PAC contributed $142,925 to California campaigns in 2009. Of that, $5,000 went to three-term Los Angeles city councilwoman Janice Hahn in her bid for lieutenant governor.[39] But after San Francisco mayor Gavin Newsom made a late entrance into the same race in 2010, AECOM gave the maximum allowable contribution to him: $13,000 total for the primary and general elections; three company executives also contributed to Newsom's successful bid.[40] AECOM has numerous financial links to San Francisco: that April, for example, the city's Public Utilities Commission approved a $26 million water-construction contract with the firm.[41]

Global engineering firms also make big campaign contributions at the local level, where it can take millions of dollars to win an election. In Houston, then unknown Bill White shattered fund-raising records in 2003, raising $8.6 million to beat out two established opponents for mayor.[42] That year, an analysis of Houston campaign contributions found that engineering firms competing for infrastructure contracts were one of the top contributors to city council and mayoral campaigns. Local firms that contributed hundreds of thousands of dollars landed millions of dollars in contracts, which the Houston City Council "has virtually unlimited discretion" in awarding because professional services aren't subject to competitive bidding requirements.[43]

All the political activity has become a point of tension within the profession. The industry finds itself in "a fundamental clash between deeply rooted ethical principles and a profession faced by the pressures of the business environment," says Professor Jimmy Smith, director of the Murdough Center for Engineering Professionalism at Texas Tech University, in Lubbock. Despite clear guidelines established by the American Society of Civil Engineers, professional engineers often complain that they are "pressured into making contributions" and that "it's a matter of survival."[44]

A review of American Society of Civil Engineers professional-conduct cases for 2000 to 2006 found that of all the ethics cases filed in those years, "improper campaign contributions" was by far the most common complaint filed.[45] The story of illegal campaign contributions at powerhouse firm PBSJ is an extreme example. But the fact that it could happen at an engineering firm that is among the top ranked in the nation reflects how a noble profession could get sucked into the ignobility of politics.

In 1959, a thirty-five-year-old engineer with the Florida road department, Howard M. "Budd" Post, was offered the chance to help create Miami Lakes, the first master-planned community in the Sunshine State. Putting up $500 each, Post and three fellow engineers formed a company that grew as fast as Florida.[46]

Along with managing the design and construction of Miami Lakes, the young men who made up what became Post, Buckley, Schuh & Jernigan, now PBSJ, engineered the sixty-five-mile Card Sound Bridge, which connected the mainland to the Florida Keys. They designed the first reverse-osmosis water-treatment plant in Florida, Aquarina, and created the Orlando Easterly Wetlands, one of the biggest wetlands for wastewater treatment. The company's blueprint for success was—and is—government contracting. Local, state, and federal taxpayers proffer more than 90 percent of PBSJ's income.[47]

In the early 1990s, Bill Randolph, then PBSJ's chairman, decided it was time to take the company national, and he began to acquire firms from the Gulf Coast to California. By the turn of the century, he'd doubled PBSJ's size and revenues.[48]

Between 2000 and 2005, two subsequent chairmen, Richard A. Wickett and H. Michael Dye, helped double revenues again, to more than half a billion dollars. As the company burgeoned, so did its political activities. In 1985, PBSJ began making campaign contributions to state and local candidates when it registered a political action committee in Florida. By 2000, PBSJ had established political committees in seven other states.[49]

The pressure to give must have been extraordinary, because around 1990, PBSJ executives began to step over the line.[50]

In 2007, U.S. prosecutors charged Wickett and Dye with felony counts related to a "long-term scheme to violate campaign-finance laws."[51] Federal elections officials who later investigated found that "PBSJ made direct corporate contributions to federal candidates and engaged in an institutionalized, corporate-wide practice of reimbursing employee contributions."[52]

A Federal Elections Commission investigation found that, starting in about 1990, Wickett and Dye set up sham bank accounts that diverted PBSJ funds to federal campaigns.[53] PBSJ employees also told investigators that their bosses routinely used company funds to reimburse them for campaign contributions; employees filed fake mileage reports to be repaid thousands of dollars. Executives also set up "bonuses" for top earners that actually "had to go to PBSJ political action committees."[54] During the heat of the 2000 elections, Dye arranged a special "midyear bonus" for certain officers and directors, then instructed them to bring checkbooks to PBSJ's board meeting so they could use their bonus money to donate to the firm's PACS.[55]

Federal officials say the scheme was "an important part of PBSJ's business strategy," and the motive was "to increase the likelihood of procuring government contracts for PBSJ."[56] They only uncovered it while investigating a $36 million embezzlement scheme undertaken by PBSJ's chief financial officer.

The CFO, William DeLoach, claimed the company's campaign-contribution scheme helped push him down a slippery slope, giving him the gumption to embezzle from his employer, and from taxpayers in the states where he overbilled on contracts. DeLoach told investigators he figured that if his superiors ever confronted him, he would "remind them of their improper reimbursement activity and could say to them, 'What are you going to do? Call the authorities?'"[57]

DeLoach went to prison for the embezzlement, with time tacked on for his role in the contributions scheme. Wickett pleaded guilty to two counts of violating federal campaign laws, Dye to filing false statements. They both were sentenced to home confinement and fines.[58] But the corporation got off the hook, much to the relief of

PBSJ's 4,000 employee-owners across the country. In a 3-2 vote along party lines, the FEC passed on the Office of General Counsel's recommendation to seek civil penalties against PBSJ for illegal corporate reimbursements.

Such action could have jeopardized the federal contracts of one of the top water firms in the United States. Instead, in 2009, the year it celebrated the 50th anniversary of its founding by young Post, Buckley, Schuh, and Jernigan, PBSJ hit record revenues despite the severe recession squeezing its clients.

More than once, I attempted to interview PBSJ's current executives about the contributions. In 2007, they said they couldn't talk about the case because the federal investigation was ongoing. After it was all over, in 2010, I tried again. Like many big engineering firms, PBSJ has both an internal public relations team and an outside firm, in its case the Conroy Martinez Group of Miami. Principal Jorge Martinez tells me PBSJ's executives did not want to discuss the issue, because "they want to put it behind them." He says, too, that neither he nor the executives could fathom how campaign contributions could have any possible relevance to the topic of water.[59]

Congress gave final approval to the American Recovery and Investment Act on February 11, 2009. A week later, President Barack Obama and Vice President Joseph Biden flew to Colorado for a bill-signing ceremony at the Denver Museum of Nature and Science. The White House chose the museum in Denver's City Park, one of the largest in the nation devoted to science, to underscore the act's clean-energy provisions. Obama and Biden toured the museum's rooftop solar array and schmoozed with solar-energy entrepreneurs. The president signed the bill in the sunny atrium as 250 business leaders, many of them from the renewable-energy industry, looked on.[60]

One floor above Obama, the museum's IMAX theatre had just opened a critically acclaimed new film.[61] *Grand Canyon Adventure: River at Risk* is so wild and beautiful, it almost belies director Greg MacGillivray's urgent message.[62] In sweeping 3-D, the Colorado River becomes a metaphor for the global water crisis. Robert Redford's narration and the Dave Matthews Band's score ask Americans and their elected leaders to pay attention before it's too late. "Whether you look at it from an environmental, economic, political, or human perspective, the high costs to the world of ignoring freshwater conservation are becoming clear," MacGillivray says of his goal in making the film. "There's got to be a consciousness on both an individual level, and at the highest levels of government."

By the end of 2009, Mary Ann Dickinson was not the only American weary of the term "shovel ready." In 2010, Lake Superior State University, in Sault Ste. Marie, Michigan, put it on its 35th annual list of suggested banished words and phrases, along with "stimulus."[63]

But the shoveling sectors of the American economy were happy. Just as the president intended, the stimulus kept them working through a severe economic recession. It proved so lucrative to U.S. engineering firms that most devoted entire teams to landing stimulus projects. As soon as the law passed, PBSJ named Vice President Mike Pavlides its "economic-stimulus program director."[64] Over the course of 2009, the federal stimulus helped drive PBSJ's revenues up 30 percent, to $798.5 million.[65] The growth was remarkable for a company that relies on taxpayers for 90 percent of its income—in a year when budget crisis gripped every level of government.[66]

The following year, though, PBSJ, a once local firm, was acquired by a British-based engineering company looking to expand its international reach, part of the increasing industrywide globalization. Other top U.S. firms continued making global acquisitions and opening international offices, especially on the big water-spending continents of Africa and Australia.

One tiny country getting a particular amount of attention for its water skill and water spending was Singapore. The island republic, with hardly any water of its own, had managed to turn a crisis of scarcity around in just one generation. Now, U.S. engineers were looking to Singapore as a twenty-first-century model for water; the American Academy of Environmental Engineers awarded the country its highest honor in 2009. Singaporeans also had some of the lowest per capita water use in the developed world, and a tangible water ethic, clear from kindergarten classrooms to the highest levels of government.

It all convinced me to make Singapore part of my search for a water ethic. I wanted to see what it looks like to recycle every last drop of water in a nation—and what it tastes like, too.

CHAPTER 7

Singapore:
Of Songbirds and Sewage

At the southeastern tip of Singapore, on a hillside overlooking a drinking-water reservoir called Bedok, showy yellow flame trees are planted in precise rows typical of the island nation's ordered landscapes. A little farther down the hill, also set in soldier-straight formation, are dozens of tall, metal poles. They look like flagpoles at a veteran's memorial, except these have hooks on top.

The poles are a uniquely Singaporean park amenity known as birdcage trellises. The most popular passions in this tiny, densely populated nation include food—spicy noodle *laksa*, chili crabs—and shopping, the best in Southeast Asia. But keeping songbirds is a traditional hobby passed down among Singapore's Chinese. Walking around the island's city center and neighborhoods, it's not uncommon to happen on an intricate wooden cage holding a beautiful, solitary songbird. During the day, bird enthusiasts hang their charges in city parks, in coffee shops, in random trees along neighborhood sidewalks. Some of the birds, like one Chinese nightingale banging the sides of its cage, seem agitated to be this close to the trees and unable to fly to them. Others—a red-whiskered bulbul with a sweet chirp, for example—seem perfectly content.

Songbird hobbyists, often older men, adore and adorn their charges as if they're mistresses. They embellish the teak or bamboo cages with jade-green beads, ivory fittings, and tiny porcelain water bowls. But this is as much competitive sport as aesthetic pursuit.

Sunday mornings, the songbird owners trot out their male zebra doves, white-rumped shamas, or Oriental white eyes—species chosen for their vigorous coos and calls—and vie to get them to sing. Male songbirds naturally try to out-sing one another as they compete for mates. Their keepers position cages as carefully as chess masters, strategizing to inspire the clearest, loudest, and longest melodies.

Traditional birdcage trellises can be found around the island, though in fewer numbers today, as songbird enthusiasts age and younger Singaporeans chase more modern pursuits. But the trellis at Bedok Reservoir is significant for a reason beyond the birds. It sings volumes about the lengths to which the nation has gone to build a water ethic among Singaporeans.

Like all of Singapore's reservoirs, Bedok was once off limits to the many residents who live near the former sand quarry. Hundreds of high-rise apartments overlook the reservoir, their small terraces bright with blooming flowers and laundry sticks hung with drying clothes. But, until recently, residents were not allowed to go near the water, much less go in for fishing, kayaking, or dragon boating (a sport featuring colorful Chinese vessels, each with a team of rowers and a drummer).

In 2004, the government and its water management and supply agency, the Public Utilities Board, called PUB, did an about-face on public access to the nation's waterways. It even changed the names: drains, canals, and reservoirs became streams, rivers, and lakes. Pushing from the outside were water-sport enthusiasts who wanted to be able to do in reservoirs like Bedok what Americans do in the reservoirs we also euphemistically call lakes: Lake Powell, Lake Mead, Lake Shasta, and the like. But there was also push from inside PUB.

"The government wants to change," says Linda Dorothy de Mello, whose job at PUB is to bring people, business, and government together on projects that build appreciation for water, "from straight drains to meandering rivers."[1]

And so, the foreboding Bedok Reservoir was transformed into a welcoming waterfront park. In fall 2004, the 100-acre park opened for the first water-sports event at a Singapore reservoir—the Wakeboard

World Cup. Today, Bedok residents jog and walk around a 3-mile track that circles the water. Kids run and shout on brightly colored playgrounds. Teen girls practice line dancing on a floating stage. (Inexplicably, in spring 2010, the nation was burning with line-dancing fever.) For the neighborhood's older residents, a beloved birdcage trellis. For the young, a $1 million aerial course featuring zip lines through forest and over water, as well as swings, rope ladders, nets, trapezes, bridges, and slides.

One hundred such projects under way around the country aim to fill not so much people's bathtubs as their hearts. The idea is to bring Singaporeans closer to water so they'll understand its value to their water-scarce home.

"It's like falling in love—everything the other person says becomes wonderful," de Mello proclaims. "Once you're engaged with the water, it becomes very easy for me to tell you something."

That concept is important to understand in the Republic of Singapore, where the government has a lot to tell its citizens about the way they should live. It also helps explain how Singaporeans have become the first people in the world to live in a "closed water loop."

That's another euphemism—one for capturing every single drop of water on the island, from rainfall to sewage, to drink over and over again.

Singapore didn't have much going for it when it became a republic just half a century ago. It had no army, no natural resources, and hardly any land. The nation is tiny—a 275-square-mile tropical island off the southern end of the Malay Peninsula, smaller than New York City and the smallest country in Southeast Asia. Its five million people also make it the most densely populated country in the region.[2]

At its founding in 1965, the new country was mired in poverty, massive unemployment, and filth. But worst of all, Singaporeans had hardly any drinking water. Their home, just north of the equator, is essentially a sandbar. It has only a few small rivers, no natural lakes, and not enough land to supply its own food.

The little island's main asset was its strategic location along the world's major shipping lanes. Singapore had been a British colony since 1824, and a primary naval base of the empire until declaring independence in 1963. It was then a short-lived member of the Federation of Malaysia, but broke off in 1965 amid painful ideological and cultural differences.

Water was the one thing Malaysia had that Singapore couldn't live without. The neighbor to the north was endowed with abundant freshwater: more than 150 river systems that help irrigate its vast rice paddies, plenty of land to store monsoon rainfall, and groundwater resources the nation hasn't had to tap.[3]

When both countries were still under colonial rule, Malaysian officials signed two long-term agreements to sell water to Singapore. But the deals, which expire in 2011 and 2061, stew resentment and diplomatic tension. Political conflicts have brought public threats by Malaysian leaders to cut off the tap.[4]

In the nation's early years, Singaporeans were well aware of the fragility of their water supply. In the countryside, women and children would line up along dusty roads awaiting a water wagon to fill their family buckets. In the 1960s, drought dried up reservoirs and the Tebrau River in Malaysia's state of Johor, where water is exported through three large pipelines across the mile-long causeway that separates the countries. Urban Singaporeans endured severe rationing, unable to turn on their taps during 12 hours of the day.

What little water the country had was largely unfit to drink.

Then, as now, Singaporean commerce gravitated to a south-central wedge of the island at the convergence of the Singapore and Kallang Rivers. The nation's industry revolved around serving huge ships anchored out at harbor. Warehouses and marine shops thrived on the riverbanks, as did street hawkers, squatters, and markets selling produce, fish, and meat. Squatters' homes had no sewer access, just overhanging latrines that opened directly into streams. The markets and the hawkers tossed their leftovers into the river. Pig and duck farms added to the filthy flotsam. Bumboats—which ferry supplies between the ships and the warehouses—motored through the mire, leaking oil and dumping other waste.[5]

"It was the smell that hit you—pungent, like raw sewage," remembers Tan Seng Chai. He grew up in Singapore in the 1950s and

'60s and is based there now as vice president for water projects in the Asia Pacific region for U.S. engineering firm Black & Veatch. "Always smelly, always dirty, and always had something floating in it—boxes, bottles, and chicken fat."[6]

From postcolonial pigsty to one of the world's most successful economies, Singapore has managed a fairy-tale turnaround. But the transformation would not have been possible without the change in Singapore's water fortunes.

The country's charismatic first prime minister, Lee Kuan Yew, was a visionary leader who described a future Singapore as an "oasis." Engineering the society and developing the economy over more than three decades, Lee spoke and wrote the word frequently, whether calling for his anti-spitting campaigns or his massive tree plantings.[7]

Lee was a political Janus—a shrewd capitalist who worked tirelessly to lure multinational corporations from the outside world, and a socialist dictator controlling the lives of Singaporeans inside. "After independence, I searched for some dramatic way to distinguish ourselves from other Third World countries," Lee writes in his memoir, *From Third World to First*. "One arm of my strategy was to make Singapore into an oasis in Southeast Asia, for if we had First World standards, then businesspeople and tourists would make us a base."[8]

In other words, international bankers weren't going to set up offices in a central business district that smelled of pig shit. Manufacturers that needed water to produce goods couldn't operate in Singapore without a more dependable supply.

Oasis seemed a curious word choice: it connotes a fertile, green splash in the desert, made so by the presence of water. Singapore didn't have any water. But Lee repeated his mantra until it came true. Today, Singaporeans live on a lush, green island with plenty of water. The government is set to let the 2011 deal with Malaysia expire without renegotiating, weaning itself from some of the wetter nation's water. By the time the second agreement expires in 2061, "we can be totally self-sufficient," says the current prime minister, Goh Chok Tong.[9]

To get there, Lee and officials of his People's Action Party first set out to clean up their young country's water.

Later, they would figure out how to make more of it.

◆   ◆   ◆

In Singapore's Cinderella tale, Lee and his fellow socialists had no fairy godmother to wave a wand and make filth disappear from the rivers and streams. But they pulled off quite a vanishing act on their own. Between 1965 and 1985, they essentially moved everyone and everything they perceived in the way of Singapore's economic progress. The clean-up program began with the squatters whose homes were without sewers—46,000 of them. The government relocated tens of thousands of families, thousands more "backyard tradesmen," 5,000 street hawkers, 610 pig farmers, and 500 duck farmers out of Singapore's central business district along the riverfront.[10]

The Singaporean squatters got minor compensation and access to public housing. Malaysian squatters got nothing but an invitation to rent flats. The government initially relocated the pig and duck farmers to a thriving agricultural district called Punggol. But then officials decided the island was too small for pigs and ducks, and they phased out these and other livestock completely.[11] Today, Singapore must import all its meat, and Punggol is home to a new town full of high-rises.

The Urban Redevelopment Authority booted the whole mass of street vendors out to "hawker centers" in Boat Quay, Empress Place, and Chinatown. Vegetable wholesalers reestablished their trade a little over a mile south, across the Ayer Rajah Expressway and along the green hills at the Pasir Panjang market, long ago the center of Singapore's state-controlled opium trade. Today, retailers and cooks rouse the market at wee, dark hours, shopping for the day's produce and fish. Bumboat operators and their families went to Pasir Panjang as well. Boat builders and related industries retreated across the island to Jurong, a town forested by the red-and-white-striped smokestacks of heavy industry, far from residential areas and the dense but now immaculate central business district.[12]

As the government carried out the painful human relocations, its dredges spent years scooping tons of rubbish and flotsam from the rivers and excavating mud from their beds to be replaced with sand. The parks department landscaped riverbanks. Public works tiled worn riverside walkways. The Environment Ministry engineered massive pollution controls. The price tag for the cleanup, not including resettlement compensation, was $300 million, or $1.6 billion in today's dollars.[13]

Tan Seng Chai, the engineer who recalls from childhood the putrid smell of the Singapore River, now has an office overlooking the river, in what was once the warehouse district. His view is a postcard: a tropical waterway, set off with lush palm trees and a gazebo in the foreground, winds its way to a modern cityscape of skyscrapers on the horizon. "When I watch my children run around in the clean water and in the canals, I tell them, 'You have no idea,'" he says. "It's incredible that this happened well within a generation."

Indeed, the sanitization of Singapore, along with the government's openhanded economic incentives to lure industry, succeeded beyond all Lee's expectations. The nation's sweet spot in the heart of Asia's shipping lanes makes it an ideal place to import natural resources to refine or manufacture goods and send them back into the world. The country has no oil of its own yet refines more than a million gallons a day.[14]

Shining skyscrapers grew in the central business district like the bright-blooming trees and shrubs Lee ordered planted in precise formation along the highway from Singapore's ultramodern airport. With the multinational corporations came the banks, drawn to the island nation in part by advantageous secrecy laws. By the turn of the century, *Barron's* was calling Singapore the new Switzerland.[15]

Lee's intense pro-business, pro–foreign-investment strategy helped drive 8 percent annual economic growth between 1960 and 1999. More than 7,000 multinationals from the United States, Japan, and Europe eventually settled there, along with 3,000 more from China and India.[16] Singapore's position along the sea-lanes helped make its port one of the busiest in the world. Office towers, five-star hotels, and upscale shopping malls filled in downtown's Orchard Road and beyond. And as the money rolled in, government worked to better the lives of Singaporeans, replacing slums with tidy high-rise housing complexes, and training young people for jobs in the global economy.

By the time of the worldwide financial crisis, when the United States was hit by double-digit unemployment in the last quarter of 2009, Singapore's jobless rate was 2.1 percent.[17] Today, Singapore has the tenth-highest per capita income in the world based on international purchasing power, ahead of the United States at eleventh place and Switzerland at twelfth.[18]

But Singaporeans made some profound trade-offs for the prosperity. Concrete now covers the country's central fruit- and vegetable-growing regions and fishponds. Singapore's Orchard Road was once fragrant with nutmeg and fruit orchards. Now, its sole crop is shopping malls like the ION Orchard, an eight-story "multisensory experiential shopping and lifestyle mall,"[19] anchored by Cartier, Dolce & Gabbana, Giorgio Armani, Louis Vuitton, and Prada.

Aging farmers never quite figured out what to do with themselves and their government compensation. Living in high-rise apartments along with the majority of Singaporeans, the farmers miss their ducks and chickens, their fruit trees and garden plots—and the opportunity to pass down what they know about the land to the next generation.[20]

The next generation, when not shopping, is overworked. Singaporeans report that their devotion to the global economy makes family life difficult; the fertility rate has plummeted to 1.25 children.[21] Financial penalties that discouraged more than two kids, along with public "Stop at two" campaigns, backfired against the consumer economy. The government replaced them with "Have three or more if you can afford it" campaigns. But Singaporean families still don't have enough babies to replace their aging population.[22]

Government is similarly involved in most aspects of life, from personal finance to housing to behavior. Lee offers no apologies for making Singapore a "nanny state," the moniker foreign correspondents gave the nation as they reported on its anti-gum, anti-spitting, anti-littering, and anti-other campaigns. "We would have been a grosser, ruder, cruder society had we not made these efforts to persuade our people to change their ways," Lee writes in his memoir. "We did not measure up as a cultivated, civilized society and were not ashamed to set about trying to become one in the shortest time possible. First, we educated and exhorted our people. After we had persuaded and won over a majority, we legislated to punish the willful minority. It has made Singapore a more pleasant place to live in. If this is a 'nanny state,' I am proud to have fostered one."[23]

When time came for Singapore's next grand water plans, the nanny state would be a handy state. After Singapore had cleaned up its waterways, the government turned to bolstering the nation's anemic water supply. As early as the 1970s, city-state engineers had studied the idea of turning sewage into potable water. By the turn of the century, Singapore had become known worldwide for perfecting the technology that now treats enough wastewater to meet 30 percent of the island's freshwater demand.[24]

In other parts of the world, including the United States, the idea of turning wastewater into tap water has been a tougher sell. The problem isn't technology: the ultrafiltered water beats any health standard on the planet. The problem, Singaporeans determined, is psychology—getting people to drink it. In the nanny state, that wasn't hard to do.

Singapore's small size, along with the perceived political vulnerability of the Malaysian pipelines, led government engineers in the 1970s to begin scrutinizing every drop of water in the country as a potential source of new supply.

They began with Singapore's abundant rainfall. Nearly 100 inches annually drench the island in warm, tropical showers all year, and especially during two monsoon seasons. The cleaned-up rivers meant that Singapore could lean more heavily on its own surface waters for supply, and put them to work capturing rain.

Lee Kuan Yew charged a civil engineer named Lee Ek Tieng with a plan to dam up every single stream and river in the country. By 1980, Singapore's water utility, PUB, was capturing about sixty-three million gallons a day from those sources, then about half the nation's daily needs.[25]

But demand for water was rising along with the number of computer wafer-fabrication plants and other thirsty industries moving in. Lee Ek Tieng, who had to turn Lee Kuan Yew's frequent big ideas into tangible engineering solutions, got to work building reservoirs as well.[26]

He also laid an underground sewer network for the entire island, a difficult job in the heavily built-up city center. Today, 100 percent of Singapore's five million residents have access to clean drinking water and to sanitation hooked up to sewers, a feat unheard of elsewhere in the industrialized world. The entire water-supply system, including every business and home on the island, is also metered.[27]

It's worth noting that an estimated two million Americans today either have no running water, or turn on their tap to unclean water.[28] Meanwhile, twenty million Americans aren't hooked up to sewers; instead, they rely on septic tanks or cesspools. Another 900,000, according to the U.S. Census Bureau, still use outhouses or privies. California has the highest number of homes with outhouses, at 67,865.[29]

Coming up with half the nation's daily water needs, of course, was not good enough. To augment the half supplied by dams, PUB had pondered sewage as a possible source of high-quality drinking water. In 1974, PUB built a pilot reclamation plant to study whether reverse-osmosis filtration could make wastewater clean enough to drink. The plant worked, but with a price tag more apropos to fine wine than municipal water. Steep costs shuttered the facility after only fourteen months.

But PUB's engineers never gave up the idea. "We knew that any water could be a potential source of water supply," says Harry Seah, an affable civil engineer who spent much of his early career with PUB working to perfect filtration. "If only we could find the right technology."[30]

Singaporean leaders believe in nothing so strongly as the power of technology to forward national goals. (The government was the first to give citizens free nationwide broadband and subsidized laptops for the poor.) They waited for advances in membrane technology to bring costs down. That took twenty-five years. They dusted off their sewage-reclamation plans in 1998, in a joint project between PUB and the government's Ministry for Environment and Water Resources. They sent Seah and another young colleague to the United

States to study Factory 21, in California's Orange County, and the Upper Occoquan Sewage Authority, in northern Virginia, both of which had used treated wastewater to recharge aquifers since the late 1970s.

This time, leaders felt confident enough in the science to build the world's first major waste-to-drinking-water plant. The "right technology" turned out to involve just what you'd expect: filtering wastewater over and over again, a process known as multibarrier water treatment.

Just as important was making Singapore's new source of water psychologically palatable. Playing around with the words *new* and *water*, a committee chaired by Lee Ek Tieng came up with the perfect name for the stuff: NEWater.[31] (PUB officials make a conscious attempt never to utter the word *wastewater* in the context of NEWater. They instead say "used water," to "reflect the new mindset that water is a precious resource that can be reused," says PUB's Teo Yin Yin.)[32]

NEWater is the Zen of water purification. Seah and his colleagues came up with three essential steps that free water molecules from waste on a transcendental journey that leads to isolation and cleanliness.

The original state isn't raw sewage, but treated wastewater. This used water has been run through primary and secondary sewage treatment: First, it's separated from sludge. Then, pumps push it through fibers that block small particles like suspended solids and bacteria. The resulting effluent is just like what we in the United States dump back into our oceans, rivers, and wetlands.

The tea-colored effluent's first step to transcendence is known as ultrafiltration. It's pushed at high pressure through racks containing millions of microscopic, hollow fibers. These tiny straws have teeny pores in them, 1/1000th the width of a human hair. Water molecules pass through with ease, but larger fellow travelers like suspended solids and protozoa get left behind.

The next step is reverse osmosis. Pumps now push the water through tubes that contain membranes so tightly woven that only water molecules can squeeze past. The membranes trap contaminants such as endocrine disruptors from pharmaceuticals, plus bacteria, viruses, and other pollutants.

The result is crystal-clear, über-clean, and drinkable. But Seah and the ever antiseptic Singaporeans wanted better. He and his team added a peace-of-mind component, ultraviolet disinfection. In this last safety stage, a mercury arc lamp zaps the water to sterilize any microorganic hangers-on.

PUB officially launched NEWater in early 2003. But the government spent the two years prior working on its acceptance. More than 200 stories about NEWater appeared in the national and international media between January 2001 and the February 2003 launch.[33] An oft-told narrative in Singapore's national daily newspaper, the *Straits Times*, described used drinking water as common and widespread in the United States: "For millions living in communities in California, Arizona, and Virginia in the U.S.," said one piece, "reclaimed water has become as ordinary as storm sewers and summer droughts."[34]

The stories were heavy on propaganda. Those projects were the only ones of their kind in the United States at the time, and moreover treated small amounts of reclaimed water to recharge aquifers. Singapore's plans were much bolder, blending NEWater into its drinking-water reservoirs, even bottling it as a crystal-clear symbol of the nation's technological prowess.

At Singapore's National Day Parade in August 2002, the standard goodie bags, tens of thousands of them, included the usual national mini-flag and other novelties, but also a 1.5-liter bottle of NEWater, festively decorated for the occasion. Declaring "Yam seng" (Chinese for *cheers*), Prime Minister Goh Chok Tong led 60,000 Singaporeans in a mass toast of NEWater. (The next day's headline in the *Straits Times*: "Cheers! to 37 years . . . and NEWater.")[35]

The water does taste fine, at least served chilled at the end of a tour of Singapore's first NEWater plant, christened by the prime minister with the turn of a giant spigot. As part of its public-education campaign, PUB built a visitor's center alongside the plant on the southeast side of the island. The modern building, with its glass walls, wave-shaped roof, and water gardens, has become a tourist attraction that draws more than 100,000 visitors a year.

Weaving through the center's multimedia mix of national pride and water science, it's easy to see how the government convinced Singaporeans to accept NEWater. In the opening exhibits, black-and-white photos from the 1960s recall the era of water rationing and once filthy waterways. In the closing ones, international headlines and awards laud the Singaporeans for their water wisdom.

Before the first plant opened, NEWater had a 98 percent acceptance rate, with 82 percent of respondents saying they'd drink it directly and another 16 percent saying they'd do so if it were mixed with reservoir water.[36] As Seah points out, "Singaporeans trust their government." Why wouldn't they, when the current generation has it so much better than the last?

The government's water ambitions didn't stop with NEWater, for the loop was not yet closed. The next bold project, first envisioned by Singapore's benevolent dictator more than two decades ago, would turn two-thirds of the island into a water-storage area.

Ultimately, the idea is for the entire nation to work as one giant cistern.

In 1987, after the last glob of chicken fat was finally cleaned up from the Singapore River, Prime Minister Lee Kuan Yew outlined his dream for a structure that would someday eliminate tides at the mouth of the river where it meets the sea, controlling Singapore's monsoon-season floods and providing the country with "a large, strategic reserve of water—freshwater—for use in an emergency.

"In 20 years, it is possible that there could be breakthroughs in technology," the ever aspiring leader declared, "and then we dam or put a barrage at the mouth of the marina—the neck that joins the sea—and we will have a huge freshwater lake."[37]

The neck that joins the sea, of course, was an estuary—where the Singapore, Kallang, and Geylang rivers met to create a brackish bay. Even in the age of sustainability, Singapore's leaders view their natural waterways as enemies to overpower rather than allies providing life—in this case, an ecosystem that was home to 182 species of fish, along with the birds and marine mammals that depend on them.[38]

In 2004, PUB put out bids for Lee's barrage. It awarded the project to Singaporean construction and civil-engineering giant Koh Brothers for $226 million. And four years later, Singapore was toasting another bold water project. The Marina Barrage, essentially a sophisticated dam, now stretches across the mouth of the bay. In a years-long process of dilution—rain falls in, seawater is pushed out—the barrage is slowly replacing the bay with an enormous freshwater reservoir.

Visitors can walk across the barrage atop a wide, concrete bridge and gaze down at its nine steel gates, each a hundred feet wide and weighing seventy tons. When rains pound Singapore during low tide, the gates are lowered to release excess water from the reservoir into the sea. When the monsoons hit at high tide, the gates stay closed and seven drainage pumps push the water out. Designed for the sinking Netherlands, the super-sized pumps can displace 75,000 gallons of water a second.

The barrage is creating Singapore's fifteenth reservoir, the first inside the city center. Combined with two more reservoirs now under construction, it will help increase the nation's water-catchment areas from one-half of the island to two-thirds. The Marina Barrage has also brought kayaking, dragon boating, and many other public events back to the mouth of the Singapore River. But, kind of like those kids at America's largest water park, kayakers at the barrage don't have to fret over waves or even tides—PUB's water controls eliminate them. They don't have to worry much about wildlife, either. The freshwater reservoir is replacing the tidal estuary. Scientists from the National University of Singapore found some thirty fishes that will no longer be able to breed as a result of the barrage, including snapper, Asian sea bass, and Indo-Pacific tarpon.[39]

While barrage construction was under way, they also built the island's first desalination plant, which wrings thirty million gallons of freshwater each day from the sea. PUB officials consider other countries' desalination wasteful "because you treat it at great expense, use it once, and return it to the sea," says Harry Seah. "But if you are recycling, it can make sense."[40]

Indeed, at half the cost of desalination, PUB officials have put their faith primarily in NEWater. They recently unveiled the nation's fifth NEWater plant, bringing the island's capacity to more than a hundred million gallons a day. That's about a third of Singapore's daily water demand.[41]

Finally, to capture the main ingredient for all those NEWater plants, Singapore is building a sewage superhighway deep underground. The so-called deep-tunnel sewerage system, 200 feet below the island's surface, is part of the largest wastewater-treatment project in the history of the world. A massive tunnel, larger than those that carry Singapore's subway trains—20 feet in diameter compared with the 19-foot-wide train tunnels—runs under the island below the trains.[42] This tunnel and a second one planned for the future will replace smaller pipelines, pumping stations, and reclamation plants across the island to free up precious land for other projects. Gravity pulls used water from homes and industries, concentrated in the northern and eastern part of Singapore, through the tunnels and into giant, centralized water-reclamation plants on each end of the island. The first, Changi, at the east side, can treat 176 million gallons of wastewater a day. (Singapore built its fifth NEWater plant on Changi's roof.) In the future, PUB plans another such plant on the west side of the island. The scheme allows "every drop of used water to be collected, treated, and further purified into NEWater," says Yong Wei Hin, assistant director of the Changi plant.[43]

By the last decades of the twentieth century, Singapore was broadly recognized as having the most advanced water-supply technology in the world. But as it turns out, the nation had gotten almost too good at providing water. PUB officials began to notice an unintended irony: water had become so accessible, and its protection and production so invisible, that people were taking it for granted—at least by Singaporean standards.

Per capita water consumption grew steadily in Singapore during the 1970s, the 1980s, and especially the 1990s. Elaborate "Save Water" campaigns in each of those decades didn't make a drop of difference. Nor did a water-conservation tax in the 1990s that charged more to Singaporeans who used more.[44] Ultimately, one strategy has worked best to lower consumption, says Seah and others. The government set out to instill a water ethic in citizens. PUB officials say the effort to build a personal connection to water has spurred more conservation than either publicity campaigns or price incentives. Since the mid-1990s, per capita consumption has declined steadily from nearly fifty gallons a person to forty gallons a person in 2010. The government's goal is to hit thirty-six gallons a person by 2030.[45]

The strategy to "bring people closer to water so that they can better appreciate and cherish this precious resource" was much more than public relations.[46] The most ambitious piece was making the Marina Barrage a waterfront public attraction. It is a very successful one, judging by the hordes of children in bathing suits running, jumping, and laughing in its fountain park on a recent hot day. Aside from fountains, sculptures, and gardens, Marina Barrage has a two-story, circular visitor center shaped like a seashell. The center houses the pumping station behind glass walls, a popular Chinese restaurant called the 7th Storey, and the Sustainable Singapore Gallery, with artwork and hands-on exhibits meant to educate the public on environmental and especially water issues. Its roof is a grass play area as big as four football fields, where families picnic and fly colorful kites.

At both the Sustainable Singapore Gallery and the NEWater Factory, hands-on displays are high tech, flashy, and interactive, designed to appeal to young Singaporeans' love for technology. Uniformed schoolchildren wind through the exhibits, many of them filling out classroom assignments. PUB works closely with both public and private schools on water curriculum. Beginning in kindergarten, kids learn all about Singapore's "four national taps": the imports from Malaysia, NEWater, desalinated water, and the increasingly important idea of local catchment areas. "We're not asking them to name every reservoir and the average annual rainfall," says PUB's Linda Dorothy de Mello. "We just want them to make the connection."[47]

The most direct new connection between Singaporeans and their water is the one that gets them wet—the kayaking at the Marina Barrage, the public park back at Bedok Reservoir and similar projects under way all over the island.

At a public housing neighborhood called Kolam Ayer, nondescript high-rise apartments once overlooked a drab, razor-straight canal. Today, the waterway has been restored with trees and aquatic plants on its banks and a river walk with floating decks and hands-on projects for neighborhood kids. A toddler yanks a giant Archimedes screw meant to teach children an ancient method of moving water. An elderly man enjoys two hobbies at once: as he fishes with a cane pole at the edge of the canal, his songbird hangs in a willow behind him, silent in a tiny, teak cage.

Living in their small, high-rise apartments, well cared for by a government that has convinced them to drink recycled water and celebrate how skillfully their nation captures every drop, the Singaporean people may seem like those songbirds in their lacquered cages. The birds have benevolent caretakers, clean water in hand-painted bowls, beautiful venues for singing.

But it's not quite how you'd want to live, if you were a songbird.

Water officials in Singapore like to say they've closed the water loop: Every river is dammed, with significant impact to fish and other wildlife. Every bit of water is collected, whether rainfall or sewage. Seawater and wastewater alike are squeezed into freshwater.

Singaporeans had no choice but to close the loop. They live on a tiny island with hardly any freshwater supply. They fear reliance on a political rival for their lifeblood. In the United States, this is not the case. We're blessed with more than 250,000 rivers—3.5 million miles of them. The longest, the Missouri, flows for a stunning 2,500 miles. The largest, the Mississippi, at its mouth gushes 593,000 cubic feet per second.[48] We've got the largest single source of fresh surface water on the planet, the Great Lakes, which hold a fifth of the world's supply.[49] Another 60,000 trillion gallons or so course underground in aquifers, recharging to the tune of about a trillion gallons a day.[50]

Singaporeans deserve global admiration for the breathtaking turnaround of their economy in just one generation. They deserve deep respect for giving every person in the country access to clean water and sanitation. And they deserve credit for becoming the world's ultimate water conservationists, reusing every drop on their tiny island.

Some American communities have so overtapped their natural supply that they're being forced to do the same. But for those that still have options, the best one happens to be the easiest and the cheapest: keeping as much water as possible in natural systems—rivers, lakes, and streams—and valuing every drop like the treasure that it is.

Singapore's water lesson is not NEWater, the barrage, or the other technological breakthroughs piling up engineering awards from the United States and other parts of the world. The crucial lesson is that the island nation managed to build an ethic among a citizenry that had stopped caring about water.

Most Americans want to see wild rivers. We want to put up rain barrels and keep chickens in the backyard—or at least have the right to do so. We don't want to see the raising of pigs and ducks phased out completely. We don't want to be fined for forgetting to flush the toilet. We don't want to be told not to chew gum.

We have the engineering prowess to harness every river. We have the technology to wrest freshwater molecules from sewage. In fact, the semipermeable membranes central to the first step of NEWater come from Pennsylvania-based GE Water and Process Technologies. Continuing to build our way to water supply will certainly enrich the contractors who land the projects. It will further empower our water bureaucracies à la Singapore, where no one is allowed a cistern because water managers must capture every drop of rain.

But if we took better care of our abundant water resources, and if we used them wisely, *we wouldn't have to.*

The Big Dipper

If the notoriety of a public figure may be measured by the number, range, and sheer juiciness of nicknames bestowed, then Patricia Mulroy, general manager of the Southern Nevada Water Authority for more than two decades, is the most notorious water manager in America.

The *New York Times* calls her the Vegas Water Czar.[1] Her local newspaper, the *Las Vegas Sun,* anoints her the Chosen One.[2]

Following that biblical theme, the trustworthy WaterWired blog, produced in Oregon, calls her Moses—but actually, it's in honor of Robert Moses, the power broker of New York City who bullied through bridges, tunnels, and parkways in the mid-twentieth century, wiping out urban neighborhoods to shape the modern suburbs.[3]

Inevitably, sexist monikers cling to a woman in power. Mulroy is reviled as the Water Witch of the West.[4] I've heard her called the Water Czarina, the Alpha Female, and this twist: the Alpha Female with Cojones.

In her Las Vegas home, Mulroy also picked up the nickname Scarlett. Water journalist Emily Green describes this comparison with the "ruthless, scheming, tough, histrionic, and beautiful" heroine in *Gone with the Wind* who cries, "As God as my witness, I will never be hungry again!"[5]

Mulroy's job is to make sure Las Vegas, the driest city in the driest state in the nation, will never, ever be thirsty. The reason she's racked up so many nicknames is because she's very, very good at it.

◆　◆　◆

No member of America's water-industrial complex thinks bigger than Patricia Mulroy. She wears ambition like the signature turned-up collars on her blouses; she has since her twenties, when as an assistant administrator in Clark County government, she helped fend off annexation of the lucrative Las Vegas Strip by city government. Mentally quick and physically fit, she bounded up the local-government ladder. In less than ten years, she was running the Las Vegas Valley Water District as deputy general manager. Her determination did not go unnoticed by the water-loving Strip. When the water district's top position opened up, the wizards of illusion who make fountains dance in the desert pushed Mulroy in preference to an archetypal water-management candidate, a former commissioner of the U.S. Bureau of Reclamation and assistant secretary of the interior who was looking to come home to Nevada.[6]

Las Vegas didn't want a water manager steeped in arcane western water law, accepting of the historic compact that gives Nevada the least water of all the seven states that share the Colorado River. When the river was divvied up in 1922, southern Nevada was nearly deserted; the entire state received 4 percent of the Colorado allocation.[7]

In the 1990s, Las Vegas became the fastest-growing metropolitan area in the country.[8] It fancied itself the glittering symbol of the New West. It wanted new ways to find new water.

Mulroy got off to a promising start. She began by taking on the fountaineers themselves. She convinced Steve Wynn—the Strip's best-known resort developer, the conjurer of flamboyant public water shows at the Mirage, the Bellagio, and Treasure Island—that he and fellow casino developers would recycle the water in their choreographed fountains, or lose them. She also began to help residents reduce what was then a 350-gallon-a-day water habit, targeting their irrigation of subtropical lawns in the Mojave Desert.[9]

But Mulroy's job was, and remains, to secure more water so the city can continue growing residents, real estate, and resorts. The new position gave her control over just one of seven rival water companies that serve southern Nevada's Las Vegas Basin. Almost immediately, she began to work on the other six, trying to convince them to pool their water under a new mega-agency. Her argument: having tapped out Nevada's original allocation of the Colorado, Vegas must become a bigger player to land more water. By combining resources, the water purveyors could develop regional supplies. They also might be able to win more clout at the negotiating table with the other states vying for water from the Colorado.[10]

Less than a year into the new job, Mulroy made one of the biggest urban water grabs in western U.S. history. After quietly prospecting to figure out how much groundwater could be pumped up from the rest of Nevada to serve Las Vegas Valley, Mulroy's district filed applications for all the unclaimed groundwater in about half the state. Her local rivals liked what they saw. They agreed to merge into Mulroy's mega-agency. After just three years as head of the Las Vegas Valley Water District, she was also named general manager of the Southern Nevada Water Authority.[11]

Ranchers and residents of the rural counties where Vegas made its claim for every last drop of groundwater were furious. They saw Mulroy as "foreclosing" on their future, by tying up all the available water rights in the four huge counties. Their battle cry became "Remember the Owens Valley!"[12] The Owens, just east of the Sierra Nevada in California, was once fertile home to orchards, farms, and ranches, but it dried to a near dust bowl after William Mulholland, chief of the Los Angeles Department of Water and Power at the turn of the twentieth century, carried out a quiet plan to acquire Owens water and send it by aqueduct 235 miles to LA. The shadowy deal was fictionalized in the 1974 film *Chinatown,* with a character based on Mulholland named Hollis Mulwray.

In 1992, when the late environmental writer Marc Reisner updated his classic book on western water, *Cadillac Desert,* he'd recently come across the "forceful" Patricia Mulroy, and he wrote about her in the promising context of urban water alliances taking shape in the New West. But in either a Freudian slip or a sly nod to her potential, Reisner referred to her as Patricia Mulwray, using the last name of the *Chinatown* character.

The new nickname may turn out to be the most apt of them all.

For the woman who definitely had the cojones to forge a bold, new path for water in the New West instead has become the nation's most ardent champion of the old.

Mulroy has indeed helped redirect the flow of Colorado River water for the good of her city. She's prevailed in her argument that Las Vegas, with its $60 billion economic output, is at least as valuable as the 400 farms in California's Imperial Valley that were getting as much Colorado River water as all of Nevada and Arizona combined.[13] In 2001, Mulroy negotiated water-banking agreements with Arizona and California that let Nevada pay to store water in those states, then pull extra from Lake Mead. In 2007, when the Colorado River Basin states agreed to a new pact for how the river should be divvied when it runs low, they also let Mulroy's agency build a $172 million reservoir in California to store any Colorado River water unclaimed by U.S. agricultural users (say, in case it rains and the farmers don't need it) to keep it from flowing to Mexico. Again, the deal lets Nevada withdraw more than its meager allocation from the Colorado.[14] (Mexico is allocated 1.5 million acre-feet of the Colorado under a 1944 treaty with the United States in which Mexico agreed to send water the other direction from six tributaries that feed into the Rio Grande. Mulroy also has proposed funding desalination plants for Mexico in exchange for some of the country's allocation.)

And despite her crusade for freshwater sources, Mulroy has declared war on waste. She's championed water-wise housing developments and landscaping. She started a cash-for-grass program that pays homeowners $1.50 a square foot to tear out their lawns. That and other initiatives helped Las Vegas pinch off 20 percent of its water use between 2001 and 2008, even as the metropolitan area added 482,000 new residents in those years to reach the milestone of two million in population.[15]

"The future, foundational ethic of water agencies has to be weaning the community of wasteful water use," says Mulroy. "Some of this is easy—we're not asking you to carry your urn to Lake Mead. We're talking about, if you're going to live in the desert, live as if it's a desert, not with Kentucky bluegrass."[16]

But in some ways, Las Vegas has made water too easy. Despite rate increases during Mulroy's tenure, Las Vegas families still enjoy some of the lowest water prices in the nation. An analysis by the water-reporting consortium Circle of Blue in 2010 found that a family of four in the water-scarce city has an average $32.93 monthly water bill, while a family using the same amount must shell out $72.95 a month in Atlanta, which receives ten times Vegas's rainfall.[17] When I interviewed Mulroy in fall 2010, Las Vegas residents could still water their lawns with this inexpensive water three times a week.

This disconnect between cost and scarcity is part of the problem with the massive groundwater project to tap the aquifers beneath the Great Basin of eastern Nevada, which would pull water from under the rural Nevada counties as well as some in western Utah. It's not that rural Nevadans or next-door neighbors in Utah don't recognize the need to share the region's most important resource. But they don't want to see it siphoned to keep water cheap in Las Vegas at the expense of their own economy and ecosystems.

Mulroy argues that the Southern Nevada Water Authority has a legal right to tap water that belongs to Nevada. But say the groundwater project makes it through the courts. The country is full of water projects and compacts that were perfectly legal—or made so by state legislatures or Congress—but one hardly needs to query Ask the Ethicist to figure out if they were right.

In his book *Escaping Plato's Cave*, the four-decade Associated Press correspondent Mort Rosenblum writes about the pathetic remnants of native villages in California and Mexico that once thrived on the banks of the Colorado River near where it flowed into the Sea of Cortez. In the early 1960s, the Colorado River treaty left Mexico with so little water that the river's lush delta ecosystem shrank to a lifeless, salt-flat wasteland.[18] In the community of Al Mayor in Baja California, a Cucapa Indian chief told Rosenblum, "Our river is gone. No more fishing. Trees are dead. No one plants. The wells are dry." The villagers can use the river's salty trickle for washing. But for drinking and cooking, they are forced to buy their water in 5-gallon jugs from a traveling water salesman.[19] It was not until 1974 that the United States agreed to include water *quality* in its promise of Colorado River water to Mexico.

Local leaders in Utah worry that southern Nevada's pipeline will prevent them from growing in the way their communities envision.[20] Scientists who study Snake Valley, at the Nevada-Utah border, speculate that the project could dry up desert vegetation, not only wiping out wildlife habitat but also creating dust storms to rival those of the 1930s.[21]

History bears out the need to listen carefully to these warnings, and come up with a new, ethical framework for moving water around U.S. regions. But Mulroy doesn't see it. Even as she fashions herself the new, green water manager for the twenty-first century, challenging the conservative mind-set of the men who divvied up the Colorado River, she's dreaming of a bigger water grab than those guys ever imagined.[22]

In 2009, as Congress debated the nearly $800 billion federal stimulus bill, Mulroy served up her most audacious suggestion for how to spend the money: if the federal government really wanted to pump up job growth and stimulate the economy, she suggested, perhaps it should consider the largest water-diversion project in American history. What if the nation decided to capture floodwater from the Mississippi River and use it to recharge the massive aquifer being sucked dry underneath America's Great Plains?[23] Mississippi floods are a menace. Meanwhile, to the west, we're depleting the High Plains Aquifer. Could the problems cancel each other out?

Mulroy envisions a scheme that would dwarf the Hoover and Glen Canyon Dams, take a decade or more to build, create tens of thousands of jobs, and inject billions of dollars into the economy. Engineering firms CH2M Hill and Black & Veatch floated the idea as part of a nothing-off-the-table contract with the Southern Nevada Water Authority as drought sunk the level in Lake Mead. In their 2008 report, the firms looked at all sorts of options for bolstering the flow of water in the Colorado River. They included building a pipeline from the Columbia River on the border of Washington and Oregon, even shipping water down from Alaska. But the Mississippi plan is the one that sparked Mulroy's imagination.[24] In public appearances and in interviews, she often seems to be working on the argument. She points out that "the West is growing dryer and the East is growing wetter" under the specter of climate change.

Shipping water from the wetter eastern United States to quench the arid West is not a new concept. In the 1960s, Texas politicians hatched the outsized Texas Water Plan to capture Mississippi River water and replenish their overtapped plains.[25] In the 1970s, Congress authorized a $6 million U.S. Army Corps of Engineers study on the feasibility of transporting water west to the High Plains.[26] In the early 1980s, Jonathan Bulkley, a former water-policy professor of mine at the University of Michigan, conducted the last serious study of the question, to show how much it would cost to connect the Great Lakes to the Missouri to move water to the High Plains. The Rocky Mountains are the roadblock. Transporting water around, through, or over them makes moving water from the eastern to the western half of the country massively expensive, Bulkley says. He couldn't see the taxpayers going for it. Building the infrastructure only as far as South Dakota, he found, would cost $20 billion (in 1982 dollars). That doesn't include the energy costs to hoist the water up and pump it hundreds of miles west, which he calculated at another $7 billion.[27]

But, like a bottled-water genius on Madison Avenue, Mulroy has taken a water project long considered flat and has carbonated and sweetened it to appeal to a new generation. Mississippi water could refill the High Plains Aquifer as the first in a chain of infrastructure projects and exchanges from east to west. Suburbanites in Denver and farmers across the eastern flank of the Rockies could then tap into the Mississippi water, relinquishing Colorado River water they now pump across the Continental Divide. That would leave more water in the Colorado—and more for Las Vegas.[28]

Las Vegas has invested deeply in conservation under Mulroy, who paid her customers more than $100 million to remove grass and replace it with desert vegetation. Still, the arid oasis lives so far beyond its water means that it also comes up flat in the search for a water ethic for America.

I wanted to find a more holistic way of thinking about the ethic—beyond using less on our lawns and in our fountains, toward a shared respect for water, ecosystems, and people. I consulted a spectrum of philosophical readings, many of them conflicting. They ranged from eighteenth-century philosopher Immanuel Kant, who famously believed that nature held no moral standing at all, to Albert Schweitzer and his beautiful "reverence for life" ideas.[29] I found academic tomes that tackled the promise of a water ethic, but so densely that the average person would no more read them than Newton's *Principia*. But perhaps, with some 85 percent of Americans identifying with a religious faith—nearly 80 percent with a Christian denomination[30]—I could find some common ground for a water ethic in the Bible and other religious texts.

The arid deserts of the Middle East, birthplace of Christianity, Islam, and Judaism, gave water utmost importance in the Bible, the Quran, and the Torah.[31] Like the flood myths, the theme of water as giver of life and cleanser of sin repeats again and again. The Quran considers water the most precious creation after humankind.[32] In the Torah and in the Bible's Old Testament, the world is created from water, which symbolizes the primordial ocean from where all life flows.[33] The Bible mentions water more than any other element, and God's care for people is often revealed with the gift of water. "He watereth the hills from his chambers," says Psalm 104. "The earth is satisfied with the fruit of thy works."[34]

Outside the desert of the Israelites, there was an obvious place to look for Christian views on water: the U.S. Bible Belt—specifically, the section where water has become most famously linked to prayer, Atlanta, Georgia. Most eastern cities sit atop massive aquifers that supply groundwater to urbanites, or they're close to major surface-water supplies such as lakes. Atlanta is not one of them. The Chattahoochee River, or the Hooch, as it is affectionately known by locals, is the smallest river in the nation to supply water to a major metro area. More than five million people in and around Atlanta rely on the Chattahoochee's Lake Sidney Lanier for all their water needs.

Lake Lanier is actually a reservoir, created by the U.S. Army Corps of Engineers in the 1950s as it dammed the Chattahoochee.

The real Sidney Lanier, a Georgia-born poet who wrote lyrically of the Chattahoochee's rapids, likely would have been appalled by the impoundment's christening. The river can no longer "hurry amain to reach the plain," as Lanier wrote in his 1877 poem "Song of the Chattahoochee."[35] It is stretched too thin by Atlanta's lawn irrigation (the city's biggest residential water use), toilet flushing (the second biggest), and other household water demands—not to mention fourteen dams, sixteen power plants, and countless industrial draws, including the Hooch-filled bottles of Dasani that roll off Coca-Cola's production line in Marietta.[36] Downstream, the Chattahoochee also brings life to south Georgia, as well as Alabama and Florida, where its basin helps irrigate 780,000 acres of corn, cotton, peanut, and other crops each year. In Florida's Panhandle, the Hooch joins another Georgia river, the Flint, to become the powerful Apalachicola, which carries sixteen billion gallons of freshwater a day to the Gulf of Mexico, there creating one of the last unspoiled brackish bays in the Southeast.

During a devastating drought in 1988, federal environmental officials declared Apalachicola Bay a disaster area when diminished Chattahoochee flow killed the bay's nationally known oyster harvest—the mainstay of the local economy. But the Corps of Engineers's allegiance stuck with Atlanta sprinklers rather than Apalachicola shellfish. In 1989, the Corps came up with a new dam-and-reservoir plan to harness even more of the Chattahoochee in dry times. A year later, Alabama, worried that a dwindled flow would hamper the state's ability to grow and develop, filed a lawsuit to stop the dam. Florida joined the suit, arguing that further upstream withdrawals would destroy Apalachicola Bay and the region's signature seafood industry.

Those were the opening jabs in a water fight that has slogged on for twenty years. In 1998, Congress passed a celebrated truce: a water compact for the three states. But tristate officials failed so miserably in negotiating the compact—they missed fourteen deadlines—that it was terminated five years later. The fight then moved on to courthouses in Birmingham, Jacksonville, Atlanta, and Washington, D.C. The lawyers fared no better than the politicians in figuring out how to share the Hooch. But in just the past decade, they've managed to bill the states' taxpayers more than $30 million in legal fees.[37]

This is the problem with America's water wars, be they among cities, regions, or states: the conflicts put each combatant in the defensive mode of figuring out how to get more and more water, rather than working together to use less. They cost citizens millions of dollars in legal fees without the first drop of "new" water. And they take attention away from what's *really* important: working to keep as much water as possible in stream, and learning to live within our water means.

Georgia did not concede that last point until the water supply for its largest city very nearly ran out. State lawmakers had long refused to consider a state water plan. One big change that did make its way to Georgia's state assembly, requiring that water-wasting toilets be replaced with efficient ones upon sale of an existing home, was unceremoniously flushed by the real estate industry. Hubris gave way to humility in fall 2007, a year and a half into the worst drought to settle on the southeastern United States in modern times. Lake Lanier came within 90 days of running dry. Then Georgia governor Sonny Perdue, a Baptist, led a public prayer service on the steps of the gold-domed state capitol in Atlanta "to very reverently and respectfully pray up a storm."[38] He quoted Psalm 65, which praises God for water abundance:

> You visit the earth and water it, you greatly enrich it; the river of God is full of water; you provide their grain, for so you have prepared it. You water its ridges abundantly, you settle its furrows; you make it soft with showers, you bless its growth.[39]

The governor's prayers were answered, and then some. The next fall, Tropical Storm Fay shepherded a flock of storms that soaked the Southeast and helped fill Lanier. But the judge considering the tristate litigation over the Chattahoochee was not so benevolent to Atlanta. In 2009, U.S. District Court judge Paul Magnuson ruled that Lanier had never been authorized as a water supply for Atlanta; the Corps of Engineers had been illegally diverting it as such for fifty years. Magnuson gave Georgia, Alabama, and Florida until 2012 to come up with a water-sharing plan for the Hooch and have Congress okay it. Otherwise, he'd cut Atlanta off Lanier. His ninety-seven-page ruling ended with what may have been the most sensible statement uttered in the twenty-year legal battle:

> Too often, state, local, and even national government actors do not consider the long-term consequences of their decisions. Local governments allow unchecked growth because it increases tax revenue, but these same governments do not sufficiently plan for the resources such unchecked growth will require. Nor do individual citizens consider frequently enough their consumption of our scarce resources, absent a crisis. . . . Only by cooperating, planning, and conserving can we avoid the situations that gave rise to this litigation.[40]

Georgia's politicians began to repent. In spring 2010, Perdue signed the Water Stewardship Act, which vaulted Georgia over any southeastern state on water conservation, with water-efficient building requirements and a daytime-irrigation ban. Later that year, when Perdue moved out of the governor's mansion, he said the lack of resolution in the tristate water wars was the major disappointment of his eight years in office.[41]

Inheriting the tristate tussle was incoming governor Nathan Deal, a three-term Congressman from north Georgia whose gubernatorial election strategy included plays to conspiracy theorists. On global warming, Deal challenged the U.S. Environmental Protection Agency's finding that greenhouse-gas pollution endangers public health, charging that climate science is "fundamentally corrupted."[42]

When it came to water, Deal had tried to wean Atlanta off the Chattahoochee and Lake Lanier, but at the expense of the Flint River. During his last term in Congress, in 2008, he sought $10 million in federal funding to study reauthorization of a series of dams on the Flint that had been nixed with the help of Jimmy Carter during his terms as governor of Georgia and president.[43]

What most people outside Georgia don't realize is that the biggest water wars in the state are not with Florida and Alabama; they are between metro Atlanta and everyone else in Georgia. Besides the Chattahoochee, the Coosa and Flint Rivers also supply water to the metro region via interbasin transfers. The transfers are so controversial within the state that rural lawmakers ten years ago managed to ban water transfers into Atlanta from any basin outside the fifteen-county metro area. But Georgia was expected to change its interbasin-transfer rules in 2011, in response to both the Lanier problem and the fears in counties upstream and downstream of Atlanta that the metro area is "suckin' water out of the state," as a prime-time television commercial charged during the 2010 gubernatorial elections. "Ask the candidates for governor," the ad admonished, "who will hold metro Atlanta accountable?"[44]

The Metro Atlanta Chamber called the ad a low blow to a city that is working hard to become sustainable. But the rest-of-us-vs.-Atlanta mentality is easy to understand when gold-dome politicians continue to draw beads on rivers like the Savannah, which forms the border between Georgia and South Carolina, and the Tennessee River, which doesn't even flow through Georgia. (That inconvenient fact hasn't stopped Peach State lawmakers. In 2008, they passed a resolution directing the state to try to fix a 200-year-old surveying error they say keeps Georgia from its rightful share of the Tennessee River, which lies just a mile north of the Georgia-Tennessee border and carries some fifteen times as much water as the Chattahoochee.)[45]

Liberals laughed when Governor Perdue prayed for rain. But they should heed the moral of the story: Atlanta's Christian community has embraced water as a cause, perhaps more widely than in any other water-stressed part of the United States. Churches and religious schools alike are trying to help the city build a water ethic based on biblical stewardship principles. More than a dozen major Presbyterian churches, for example, work together under the auspices of the Earth Covenant Ministry, which developed a water initiative "to engage people of faith on the issue of water: how we use it, treat it, advocate for it, and share it with neighbors downstream for the flourishing of all creation." The ministry preaches a gospel of relating to downstream neighbors and nearby states "not as competitors with whom to be at war, but as companions in the shared responsibility of protecting water," says the organization's founder, Reverend Alan Jenkins. The far-reaching ministry gives water-conservation advice to parishioners and water-policy advice to politicians—weighing in on the transfer issue at the state Capitol Building, for example.[46]

Rural Georgians also are turning to their churches for an answer to water conflict. In Rome, in the northwest corner of the state, Joe Cook, Riverkeeper of the Upper Coosa, has been making the Wednesday-night rounds at Baptist and Methodist churches for a talk that asks, "If you had water in abundance and your neighbor was in need, would you share your abundance with your neighbor?" Sharing is, after all, the Christian thing to do. But Cook says the answer, for a majority of parishioners in Rome, is no.

It's not that they wouldn't share their water blessings (three rivers that carry through about 4.4 billion gallons of water a day, compared with the 1.6 billion gallons that flow by Atlanta in the Chattahoochee) with neighbors who were truly in need. But, like the rural Utah and Nevada interests fretting over southern Nevada's groundwater grab, they don't want to see their rivers irrigate metro-area lawns at the expense of their own growth and prosperity. "Metro Atlanta is starting to get serious about water conservation and doing the right thing, but there's still a lot Metro Atlanta can do," Cook says. "Until they do, the good Baptists of Rome, Georgia, and elsewhere are not inclined to share what they have in abundance."[47]

After the philosophers, the academics, and the Christians, there was still one crucial authority I had yet to mine for ethical truths about water. And that was YouTube. One Saturday morning, I settled in on the couch with my laptop and an expert navigator of classic cartoons on each side of me. We searched for the short, evil genius Dr. Simon Bar Sinister, who's always trying to take over the world in the *Underdog* series from the early 1960s. In an episode called "The Big Dipper," Bar Sinister creates a machine to suck up all the water on the planet. He plans to stash the contents of all the lakes, rivers, and oceans in small bottles so he can control the thirsty humans and make them his slaves.

It blew my mind that the *Mad Men*–era advertising execs who created *Underdog* on behalf of General Mills managed to so presciently predict America's twenty-first-century water strife, down to Bar Sinister's plan to sell the freshwater in small bottles at exorbitant rates. They even got the pattern of the water-industrial complex down: The first time he revs up the Big Dipper, it doesn't work—the water freezes. The second time, it malfunctions again—the water turns to steam. Third try, it fails again, causing the water to flood his house. But finally, the Big Dipper works and Bar Sinister begins to suck up all the water in the world, labeling his bottles with the sources: the Green River, Lake Michigan, the Ohio River, and so on around the planet.

The label on one of the bottles reads "Mississippi."

No doubt, American ingenuity could build a Big Dipper to suck the Mississippi River into the thirsting High Plains Aquifer. The crack water lawyers of the West could finesse it through the courts. The casino builders of Nevada could even hook up with the iPad makers of California and lobby Congress hard enough to pour on the money. But none of that changes the ethical problems with long-distance transfer of water in twenty-first-century America.

Despite its sometimes devastating floods, the Mississippi has at other times dipped so low that barges could not make their journey south. Some boosters have suggested that the U.S. Army Corps of Engineers build a system of pipes to drain water from Lake Michigan to the Mississippi to buoy the boats next time it happens.[48]

Like the reengineering in the Sacramento–San Joaquin Delta and the Everglades, the image of pipes moving Lake Michigan water to the Mississippi, Mississippi water to the High Plains, and High Plains water to the Colorado deteriorates into a hallucination worthy of a Rube Goldberg cartoon. Tellingly, the Pulitzer Prize–winning artist began his career as an engineer with San Francisco's water and sewer department.

Such sketches have been drawn for just about every untouched stretch of freshwater left from East to West. In Florida, housing developers who had helped overtap the aquifer in the southern and central regions of the state looked hundreds of miles north to the tea-brown Suwannee, the least obstructed major river remaining in the United States.[49] (Maybe they'd been watching too much *Underdog*: in the Big Dipper episode, one of Simon Bar Sinister's little glass bottles is labeled "Swanee River.")

In Colorado, Fort Collins entrepreneur Aaron Million is seeking regulatory approval of his plan for a 500-mile, $3 billion water pipeline that would traverse the Continental Divide to bring water from the Green River and the Flaming Gorge Reservoir in southwest Wyoming to the fast-growing cities of Colorado's Front Range.[50]

In a scheme to outdo Patricia Mulroy's Mississippi, seemingly eternal American presidential candidate Lyndon LaRouche is building a small following for the North American Water and Power Alliance. The alliance has taken up a 1964 plan by Ralph M. Parsons, founder of the powerhouse Parsons Corporation engineering firm, who dreamed of building dams up to 1,800 feet high in the canyons of British Columbia to turn a natural depression called the Rocky Mountain Trench into a 680-million-acre reservoir—one with three times the capacity of all of today's U.S. reservoirs combined.[51] LaRouche and his followers tout a modern-day Civilian Conservation Corps project akin to the Moon landing in its promise for renewing America's scientific prowess and its spirit. The largest infrastructure scheme in history would put 4 million Americans to work diverting water from the border between Alaska and Canada's Yukon territory into a "continental water-management system" that will "make the great American desert bloom," while stabilizing water supplies in the eastern United States and the Great Lakes.[52]

It's a safe bet the water-loving Canadians would never stand for such a plan. In 1997, Canadian entrepreneur John Febbraro, of Ontario, sparked an international incident—and then, an unprecedented Great Lakes water treaty—when he managed to acquire a permit to ship water in bulk on oceangoing freighters from Lake Superior to Asia.[53]

It's easy enough to discount LaRouche's young Water and Power
Alliance disciples, especially when they punctuate their water pre-
sentations with a peculiar obsession about the threat the United
Kingdom poses to the United States. Others, such as Mulroy and
Febbraro, paint a convincing picture of bounty—as well as the flood
dangers that may be aggravated by climate change—to argue for
shifting water around regions, the country, or the world. Lake Superior is so large that astronauts could see it from the Moon, along
with the familiar outline of the rest of the Great Lakes—Michigan, Huron, Erie, and Ontario. The five lakes and their connecting
channels form the largest fresh surface-water system on the planet.
Only the polar ice caps hold more.[54] Like the Mississippi, the lakes
look to have more than their share. But environmentalists on both
sides of the U.S.-Canadian border point to the cautionary tale of the
Aral Sea.

Once the fourth-largest inland body of water in the world, the
Aral has gone from bountiful to pitiful in one generation. In the heart
of Central Asia, the Aral once spread across the border of Uzbekistan
and Kazakhstan for 26,000 square miles. Beginning in the 1960s,
the Soviet government began to divert the two freshwater rivers that
feed the sea—the Amu Darya and the Syr Darya—to increase cotton production in the desert for Russian textile mills. In fifty years,
the project has shrunk the Aral to one-quarter of its former surface
area, and just one-tenth of its former volume. Great Lakes journalist
Peter Annin traveled to deserted fishing villages in Uzbekistan and
described thirty-foot cliffs "overlooking a sprawling scrub-brush desert that stretches for miles beyond the horizon, with no water in sight.
The cool sea breeze has been supplanted by a hot desert wind; the
crashing waves have been replaced by aimless drifts of desert sand."[55]

From a formerly thriving fishing community called Muynak on
the south shore of the Aral, Annin had to drive across the old seabed
for five hours to get to the new southernmost point of the inland sea.
The Aral was once a tourist mecca for fishing and hunting. Today, the
two smaller water bodies that remain of the brackish sea are so salty
that no native fish survive. Nicholai Aladin, of the Russian Academy
of Sciences, calls it "a biblical disaster."[56]

It is a disaster unlikely to be repeated in the United States or Canada, given today's scientific knowledge, freshwater protections in both nations, and the Great Lakes Compact. The document, negotiated by all eight Great Lakes states and passed by Congress in 2008, grew out of fears over the ease with which Febbraro acquired his bulk-transfer permit for Lake Superior water a decade before. It prevents bulk transport of water out of the lakes—though a loophole allows companies to transport it in plastic bottles.

America's environmental history makes clear that the biggest water fixes are more likely to lead to new and never-imagined consequences than to something we've already seen. The Soviets did not set out to create the disaster of the Aral Sea, any more than America's twentieth-century water managers planned to drain the Colorado River.

At the turn of the twenty-first century, the new Great Lakes Compact, the updated Colorado River Compact, and other efforts around the nation signaled an acceptance of this truth in regions that had battled over water in the twentieth. Water-conservation propaganda spread like grass (and often depicted bright, green grass) on highway billboards and television public-service announcements across the country. But as they asked their citizens to practice moderation, many water managers and their bosses—often elected officials—could not, themselves, kick the urge to binge. They were not Simon Bar Sinister evil. Like Mulroy, they definitely viewed water as a treasure—one to go after and count by the millions of acre-feet.

California's Delta, the Florida Everglades, the Colorado River, and Georgia's Chattahoochee all debunk the water-management myth that surplus water sloshes around in our rivers and under the ground. Western water managers know all too well that the 1922 Colorado River Compact's projections for the river flow that could be expected each year—17.5 million acre-feet—were far too optimistic. By 1965, the U.S. Bureau of Reclamation said longer-term data showed the actual flow might be closer to 14 million acre-feet.[57] Today, scientists say 13.7 million-acre feet may be a more realistic estimate.[58]

As Patricia Mulroy points out, when she took over as general manager of the Southern Nevada Water Authority a little more than two decades ago, Bureau of Reclamation computer models showed zero probability—zero—that Lake Mead could ever fall as low as it has today. "To me, probability has become meaningless," she says. "We have to function in the realm of hope for the best and plan for the worst—know what you have to do when the worst occurs, and know when to pull the trigger."[59]

The agency currently is tunneling under Lake Mead to install a third intake pipe below the reservoir in the original Colorado River channel. Mulroy says she will go forward with the groundwater project only if the level in Mead drops to 1,025 feet. The all-time low, set in 1956, was 1,083 feet.

In Washington, her bid for stimulus funding for a Mississippi River transfer study came up dry. But she says that if climate change brings increased drought in the West and violent weather in the East, "I predict it won't take too many years of destructive flooding in the Midwest for this to find its way to Congress as a flood-control project.

"I don't think the politics are ripe yet," Mulroy says. "But I've planted the seeds."[60]

CHAPTER 9

The Business of Blue

In his hometown of Milwaukee, Wisconsin, Richard Meeusen is known as a brash CEO who is highly opinionated and quick to point out the obvious—especially the painfully obvious.[1] The penchant has served him well. The former accountant was not yet 50 when he was named chairman, president, and CEO of Milwaukee-based Badger Meter Inc., the largest water-meter company in North America, which he then led to record sales of $280 million.[2]

Meeusen was able to move water meters even during the economic downturn by pointing out to utility, commercial, and industrial customers that not accounting for water is the same as not accounting for money.

But Meeusen has a more provocatively obvious statement to make about water, a twist on the aspirations of Patricia Mulroy: if areas such as Las Vegas and Atlanta are running dry, doesn't it makes sense to shift water-dependent industry—and even population—away from them, and to water-rich parts of the nation like Milwaukee?

"Most of the aquifers in America are being drained; most of the aquifers in the world are being drained," says Meeusen. "Milwaukee has water. Let's look at this realistically."[3]

This aquatic ambition hit Meeusen in 2009, when he was about halfway through reading Judge Paul Magnuson's ruling against Atlanta in the tristate water conflict. Given his line of business, Meeusen is a water wonk who prolifically reads—and often tweets about—every new report, court ruling, and analysis on the subject, particularly if it involves scarcity. About the same time as Magnuson's Lake Lanier bombshell, Meeusen had read a local report from the Milwaukee Water Works that showed it operating at only 30 percent capacity.

"The water system in Milwaukee was built to handle Miller, Schlitz, and other breweries we don't have anymore," he says. "If you're a wet business in Atlanta, you ought to be thinking about this."

Meeusen is intimately familiar with the loss of Milwaukee's storied beer industry and the consequences for the city's economy, having been born and raised in the west-side suburbs, son of a machinist on the bottling lines at Miller Brewing Company. Milwaukee was once the nation's No. 1 brewer, headquarters to companies, including Miller, Pabst, Schlitz, and Blatz, drawn there by the water bounty of Lake Michigan and the rivers running through the city. But as Meeusen grew up, he watched the beer makers leave one by one, along with other industries and families lured away by the warm and business-friendly climate of America's Sun Belt.

When Meeusen was five years old, in 1960, Milwaukee's population peaked at 740,000. By the turn of the twenty-first century, it hovered at 600,000, and only one brewer, Miller Coors, remained in Milwaukee. The tanneries, another mainstay built on large quantities of water, were gone, too.[4] As the city shed jobs, unemployment climbed; Milwaukee was one of the few metro areas in the country to have fewer jobs in 2008 than in 2001.[5]

Water, Meeusen is convinced, is going to change all that in the twenty-first century—as surely as it was the main ingredient flowing through the city's grand brick brewhouses in the nineteenth and twentieth.

In 2009, Meeusen and other business and political leaders in the city launched the Milwaukee Water Council to spark a "blue gold rush." Milwaukee is already home to 150 water-dependent industries, including heavy hitters such as Veolia, Kohler, Siemens, and ITT. Some settled here to meet demand among breweries and other manufacturers that had to comply with water-pollution regulations beginning in the 1970s; now, they are working on technologies to stretch scarce water supplies. Others are homegrown, such as Badger Meter, whose products range from simple household water meters to electromagnetic meters five feet across used in hydroelectric plants. Still others have spun off from the University of Wisconsin–Milwaukee, which houses the Great Lakes Water Institute.

In addition to drawing manufacturers that require large quantities of water for production, Milwaukee's blue-gold rush boosters envision a "Silicon Valley of water" in the Midwest that also caters to those industries as it serves a world searching for new technologies in water quality and efficiency. They see Milwaukee as a global water hub like Singapore or Delft: water professionals gather at Lake Michigan for international conferences, and college students are drawn to UWM's new School of Freshwater Sciences, which is offering the nation's first doctoral degrees in that discipline.

Milwaukee's blue awakening reflects that of the global private water business, which includes manufacturers, water-technology firms, utilities, and engineering and other consultants—the companies that monitor, manage, and improve water supplies. This sector still lags far behind energy when it comes to the private investment, industry standards, and government incentives that drove the green revolution. For example, the U.S. Green Building Council paid scant attention to water in developing its vaunted LEED certification program for buildings. Of sixty-nine possible points that builders could earn for sustainable construction, only five were available for water efficiency.[6] (A new draft of the standards proposed for 2012 makes a leap, with new water credits, including one for recycling water in cooling towers.)[7]

But now, investors are beginning to flock to the $400 billion sector as it is buoyed by global shortages, growing population, and rising living standards.[8] As scarcity forces customers in regions ranging from the American Southwest to Saudi Arabia to make operational shifts—using wastewater rather than freshwater in manufacturing, for example—companies such as GE that helped market innovations in the green-energy sector are turning to water.

Make no mistake: many of the players in the blue-gold rush remain overly enamored of the mega, energy-intensive solutions of the past. Desalination is the big fix du jour, though water-savvy Singapore has shrunk ambitious plans for desalination in favor of island-wide water recycling. The blue revolution is a treasure chest of *small* technologies: nanotechnology, microfiltration, aerators, and waterless everything; waterless urinals and car washes that substitute a small amount of chemicals; even new waterless woks for Chinese restaurants. These are the innovations that make the water ethic easy—helping us consume much less, and keep much more in aquifers, rivers, and streams.

The newest computer-controlled irrigation sensors have large farms slashing as much as three-fourths of their water use from traditional flood irrigation. Filtration advances make recycled water an option for even those industries that require the purest water.

A building with water-efficient designs and products averages 15 percent lower water use, 10 percent less energy consumption, and operating costs reduced by 12 percent.[9] The financials are convincing major corporations to make water conservation a key part of sustainability programs. U.S. food giant Kraft slashed global water use more than 20 percent—by three billion gallons—in less than three years with operational changes and employee awareness. The company's switch to recycled water to cool coffee grinders at its Maxwell House plant in Jacksonville, Florida, means twenty million gallons a year stays put in the St. Johns River.

IBM and the Dow Chemical Company are working on smart metering projects to give homes, businesses, and cities precise insights into water use, raising consciousness and lowering demand as they pinpoint leaks and inefficiencies. This will be especially useful to those municipalities still losing as much as half their water through leaky pipes and to those that don't yet meter water use (currently charging a flat rate no matter how much residents run the tap).[10]

The water sector also is moving beyond real-time analytics to prediction tools that report how much water to expect in our aquifers, rivers, and soils on a given day. Such data is as vital as the weather forecast for water utilities, farmers, and others. But until now, we never invested in the technology to gather it. These tools, known as advanced hydroinformatics, also could better inform the public about water quality: we could tell shrimpers along the Gulf Coast when and where to expect Gulf hypoxia, help tourists skirt red tide outbreaks, and warn water-plant operators about *Giardia* pathogens coming downriver.[11]

The blue revolution gives new meaning, too, to blue-collar jobs. There are lots of them—including in manufacturing plants that produce water-efficient products, wholesalers and retailers who sell them, and the local contractors who install them. An Alliance for Water Efficiency analysis found that $500 million invested in a national water-efficiency retrofit program for homes would create nine thousand jobs as it saves billions of gallons of water—and the electricity required to produce those billions.[12]

Jobs were already on the rise in Milwaukee when I interviewed Richard Meeusen and other members of the Milwaukee Water Council in fall 2010. Their efforts had just landed a water-testing tech company out of California. An Ohio uniform supplier had erected a large industrial-laundering plant on the northwest side and hired eighty people. In a cavernous building abandoned by a heavy-equipment manufacturer, a local company called Sweet Water Organics had launched the first commercial spin-off of Will Allen's innovative urban aquaculture/agricultural model. Where industrial cranes had been pieced together last century, thousands of perch were fattening in ten thousand–gallon rectangular pools stacked in vertical systems. Lettuce, basil, tomatoes, chili peppers, and watercress grew among the tanks, filtering the fish waste, which fertilized the plants. Sweet Water was already doing a brisk business peddling veggies to area restaurants; the perch would soon be selling size. "We want Milwaukee to be the aquaculture center of America," says Fred Binkowski, a fisheries biologist at the Great Lakes Water Institute who is assisting the company. "Perch is the icon of the Friday-night fish fry."[13]

This future sounded so inviting, I could almost smell the perch frying. It all made a lot of sense for Milwaukee—except for one detail: to help recruit water-dependent industries from out of town, Milwaukee's leaders decided to hold out the promise of cheap water. In this place of blue abundance, that may not sound like a problem. But when you consider that water giveaways are what landed us in such a fix to begin with, it could be a big one.

Priceless

Of all the mysteries surrounding water, all its complexities, all the ways water can make us downright irrational, perhaps none is more mysterious and complex than the price of water. Consider just some of the madness: Globally, the poor pay much more for water than the rich. In the United States, we subsidize water the most for the sector that is doing most to deplete it. Individually, we pay a thousand times more for water in little plastic bottles than for the exact same water that flows out of the tap.

The illogic goes on. Americans who live in the regions of greatest scarcity often pay the least for water. The average family of four in Phoenix, the ultradry southwestern city in the middle of the Sonoran Desert, pays monthly water bills of $34, while a Boston family shells out $65 for the same amount of water.[14]

When we sit down each month to pay the bills, the check to the water department is usually the smallest we write. This is why we don't worry about the tap in the same way we fret over edging up the thermostat each summer to shave a few bucks off the electric bill. Meanwhile, when some external factor inspires us to use less—like the drought that has plagued much of the United States in the twenty-first century—we feel punished by water utilities. When we conserve, they lose revenues, and often hike prices.

The same is true for private industry. One reason investors and businesses have been slow to embrace the blue revolution and start paying closer attention to efficiency is because cheap water meant they didn't have to. Subsidized irrigation helped make it rational for farmers to flood their fields. Likewise, the largest industries had no incentives to recycle water because fresh, treated drinking water cost them so little.

Our aquifers, rivers, springs, and streams would be a lot better off if everyone simply paid a fair price for using America's most valuable treasure. But with money and water, it's never simple. Milwaukee is a prime example. To hurry the blue-gold rush, the city is slashing water rates for any company that brings in at least twenty-five jobs. But Milwaukee's commercial water rates already were low compared with other utilities. In one study, Wisconsin's Public Service Commission found that an industrial customer such as Cargill Meat Solutions pays $41,151 per quarter for water in Milwaukee but would pay $157,557 in San Diego, $172,367 in Pittsburgh, $174,405 in Phoenix, $209,482 in Seattle, $251,984 in Atlanta, and $274,000 in Los Angeles.[15]

Moreover, the Milwaukee Water Works already was operating in the red because of declining water use in the city and rapidly rising water-treatment costs. In fact, just as the city planned to subsidize water to bring in new industry, it had to *hike* rates for current businesses and residents.

As Milwaukee looked forward to building a new, blue economy, local leaders said all the right things. They rhapsodized about water in the Wisconsin tradition of the Leopolds, John Muir, and Gaylord Nelson. They partnered up with Veolia on a Water Impact Index—a carbon footprint for water—for Milwaukee and began working on projects to lessen the city's impact on water, such as more wetlands development and conservation. But in practice, they undersold Wisconsin's water in exchange for growth. It was just the sort of giveaway that led other states—once water-rich Florida, for example—to water crises their boosters never would have imagined.

Milwaukee's business leaders could be right that the nation's water woes will create regional economic shifts, forcing those industries that rely on large amounts of water, from manufacturers to food processors and bottlers, out of the Sun Belt. If so, it would not seem the time to make water cheap. Instead, it's the ideal opportunity to get the price of water right, ensuring its value to residents and old and new industries alike.

◆   ◆   ◆

In spring 2010, an economist named David Zetland, a postdoctoral fellow and a lecturer at the University of California at Berkeley, filled out an application to serve on the California Water Commission. For the answer to question 37, "Please explain why you wish to serve in the Schwarzenegger Administration," he wrote, "The State's water should be allocated to the highest and best use, for the benefit of all Californians. I have a long and public record of writing and speaking on this question, and I feel that I can be a useful member of the State's Water Commission." Zetland slipped the application in an envelope, stuck on a Homer Simpson stamp, and put it in the mail to the governor's appointments office.[16]

Zetland never heard back. When the governor's staff announced the appointments, they included two members of the state's construction industry, two representatives of water agencies, two environmentalists, a state senator, a water lawyer, and a farmer.[17] This was no big surprise. For the most part, water management has avoided economists, who tend to point out pesky truths such as the cost inefficiencies of desalination, or the opportunity costs of the bulk water we give away to mining companies or other large users. Economists see these latter costs as lost opportunities: every gallon extracted to, say, grow alfalfa or to manufacture bottled water is one *not* used for some possible alternative—producing electricity or growing a boxful of tomatoes or restoring a wetland.

Politicians steer clear of economists, too, because their answer to water woes is usually "Raise prices," which voters don't want to hear. Admittedly, journalists don't often seek them out, either, because it's hard to translate their language of externalities and long-run marginal costs.

There is another important group of people who don't like what economists have to say. The idea of putting a price on water is anathema to many environmentalists and human rights activists who feel strongly that water should be free.

The tradition of free water has been fundamental since ancient times—as absolute as free air, or the right to take in mountain vistas. In the sixth century, the Byzantine emperor Justinian declared that "by natural law," air, running water, the sea, and the shores were "common to all." [18] The free flow of water is also sacred, coursing through every religion—from Judaism's ritual washing to the "living water" of Jesus to Mohammed's declaration that all people have free access to water.[19]

As economic developers and venture capitalists champion a blue gold rush, water activists such as Canadian author Maude Barlow turn the phrase upside down to describe a dangerous idea that fails to acknowledge water as a human right to be shared by all people. In her book *Blue Gold: The Fight to Stop the Corporate Theft of the World's Water*, Barlow argues that the planet's water is being privatized, rapidly moving from a public good to a private commodity bought and sold like pork bellies.

Barlow believes we should hold freshwater as part of "the commons." This, in the words of journalist Jonathan Rowe, is the "vast realm that lies outside of both the economic market and the institutional state, and that all of us typically use without toll or price. The atmosphere and oceans, languages and culture, the stores of human knowledge and wisdom, the informal support systems of community, the peace and quiet we crave, the generic building blocks of life—these are all aspects of the commons."[20]

Advocates' work to bring water to the poor could not be more urgent; before you finish this paragraph, a child somewhere will have died from lack of water or a waterborne disease—one dies *every twenty seconds*. More than 900 million people on the planet still lacked access to clean drinking water in 2010, and 2.6 billion did not have adequate sanitation.[21]

The United States, however, has a different set of problems. American water activists, for the past several years, have locked their sights on bottled water. They decry bottlemania for commercializing our freshwater reserves at the rate of some 9 billion gallons a year in the United States.[22] But federal and state governments have handed public water to private interests since the Swamp Land Act of 1850. Challenging America's water giveaways in twelve-ounce servings is like confronting climate change on the basis of lightbulbs alone, with no mention of coal-burning power plants, the largest U.S. source of carbon dioxide pollution, or cars, the second-largest source. A water ethic would take stock of *all* use, including that of the beverage brokers and their unique water trade. Thermoelectric power pulls in 201 billion gallons of water a *day*. Agricultural irrigation diverts 128 billion gallons daily. U.S. industries tap 18 billion; mining, 4 billion. We also must look in the mirror, at water for public supply— 44 billion gallons a day.[23] Free and cheap water in America has cost our freshwater ecosystems—and us—too much.

It's time to at least *listen* to what the economists have to say.

One of the reasons I decided to call Zetland is that he aims to be a "people's economist." Zetland blogs at Aguanomics.com—career-wise, he says, "the longest suicide note in history."[24] Plus, he makes bumper stickers: "Nature Makes a Drought . . . Man Makes a Shortage" and "Some Water for Free . . . Pay for More." I decided he'd be a good one to listen to on the topic of why no one wants to listen to economists.

First, a brief history of how Americans have come to pay some of the lowest prices for water in the Western world. The federal government created the illusion of abundance with the massive water-supply projects of the twentieth century. In the West, for example, the Bureau of Reclamation built more than a hundred major water-supply projects between 1902 and 1994, including projects for irrigation, at a cost of $22 billion. Under reclamation law, these were supposed to be reimbursed by beneficiaries—the vast majority of them farmers. The government billed them about $17 billion. Over time, various relief acts and grants knocked that figure down to $3.4 billion—no interest required. Most has not been repaid.[25]

The moving of so much water left the impression that no one really had to worry about the efforts and costs involved in turning deserts into oases. Nationwide, as the feds picked up the tab for more than 600 dams and reservoirs and 55,000 miles of irrigation canals and conduits, tens of millions of people considered it perfectly rational to live, work, and farm on some of the most inhospitable land in the country.

The next wave of subsidies came in the 1970s, this time for the water in our taps. After passage of the Clean Water Act and the Safe Drinking Water Act, the feds doled out billions of dollars to local communities to help upgrade their waterworks. So, ratepayers didn't feel these costs, either. It was still perfectly rational to use treated drinking water to flush toilets. Nor did we begin to pay what economists call the long-run costs of supplying water to growing communities. The next source of water always costs more than the last one. Desalinated water, for example, averages 10 to 300 times more than groundwater—at about $1,000 per acre-foot versus $3 to $100 per acre-foot.[26]

Utilities didn't work in these costs the way a private business would, because most are run by local elected officials who face the wrath of voters for raising rates. They also assumed the feds would continue to cough up money. But the opposite happened. The big dollars dried up during the Reagan Revolution, when the feds tried to shift costs back to local utilities. Instead, many utilities simply did not do as many upgrades, in part because they didn't want to raise prices. The result is today's water-infrastructure breakdown, which the American Society of Civil Engineers claims will require $255 billion to fix. (A blue revolution, of course, would be cheaper.)

Though many people worry about the privatization of local utilities, the truth is that private utilities have both botched and improved U.S. water services—and so have government utilities. About 25 percent of U.S. water utilities are run by private companies, a proportion that is growing as cash-strapped local governments try to figure out how to upgrade aging systems. Cities unhappy with privatized utilities include Atlanta, which wrested control of its system back from United Water amid cost overruns and poor service.[27] But the trick for local communities is to look beyond the two extreme views of privatization—it is neither evil nor a panacea—and analyze the providers' financial health, experience with similar-sized systems, customer-service records, and commitment to conservation.[28]

Part of the water ethic means valuing water enough to pay for it—whether it is the water keeping our wetlands alive, the water that grows our food, or the water we drink. Water subsidies for the faucet have the same result as irrigation subsidies for agriculture: they encourage us to use much more than we really need. Zetland argues that we've reached "the end of abundance," the point at which the price of water should now rise and fall based on scarcity.[29] Currently, when drought hits, water managers ask customers to use less, or force them to. When we do, utility revenues decline, so we get hit with a rate increase the following year—in effect, a punishment for conserving. New Yorkers used 5 percent less water in 2009, a goal championed by the city's water agency. But the decrease caused a revenue shortfall of $110 million, which helped lead the agency to hike water rates 13 percent in 2010.[30]

Instead, Zetland says, utility managers facing scarcity should charge at rates "worthy of attention." In the short run, people would no longer sprinkle the sidewalk. In the long run, they'd shift other habits. Paying the true cost of water would naturally shrink lawns, just as $4-a-gallon gas lowered Hummer sales. But it also would let people use water in the way we choose, rather than prompting government to hire water cops or set up hotlines for neighbors to nark on each other for surreptitious sprinkling. Some citizens would let the yard turn brown. Others growing food in the backyard could water judiciously or invest in rainwater catchment.

But back to Maude Barlow and our right to water: won't higher prices hurt the poor, who might not be able to afford water for their basic needs? Zetland's solution goes back to the bumper sticker: "Some Water for Free . . . Pay for More." He thinks we should all receive a predetermined, essential amount of water each month dirt cheap. Only those who use more would pay the higher prices.

On one urgent matter, Barlow and Zetland agree: the need for citizens to pay more attention to water. For too long, management of this public treasure has been overly influenced by the large users that helped turn America's water plenty into paucity in just half a century. "Really, what matters more than anything is that people get involved," says Zetland. "Water managers will do a better job if people are paying attention."[31]

◆   ◆   ◆

Economists do have a blind spot: many cannot seem to see that price isn't everything. Putting the right price on water not only for utility customers at home but also for businesses that use water in their processes and products is an important part of the blue revolution. But it's not the sole solution to America's water woes. We humans don't behave in the rational ways economists would like us to—and that's particularly true when it comes to water. Singapore, for example, raised water prices and saw demand fall over time. But water officials there told me that when price was their *sole* strategy, it didn't help. A water-conservation tax introduced in 1991 charged an additional 5 percent for households that used more and an additional 10 percent for excessive commercial water use. The hike helped lower consumption in the commercial sector, which makes up about half the island's water use. The government also phased out certain industries, such as pulp mills, with particularly intense demand. But the conservation tax—and subsequent increases in 1992 and 1993—didn't put a dent in Singaporean residents' water consumption. Water use continued to grow, even on a per capita basis. Likewise, puffy "Save Water" campaigns in the 1970s, '80s, and '90s didn't change the water-use culture.[32] What finally did was the water ethic taking hold—the reconnection between Singaporeans and their water that had been left behind and forgotten in the country's mad race from the Third World to the First.

The rainwater tank is another good example. In Australia's backyards, this latest garden must-have is so ubiquitous that *Australian Geographic* named it one of its "100 Aussie Icons," right up there with the boomerang and the didgeridoo. But economists and water managers are often skeptical of the widespread adoption of rainwater catchment in the United States, particularly for utility customers, because of cost. It's usually cheaper for citizens to pay the utility and sprinkle the garden with drinking water than to install a tank. (Rain barrels can run less than $100, but the larger-capacity tanks popular in Australia, often professionally installed and plumbed to the toilets and the laundry, can average $2,700 to $4,900, depending on size.[33]) What the water managers and economists don't see is that the value we derive from harvesting our own water has little to do with money.

Especially for urbanites, rainwater catchment, much like home gardening and backyard composting, is a way to feel closer to nature, and to water. Taking that small step off the water grid also gives a satisfying taste of self-sufficiency. But more than anything, it makes citizens part of the solution.

Pricing water to reflect its value, from getting our household water bills right to eliminating subsidies for the agricultural operations that do the most damage to our aquifers, is key to unmaking America's water crisis. But it is not the only key, any more than money unlocks the door to happiness. Price is not enough; technology is not enough—even Luna Leopold's "reverence for rivers" is not enough. What America needs most is a water ethic, flowing seen and unseen throughout the culture like the lifeblood that courses through our rivers and underground.

In 2008, a strange thing happened in Milwaukee. The city began to gain population. The four-county metropolitan area grew that year by the exact same number of people Las Vegas lost—10,000.[34] Across the Sun Belt during the housing collapse, Nevada and other retirement hot spots from Florida to California lost more residents than they gained from other states for the first time in their modern histories. At the same time, several long-declining regions in the Midwest began to expand.

There were some good reasons to believe the trends might be temporary: the recession forced construction workers to leave cities such as Las Vegas with moribund real estate markets. Meanwhile, it kept a number of people who would have left the Midwest stuck in place. There was no evidence, yet, of a reversal in the migration patterns that shifted America's economic and political power to the Sun Belt in the late twentieth century. After all, while the Midwest has seen its annual stretch of frost reduced by about a week, shoveling snow is never fun.

Still, the blue-gold boosters were convinced they were onto something. "There's nothing you can do about the weather," Dean Amhaus, the Milwaukee Water Council's full-time director, told me.

But if you own a business "dependent on an abundant, reliable water source," he says, you probably aren't thinking about building a plant in Las Vegas, Phoenix, Albuquerque, or Atlanta these days.[35]

In sunny Las Vegas, Patricia Mulroy says Milwaukee can have the water-dependent manufacturing companies; she doesn't want them. She also agrees that climate change will spur population migrations around the United States, some we aren't able to imagine today. But despite the half-built condos, subdivisions, and other architectural wounds that scar her city after the housing bust, she is convinced that Las Vegas will rebound at some happy medium between the unsustainable boom years and the current collapse, which has wrought the highest foreclosure rate in the nation.

Its choreographed fountains dancing as Lake Mead continues dropping, Las Vegas proves irresistible to prophets of doom. The doomsaying is familiar to people along the next stop in my search for a water ethic—Perth, capital of Western Australia, the driest state on the driest inhabited continent. In 2004, Tim Flannery, one of Australia's best-known scientists and a onetime Australian of the Year, made this shocking public statement: "I think there is a fair chance Perth will be the twenty-first century's first ghost metropolis," its population forced to abandon the city for lack of freshwater.[36]

So far, though, no Aussie mass of humanity is fleeing Perth, which grew vigorously during the global economic collapse. Instead, Western Australians have responded to an epic crisis with a new water ethic, one that has them adapting to their dry surroundings for the first time in modern history. Perhaps more remarkably, helping lead the way is the woman in charge of selling them water.

CHAPTER 10

Australia:
Dry Down Under

Most every kid in America has heard, while digging at the beach or in a backyard hole, that if she tunnels far enough, she'll eventually hit China. Actually, a straight bore through most of the United States would pop out in the Indian Ocean, offshore from the coast of Western Australia.

From most American backyards, including that of the White House, the city farthest round the earth is called Perth.[1]

Our geographic antipode is a notoriously isolated perch on the far western edge of Australia. The Indian Ocean lies west; Australia's Great Victorian Desert, to the east. The 1.6 million people in this tidy, green city make up 70 percent of the otherwise sparsely populated state of Western Australia, which spans the entire western third of the continent.[2]

That locus, in the driest state of the driest inhabited continent, makes Perth one of the most parched metropolitan areas on the planet. But you'd never know it looking at the tropical foliage and public parks, set like fine emeralds in riverfront strands and city-square solitaires.

Australia is America's geographic mirror on the other side of the globe, and Perth's development reflects our own in portentous ways: the city's colonists overgrazed grasslands, and its latter developers overdrained wetlands. They insisted on classical gardens in a climate more suited to sagebrush. They extirpated native people and ignored their predecessors' adaptive ways of living with land and water.

Southwest Australia's Aboriginal inhabitants, the Nyungar, re-
vered water. Their ancestral songs and stories taught that a water
snake, Waakal, made waterways such as the placid Swan River,
which runs through today's Perth. Since the snake created water, it
created life.[3] Water holes were sacred because they were Waakal's
home. The Nyungar hunted and foraged their territory with little
disturbance to water sources. They survived dry periods by know-
ing "all the locations of even the smallest rockholes and temporary
waters" to survive.[4]

In 1827, Captain James Stirling, founder of the British colony that
would become Perth, led a short expedition up the curvy, calm Swan.
He was confident he'd hit on the one place in Australia with fertile
soils and plenty of freshwater—so much so that he planted gardens
and left behind livestock to graze while he returned to England.[5]

But Stirling made a pretty serious mistake. In fact, the area's soils
are little more than sand. And water plentiful one year can be gone
the next.

Two years later, he set out to found the Swan River Colony. He
sailed its new government officers and their families from London
aboard an overloaded ship called the *Parmelia*. The deck, hold, and
cabins were packed with the families' trunks, as well as livestock,
books, rum barrels, and three years' worth of supplies.

Stirling also made room for the indispensables that would make
the new settlement look like home: nine boxes of plants and cuttings,
from seeds and bulbs to strawberries and trees, and a government
naturalist named James Drummond (and his wife and six kids) to
take care of the water-loving plants.[6]

Upon the *Parmelia*'s arrival in 1829, Stirling found that the freshwater pools he'd seen in southwestern Australia, the gardens he'd
planted, and the livestock he'd left behind had been swallowed up
by the area's lifeless sand.[7]

Nonetheless, he blithely charged Drummond with scratching
out a government garden to cultivate plants, flowers, and fruits
and distribute them to the settlers.[8] Suffering in the parched climate, which can go months with no rainfall and temperatures up
to 110 degrees Fahrenheit,[9] the Swan River colonists were eager to

surround themselves with Arcadian gardens reminiscent of their homeland.

Thus began the long and lasting refusal of Perth's people to adapt to their dry surroundings. Today, the green-carpeted Government House gardens remain a centerpiece of civic pride in Perth. Along with the city's many other English-style parks, they represent both the cultural identity and the aspirations of Perth's citizens, who built a city of parks along the Swan to repudiate the sand below ground and the arid climate above.

If England inspired Perth's development patterns in the nineteenth and early twentieth centuries, Hollywood became the modern muse. Western Australia's booming mining, gas, and oil industries drove the strongest economic and fastest population growth in the nation in the latter half of the century.[10] Television beamed in images of what success in a fast-growing, desert metropolis should look like: a treeless carpet of lawn out front, a large swimming pool in back, per *Beverly Hills 90210*.

As if reading from the menus at the American fast food places popping up around Perth, developers began to build super-sized subdivisions with extra-large lawns and Big Gulp water demand. They franchised out the rugged Indian Ocean coastline north of the city with McMansions. All the growth made Perth very, very thirsty. By the turn of the twenty-first century, the people of Western Australia had become some of the most water wasting on the planet—not as thriftless as their U.S. counterparts, but close, with a daily per capita consumption of about 135 gallons.[11]

When most of the world fell into recession during the global financial crisis, growth in Perth pushed on. Iron ore, gold, and other natural resources held Western Australia's GDP growth above 5 percent for the entire first decade of the twenty-first century.[12] By 2009, the average size of a new home in Australia (2,625 square feet in Perth) had ballooned larger than that of any other country, including defending champion the United States (2,168 square feet).[13]

You'd think Perth's water demand would have kept exploding right along with the economy and new-home construction. Instead, it went in the opposite direction. As Perth's citizens brought bigger paychecks into bigger homes in the first decade of the century, their water use steadily dropped. The catalyst was a drought, the most devastating in Australia's modern history, along with scientific evidence that southwestern Australia is drying permanently.

Today, the people of Perth are doing something their forebears refused to do: they're figuring out how to adapt to an entirely new climate. And, as our counterparts on the other side of the globe, they're proof that we can do it, too.

In the same way that flood has defined the Dutch, catastrophic drought has defined life in modern Australia. It's the sort of drought that desiccates rivers, blows dust storms that turn day to night, and sets off raging brush fires so disastrous that they have names—like those given to the Black Friday Fires of 1939, which killed 70 people and destroyed 1,000 homes, and to the Ash Wednesday Fires of 1983, in which another 70 died.[14]

Australia was founded during such a catastrophe, the Federation Drought. It scorched from 1895 through 1901, the year the six separate British colonies of New South Wales, Queensland, South Australia, Tasmania, Victoria, and Western Australia signed off on their constitution to become the states of Australia. The Federation Drought dried up rivers and lakes, wiped out virtually the entire wheat crop, and killed 50 million sheep—half of Australia's signature livestock.[15]

The Federation Drought, and others—during both World Wars, in the 1960s, and again in the 1980s—are as indelible to Australians' psyches and their history books as the wars themselves. Historian Michael McKernan calls Australia's drought menace "the red marauder." After spending much of his career researching and writing about the horrors of World War I, he was stunned to find Aussie soldiers who'd survived both the war and the period's drought insist that "the hardship of life at war was preferable to that lived in drought."[16]

Along with the lowest annual rainfall of any inhabited continent, Australia has the lowest river discharge—about one-sixth of Europe's or Asia's.[17] Still, Australia's European settlers battled water scarcity and plagues of rabbits (introduced by the same European settlers) to spread agriculture across the colonies. They launched large-scale irrigation in 1886. The schemes were modeled on U.S. irrigation—and brought similarly devastating results to rivers.[18]

From federation on, states vied to build the biggest and best water-control projects to harness what little river water flowed through the nation.[19] In the west, an Irish civil engineer named C. Y. O'Connor built the longest water pipe seen anywhere in the world up to that point. Completed in 1903, his celebrated scheme dammed up the Helena River east of Perth and pumped it uphill to the eastern Goldfields, where men from around the world were stampeding to a gold rush.[20] (One of them, a young American engineer and future president named Herbert Hoover, made both his name and his fortune there.)[21]

In the south, Victoria, New South Wales, and South Australia launched ambitious projects to tap the Murray River, which runs through the three states. "The mighty Murray," the largest river in Australia, flowed during all but the worst droughts. Or at least it used to. Today, dams, weirs, and other schemes have overtapped the Murray to the point that only one-third of its historic flow reaches the sea.[22]

In their ongoing war with drought, Australians became obsessed with stockpiling water. In the 1960s, the Australian government even considered exploding hydrogen bombs to create gargantuan reservoirs. Boosters argued that the costs would be cheaper than traditional construction methods, and that "the radioactive contamination of the crater would be negligible after a few months."[23]

Nuclear reservoirs never came to be. But by 2000, Australia was storing more water than any other country in the world, behind five hundred large dams and hundreds of thousands more farm dams.[24] What Australia's hydroengineers of the nineteenth and twentieth centuries could not have known was that no dam was large enough to offset the drought that arrived with the twenty-first.

Between 2000 and 2010, the rain stopped falling in the very places Australians had built their cities and developed their irrigation schemes.[25] The driest period on record shriveled Australia's crops. Normally the second-largest exporter of grain after the United States, Australia had to import grain to offset a wheat shortage.[26] In the forests, eucalyptus and other drought-hardy trees died off en masse.[27] In outdoor-loving cities like Sydney, water-spoiled residents had to forgo filling swimming pools and watch lush lawns fry to a crisp brown. In rural sheepherding areas, some Aussie children who'd been born after the turn of the century reached age four having never seen rain.[28]

But most frightening was the looming failure of the five hundred massive dams on which Australians had grown to depend. Between 1997 and 2008, utilities in Australia's major capital cities reported that the flow of water into their concrete confines averaged half the long-term normal of the previous century. Melbourne and Adelaide received 65 percent of their century average. Brisbane collected only 44 percent. Sydney and Perth each got only 43 percent of their historic average over the decade.[29]

At first, researchers and water managers dubbed this a one-in-a-thousand-years drought.[30] Over time, everyone came to call it the Big Dry. But finally, scientists concluded that it really shouldn't be characterized as a drought at all. Instead, like in today's American West, it was the new normal. The rainfall deficits and higher temperatures appeared to be permanent changes to Australia's weather map. At the University of Adelaide, water expert Mike Young explained that unlike during the Federation Drought, the Second World War Drought, and others, "When the drought breaks, we will not return to cooler, wetter conditions . . . . [W]e are not expecting to return back to the old regime."[31]

When they try to crystal-ball the impacts of climate change for America's rivers, rainfall, and other resources, U.S. water managers assume that it can't be *all* bad: while some areas will see less water, they say, others that need it will see more. Water managers in Australia used to say the same. The Big Dry proved them wrong. As the consequences of climate change unfolded, utility officials were dismayed to find that "all of the surprises have been on the negative side." Extreme hot and windy summer days in Victoria, for example, led to bushfires that in turn destroyed 30 percent of Melbourne's crucial forest catchment areas, which capture and store water.[32]

Utility officials around the country also quit referring to the Big Dry as a drought. It was, instead, the future. To get a feel for it, they looked southwest, to Perth. The city of lovingly tended gardens was the first in Australia to endure long-term rainfall deficits. Nationally, utility managers began referring to Perth as the "canary in the coal mine . . . the first capital city to be impacted by climate change."[33]

Historic averages showed Perth was not, in fact, in the first decade of a drying climate. It had been drying out for thirty years.

Winter, Down Under, arrives in June. (Just as topsy-turvy for Americans who visit Australia in December, Santa Claus brings new bathing suits and water toys so kids can cool off in the dry heat that sizzles during Christmas break.)

In Perth, winter means rainfall. Most everyone welcomes the rains that cool the palm-lined streets in June, July, and August— especially because they follow the hot, dry summer that lasts December through February, and the hot, dry fall that goes on March through May. (Calling the latter season "fall" seems a stretch. It is, more accurately, summer 2.0.)

In 2001, winter did not come.[34] Jim Gill, then CEO of the Water Corporation of Western Australia, watched the bad news on a computer graph at his office in a leafy Perth suburb called Leederville. The probability graph plotted stream flows into the ten major dams the Water Corporation relied on to supply drinking water to about a million and a half customers in Perth, towns to the south, and additional communities along the iconic water pipeline built west to the Goldfields in 1903. Traditionally, dam levels sucked down during the thirsty summer and fall months would begin to rise again by July. Even in drought years, the stream-flow lines on the graph would be there. They'd just be particularly low. But that July, the stream-inflow lines disappeared—they had plotted off the probability graph.[35]

"We were very worried," says Gill, a Cambridge- and Harvard-educated civil engineer who'd been named Water Corporation's

CEO after a career building bridges and running Western Australia's railroads. "It was the winter from hell."[36]

By August, the dams held just 25 percent of their capacity. It was the smallest amount of water they'd carried since 1962. Back then, the dams had to supply fewer than 500,000 people. Now, the quarter-full conveyances were supposed to quench a million. A million of the biggest water wasters in Perth's history, and among the most wasteful anywhere in the world.

Perth's population doubled between 1970 and 2001.[37] Outdoor watering expanded exponentially during that time. In 1977, fewer than 10 percent of Perth's homes had irrigation systems to keep spreading lawns green. By 1998, the figure was more than 60 percent.[38]

Of course, the real calamity for Perth's water was the backhoe rather than the borehole—the city's sprawling development patterns. Though Perth's nineteenth-century developers had little choice but to stick to the sandy soils of the Swan Coastal Plain, the advent of heavy earth-moving machinery after World War II meant their twentieth-century counterparts could fill in the lower-lying wetlands, too.[39] To get to the wetlands, the modern developers bulldozed mile after mile of the region's bushland. By the twenty-first century, more than 70 percent of the area's famous bush was gone.[40] So were 80 percent of the wetlands.[41]

Before the Big Dry, Perth's proud new homeowners seemed to have little concept of the precious wetlands and bushland their subdivisions replaced—much less the water scarcity of their environs. Thirty percent of Western Australia's population had relocated from somewhere overseas.[42] Even longtime residents were oblivious to the biggest problem awaiting Perth. And why wouldn't they be? The government had trotted out new water-storage and water-supply projects endlessly from the day C.Y. O'Connor locked the first steel pipes together for his Goldfields water scheme a hundred years before.

Throughout the 1970s, '80s, and '90s, Water Corporation sommeliers uncorked new groundwater schemes up and down the northern suburbs to top off supply. By 2001, Perth was getting half its water from the ancient aquifer that underlies the city, the other half from the dams.

But in the dry winter of 2001, all that still wasn't enough. And Gill and his colleagues were feeling the heat. The public figured that if Perth was running out of water, the Water Corporation was to blame. Perth's media mounted a campaign against the utility, alleging incompetence for failing to adequately plan for Western Australia's water supply.[43]

As dam levels dropped, Water Corporation imposed a daytime sprinkler ban and two-day-a-week irrigation schedule based on home address to spread water demand over the week. Residents, especially business owners and workers in Perth's substantial nursery and lawn industries, decried the new rules. "No one believed the lawns and gardens could survive on two days a week," says Greg Stewart, general manager of a chain of landscaping stores called Total Eden.[44]

At the Water Corporation, Gill appointed a drought committee of senior managers who held emergency meetings as often as three times a week in a small conference room at Leederville headquarters. They called their drought bunker the Canning Room, after one of Perth's original, enormous concrete dams built in the 1940s.[45]

The name was ironic, given the fact that Perth's dams were failing.

As bad as winter 2001 seemed, the following winter was worse. In 2002, Water Corporation officials celebrated the opening of another major dam, this one on the Harvey River, in a fruit and wine region south of Perth. It's a safe bet Harvey will go down in history as southwest Australia's last mega-dam.

That winter, the dams plunged to less than one-fifth of capacity. In the precipitous drop, scientists were beginning to see the drying as long term, even permanent. They documented a 21 percent reduction in rainfall in southwest Australia in the last three decades of the twentieth century. The low-pressure weather system that used to bring the welcome winter rains has shifted slightly to the south, a feature of global warming. It's not that the rain doesn't fall anymore, explains Chari Pattiaratchi, a professor of coastal oceanography at the University of Western Australia. Instead, "the rain that used to fall on land now falls in the ocean."[46]

On a historic graph, the plot lines now showed that between 1975 and 2002, stream flows to Perth's dams had averaged under half the figure from 1911 to 1974. The average for the decade from 1997 to 2006 was lower still.[47]

The most telling fact the computers spit out, though, was that the trickle of water into dams was not just a matter of declining rainfall. As southwest Australia's rainfall decreased 20 percent, stream flow into dams decreased between 50 percent and 70 percent.[48] That meant the three-decade drying of Perth could not be blamed on global warming alone.

Stream flows dried by half in precisely the same thirty years that Perth's population doubled. Filling the wetlands, felling the bushlands, paving over the recharge areas, and pumping the ancient groundwater all had something to do with it.

Just as global warming wasn't the only factor drying up Perth, it wasn't the singular alarm that finally roused citizens from their pool lounges built from *kwila* wood to pay attention to water. Popular environmental awareness in twenty-first-century Perth was awakened in part by the Big Dry and by drought's historic imprint on the national psyche, says noted Australian landscape architect Richard Weller.[49] But the vexations of population growth, from the flattened bushland to the snarled morning traffic from the suburbs, were also wake-up calls. Another ringing alarm was scientist Tim Flannery's prediction of Perth as a "ghost metropolis." But of all the water warnings sounded in the early years of the century, none was so frightening to southwestern Australians as the threat to shut off their lawn sprinklers.

Still in the grip of the Big Dry in 2005, Jim Gill began to warn that a total irrigation ban was imminent if water levels didn't rise. State university scientists urged the ban. Representatives of Perth's $1.4 billion lawn-and-landscape industry fought it, warning that 16,000 workers would lose their jobs. But people were beginning to realize that the permanent daytime sprinkler ban and two-day-a-week watering rules, now in place for four years, had not killed off anyone's roses. Greg Stewart of Total Eden says residential irrigation sales dropped more than 20 percent in the first year. But during the second year, residents began to accept the idea of gardening with less water. By the third and fourth years, they were demanding so many new types of native plants and drought-tolerant turfs that landscape-industry sales had begun to return to their water-wasting heydays.[50]

The irrigation ban became a major issue in Western Australia's 2005 elections. Premier Geoff Gallop, a PhD economist, promised that if voters returned the Australian Labor Party to power, the sprinklers would keep spinning come summer.[51]

Labor stayed in power. And the sprinklers kept whirring under the evening-only, two-day-a-week rules. But something had changed: the level of public engagement in water. Citizens became increasingly interested in water policy. They wanted to keep Perth green with some irrigation. But their supply-side conventional wisdom was giving way. Until then, popular sentiment always had it that the state's engineers would ultimately solve Perth's water problems in the same way C. Y. O'Connor had quenched the Goldfields.

Now, community opinion began to stray from the kinds of water schemes that had helped dry out Perth. Citizens spoke out against the Water Corporation's top choice for new water supply in the new century: a plan to tap a huge aquifer called the Yarragadee.[52] Water Corporation officials declared the underground source plentiful enough to meet all the needs of the growing southwest, with "a staggering two thousand times the capacity of Sydney Harbour."[53]

Public university scientists and farmers who made their living in the region vehemently disagreed. Ultimately, state environmental regulators overturned Water Corporation's preferred option to develop the Yarragadee Aquifer. Public—and therefore political—opinion came to favor a second option, a desalination plant at the Indian Ocean that would deliver the same amount of water annually, though at considerably higher cost.

Western Australia opened the nation's first major seawater-desalination plant in 2006, in a coastal industrial town called Kwinana, south of Perth. The $385 million plant is the largest in the world powered by renewable energy. Its blue-gray exterior reflects the colors of the massive bay it overlooks. Cockburn Sound is both an abundant marine fishery and the most intensely used bay on Australia's west coast. The Kwinana plant's twenty thousand reverse-osmosis membranes wring twelve billion gallons of freshwater from the sound each year. The Water Corporation is now building another plant, this one to cost $1 billion, at a coastal village farther south called Binningup that will produce about the same amount.

When the second plant opens in late 2011, one-third of southwestern Australia's water supply will come from the sea. The costly transition from dams to desalination is now spreading across the country: Victoria, South Australia, New South Wales, and Queensland all recently opened major desalinization plants or have them under construction.

But the real sea change was not that from dams to desal; it was a cultural shift from complacency to care. Western Australians had become convinced they should lay off their remaining freshwater resources. And for the first time in the state's modern development, a water ethic began to take root in the region's sandy soils.

A few years earlier, in 1996, an analyst named Meredith Blais came to work for the Water Corporation from BC Hydro, one of the largest electric utilities in Canada. Blais had a background in commercial financial services. But her work exporting water from Canada to the United States for hydropower convinced her that grasping the soft side of the industry—the popular imagination, the values of indigenous cultures, and other intangibles—was more important than her training in risk and rate of return.

During the Yarragadee controversy, Water Corporation looked out of touch with residents who were demanding efficiency before any new groundwater wells. After it was over, in 2007, Blais helped convince executives to build the utility's long-term water-development plans around community preferences. Over two years, Water Corporation officials met with thousands of residents at shopping-center forums, public meetings, and other venues. At the beginning of the Big Dry, public sentiment ran strongly against limits to water, especially garden water. Now, as popular opinion turned against tapping new freshwater resources, the top two priorities to emerge were healthy ecosystems and water conservation.

The community-inspired water plan became known as Water Forever. Like most feel-good documents, it might have gathered dust on a shelf if not for a keen move by Blais, who hired an economist to make the business case for it. The consultant's report was dramatic: the Water Corporation would save more than a billion dollars if it paid more serious attention to conservation. An investment of $81 million in water-efficiency programs would save $1.1 billion in new-source costs and another $136 million in wastewater-treatment costs.[54]

The numbers were "too big to ignore" for the Water Corporation's new CEO. Sue Murphy was a civil engineer who'd made a name for herself managing construction projects in the rugged gas and oil fields of northwestern Australia. Jim Gill recruited her to Water Corporation in 2004 to manage the capital side of the desalination work. When he retired in 2008, she was named CEO.

Murphy accepted the economic arguments for efficiency as "a no-brainer." "It's not about reducing revenue," she says. "It's about deferring capital spending."[55] Indeed, as Western Australians' water use continued to plummet, the Water Corporation's revenues rose every year of the Big Dry, to $1.7 billion in 2008–2009.[56]

By the time the Water Forever plan got under way in 2009, the average resident's daily water use had already dropped from 135 gallons a day to about 100 a day, a 25 percent reduction in the decade of the Big Dry.[57] As French engineers worked on the mega-technology of desalination, Perth witnessed a revolution in individual technologies like rainwater tanks, 44,000 of which were installed in city homes by 2007.[58] Businesses saw the most dramatic savings, like the fish-filleting operation that installed foot-operated taps to slice 80 percent from its daily use.

Water Forever aims to reduce overall water demand by another 25 percent. The program sends "water-wise specialists" door-to-door to build personal relationships with citizens and help them use less water. It employs four full-time teachers who develop water curriculum and work to understand how children influence the way their families use water. It calls for recycling 60 percent of southwest Australia's wastewater to irrigate everything from parks to food crops. Already, treated wastewater irrigates agricultural areas to the south, including tree plantations and wine grapes. (Maybe *that's* the secret to Omrah's award-winning chardonnay.)

Perth's water savings were not the most dramatic in Australia during the Big Dry. Some Australian cities slashed water use by nearly half with emergency irrigation bans that carried fines of up to $5,000 for citizens and $10,000 for businesses.[59] The difference was that Perth was learning to live permanently with less water. In 2010, as heavy rains pounded the country, headlines in every state but Western Australia announced that water restrictions were being eased.[60] In Perth, the state water minister used the occasion of rain to announce a permanent winter-sprinkler ban. Ten years earlier, a permanent ban would have been political suicide.

Perth is still lush with vegetation. Kingly palm trees line the streets. Soccer fields stretch for miles along the riverfront. Terraces sag with large, old hibiscus and other flowering tropicals more suited to the South Pacific. That all the green survives is proof no one needed to water more than two evenings a week in the first place.

These days, Murphy is pushing beyond the tap to help Western Australia figure out new development patterns more appropriate to its dry climate. "We're only going to get so far turning the shower off after three minutes," she says. "The next step is, How are we going to become adults and have a mature relationship with our surroundings?"[61] She's brought in academics, including Richard Weller, the landscape architect who is a longtime critic of the status quo. He calls her "absolutely genuine about change,"[62] pushing the Water Corporation far beyond its traditional role.

"The black-letter law of the role of a water utility is to just track demand up and supply more," Murphy says. "But if we do that we've missed the point. We've missed the point altogether."[63]

Building a jetty on Western Australia's coast in one of her first major management projects as a young engineer in the 1970s, Sue Murphy became the butt of jokes for likening big construction jobs to organizing a dinner party. She was quoted as saying, "It's about sequence, it's about budget, it's about getting the right people and the right ingredients and making it all happen." Her male colleagues gave her a copy of the *Woman's Weekly Cookbook*. They inscribed it, "Every Girl's Guide to Jetty Construction."[64]

But Murphy's recipe is resonating in Perth, where she is pushing three ingredients to a sustainable future. She calls them Water Forever, Zero Footprint, and Great Place—a three-part goal to lower Perth's water and carbon footprints in a way that allows the community to grow and maintain the quality of life for which it is known. "It's a triangle held together with plastic bands," she says. "If you pull Great Place too far, and people have an affluent lifestyle and disregard their surroundings, you distort the whole triangle. Similarly, if you pull the Zero Footprint too far, and have a cloth-and-ashes approach to everything that doesn't allow development, you distort the whole thing. It's a matter of keeping them all in tension enough to keep moving."[65]

To hear a gas-and-oil engineer rhapsodize on sustainability is enough to make you wonder whether Sue Murphy's male colleagues were right: perhaps Murphy's gender is worth noting. In Australia, just as in the United States and elsewhere around the world, water professionals tend to be engineers, who tend to be men. The generalization may not be fair to women engineers and their male counterparts working to diversify the profession—and the many firms, universities, and professional organizations supporting the efforts. But the fact remains that the engineering workforce has the greatest underrepresentation of women of any profession. In the United States, only 11.5 percent of working engineers are women.[66] The future doesn't look much better: while the number of women undergraduates on college campuses has increased in recent years to more than half, the number of women engineering undergraduates has declined slightly, to less than one-fifth. Women comprised 18.5 percent of engineering undergraduates in 1995. A decade later, 17.2 percent of engineering undergrads were women.[67]

Drill down into the U.S. utility-workforce data, and the picture is much worse. The U.S. Bureau of Labor Statistics reported that in 2009, water-utility workforces were still 90 percent male.[68]

Florida Everglades champion Marjory Stoneman Douglas, before she became an environmentalist, advocated as a suffragist and journalist for women to crack male-dominated careers. In a *Miami Herald* column in the 1920s, Douglas wrote that men working alone were not as sensitive to the broader needs of society.[69] As an older activist—she did not devote herself full time to the Everglades until age seventy-nine—she connected that dynamic to the interplay of engineers and nature in America's greatest wetland.

Douglas memorably described U.S. Army Corps engineers as emotionally arrested boys who played in south Florida's muck as if it was their own mud pie.[70] She once wrote in the *Herald* that men are "chiefly interested in the material improvement of . . . roads, bridges, deeper harbors, no-fence laws, and such excellent measures, all related in some way to their earning capacities. Now the women voters are interested in these things also, but when they sponsor especially a bill in the legislature you may notice that it is not material improvements which they desire for the state or their locality. The thing that interests them is the welfare and advancement of people."[71]

Those statements seem archaic in our egalitarian, modern age; at this writing, the American president's most urgent priority is to give everyone in the country access to health care. As well they should: it's been nearly a century since Douglas wrote them, in 1923. Yet in the U.S. water sector, Douglas's words are still disturbingly timely. The sector is neither egalitarian nor modern. Utilities have been among the most stubborn holdouts in America's slow turn toward corporate sustainability and its truism that conservation can lead to higher profits. James H. Miller, CEO of the global utility PPL Corporation, which runs hydropower plants throughout much of the United States, from Maine to Montana, may have summed it up best when he lectured electrical-engineering and computer-engineering students at his alma mater, the University of Delaware, in 2010: "There's an awful lot of talk about conservation driving down the need for electricity, but to me that's counterintuitive to the continued progress of our country," he told the students. "We want to make things, and that takes power."[72]

Water scholars in the United States and abroad spend a lot of time thinking about how the lack of women in water management in the developing world exacerbates global water problems. American environmental lawyer Kathy Robb, cofounder of the Women's Network for a Sustainable Future, points out that water engineering in developing parts of Africa and Asia "tends to emphasize providing water facilities, leaving the social issues to be sorted out over time." She notes that involving women in the earliest stages of water planning makes facilities much more relevant. Bringing women into decisions about where to put new wells, for example, helps reduce the distance girls must walk to collect water, enabling more of them to attend school.[73]

America's water problems in no way compare with a global crisis that has half the world's hospital beds filled with patients suffering waterborne disease.[74] But the more I study American water management, the more I wonder whether the First World would gain from more women in the sector as well. The U.S. sector is dominated by forty-five-to-sixty-four-year-old men who came of age during an era of gallantry for civil engineers, when the job was to "announce and defend" projects, not engage the community in them. Those general demographics are hanging on as the baby boom generation forestalls retirement and the percentage of younger workers—male and female—who've been trained in the people side of water declines.[75]

The Water Corporation is no doubt still an engineering organization; its desalination strategy is sharply opposed by environmentalists and economists who argue Perth should have taken water efficiency much more seriously before embarking on such energy-intensive and costly technology. But there's no question the utility is one of the few to have made the shift from announce-and-defend to community engagement. It's hard to say whether Sue Murphy's gender has a whit to do with it. Patricia Mulroy of the Southern Nevada Water Authority may be the best evidence that it does not.

What is clear is that Murphy is helping launch a brand-new role for water utilities globally. Murphy wants the Water Corporation to

"influence outside our mandate," helping Perth citizens build a water ethic as they figure out who they want to be in the twenty-first
century, if not the English gardeners of the nineteenth or California
suburbanites of the twentieth.

"Neither of those visions was right for Western Australia,"
says Murphy, a mother of three daughters who likens the challenge to helping children grow up to become precisely who they're
meant to be. "The white population of Perth has been in a battle
with the environment ever since we arrived: cut down the bush,
plant the grass.

"Until we make peace, the battle keeps going."[76]

One beautiful Sunday morning under pale blue skies in Perth, I
rented a car and set out to find C.Y. O'Connor's century-old water pipe to the Goldfields. My friend Ros, who comes from Perth,
had Google mapped my day. Ros was ambitious—one of those small
numbers of women I just talked about, with her engineering doctorate. The 76 turns she had dictated for me were not easy for someone
unaccustomed to driving on the left.

If Australia has Sunday drivers, I was the worst that morning as I
headed east through the hills of Perth and the area's endless roundabouts. Stressed out trying to keep left, navigate the roundabouts,
and read Ros's map, I had to pull over to check out yards. I saw few
English gardens in these outskirts of Perth, but lots of rainwater
tanks, rock gardens, and native plants, from peppermint trees to kan-
garoo paws, with their red-and-green blossoms.

The farther I traveled from the city, the more I relaxed my grip
on the right-side steering wheel. Literally and mentally far from the
coastal crowds and the generic suburbs north and south of Perth, I
could see why the metro area was growing farther and farther out.
I drove through historic villages with cozy cafés and old willow trees
dripping their shade over sidewalks. Once I'd passed the villages and
begun to wind up Mundaring Weir Road toward the dam that feeds
the Goldfields pipe, I was driving well enough to enjoy the deep eucalyptus forests that stretched on both sides of me.

In 1903, the year O'Connor's pipe began to send water from the hulking dam to the Goldfields, the state had ring-barked and burned these forests, killing more than twelve thousand acres of trees. Public-works engineers were convinced that getting rid of the trees would speed up stream flow into the dam. Some years later, they saw the opposite was true: deforestation led to lower stream flows and rising salinity in the weir.[77]

Now, as I drove through the forests of tall jarrah and smooth-barked wandoo, frequent signs—posted by the Water Corporation—reminded me that these trees are protected. The utility had learned that conserving forests is one of the best ways to save water. Going a step farther, its scientists had identified catchment management—letting trees grow larger to increase the amount of rainfall the forest captures—as a key water-supply strategy for the future.

In a 5 million–acre forest to the south near a dam called Wungong, a twelve-year trial is under way to see how much water catchment management could yield. Scientists are thinning 10,000 acres of jarrah and white-flowering marri to let trees grow to their pre-European density. The larger the trees, the more water per acre percolates into the soil, aquifer, and streams, and then to dams. Early results from the small area indicate two million more gallons a day flowing into Wungong Dam.[78] If the trial continues to succeed, Water Forever plans call for multiplying those numbers across Western Australia's forest catchment areas.

The transcendentalist cliché about journey over destination proved true when I finally made it to the pipeline. I walked the hundred-foot-high wall of Mundaring Dam, its still reservoir on one side, the dusty Helena River bed on the other, so long dry that clumps of bush were spreading over the bottom. I wandered through the brick steam-pumping station that still chugs water to the pipeline.

Then, I found the first links of O'Connor's pipe. I thought it was sad he never knew how Western Australians came to celebrate him as a hero. Beaten by vicious political and press criticism, he rode his favorite horse into the Indian Ocean and put a bullet in his head. Less than a year later, water began to gush to the Goldfields.

At the turn of the last century, it was no less than revolutionary to lay pipe nearly four hundred miles uphill and turn water into gold in a dry and isolated land. This century, it is equally revolutionary that one of the most wasteful cultures in the world is learning to live with less water—adapting to its dry and isolated land.

The impressive part of my day trip was not O'Connor's pipeline. It was his descendants' water ethic on display along the way: Abundant rainwater tanks. English gardens converted to native landscapes. A water utility trying to save as much water as it is trying to make. Catchment forests that affirm the importance of keeping as much freshwater as possible in nature: soils and streams, wetlands and woods.

In February 1962, another American took a much more spectacular day trip, maybe the best one ever. Astronaut John Glenn blasted off from Cape Canaveral aboard the *Friendship 7* in the country's first orbital space flight. Glenn spun east at 17,500 miles an hour in the cramped space capsule. He experienced "nothing novel" in the first forty minutes, from Florida to Africa, writes Tom Wolfe in *The Right Stuff*. Everything Glenn saw, felt, and did was precisely the same as he had experienced in NASA's simulators.[79]

But wonder took hold as he sailed into the night side of Earth, over the Indian Ocean. He saw stars and the atmosphere's haze, and then, over Western Australia, lights. "Off to one side he could make out the lights of an entire city . . . an absolute mass of electric lights, and south of it there was another one, a smaller one," Wolfe writes. "The big mass was the city of Perth and the smaller one was a town called Rockingham."

It was midnight in Perth and Rockingham. "But practically every living soul in both places had stayed up to turn on every light they had for the American sailing over in the satellite."[80]

Half a century later, America's longtime friend around the night side of the globe has something new to show us. We've long shared with our geographic antipode the poles of prosperity and waste. We've imported Western Australians' outback kitsch and chardonnays.

Now, it's time to do the same with their water ethic.

CHAPTER 11

An American Water Ethic

To find hope for a water ethic in the United States takes some serious searching, and in some pretty unlikely places. Like the hot-as-blazes roof of a commercial office building on the sprawling north side of San Antonio, Texas, in the middle of summer.

When he used to clamber up to this roof just a decade ago, Rex Poppy, the chief building engineer for local commercial developer Concord Property Corporation, looked out over a vista of trees and cow pasture—with plenty of deer darting through—as far as he could see. Today, in every direction, buildings and highways spread to the horizon. To the north, new housing developments are stacked like terrace steps to the heaven that is Texas Hill Country. Military personnel, immigrants from nearby Mexico, and retiring baby boomers have helped drive the third-highest population growth in the nation to San Antonio, behind New York City and Los Angeles.[1]

The flow of moving vans has more than doubled the population since 1970, to 1.4 million.[2] But the flow of the city's historic water source, the once prodigious Edwards Aquifer, cannot keep up.

Until recently, San Antonio was the only major city in the United States to derive its entire water supply from a single aquifer. The 180-mile-long Edwards quenches 2 million people and provides nearly all the agricultural and industrial water in the region. It is home to fourteen endangered or threatened aquatic creatures and fills thousands of springs, as well as the Guadalupe, Nueces, San

Antonio, and San Marcos rivers. But so many users revved up so many pumps that the Edwards could no longer meet all the human and natural needs. Just twenty years ago, the situation seemed as intractable as those in California's Delta, the Everglades of Florida, or Atlanta, where federal judges have declared that water conventions must change to protect endangered species, halt pollution, and save an overburdened river.

"All those places are calling out 'Armageddon,'" says Alexander Briseño, chairman of the board of trustees of the San Antonio Water System. "But it's not—we're living it here."[3]

Briseño was city manager in San Antonio in 1993, when U.S. District judge Lucius D. Bunton III ordered Texas to back off the Edwards and make a "fundamental change" in its approach to water.[4] Around the same time, San Antonio voters halted the city's only backup plan: a controversial reservoir and dam project on the Medina River the city had spent the past decade permitting.

"We were thinking 'Armageddon,' too," Briseño says.[5]

San Antonio had no choice but to dramatically cut waste. In the early 1980s, citizens used an average 225 gallons of water every day. Twenty-five years later, that number had been slashed in half, to 115 gallons. The San Antonio Water System now pumps less from the Edwards than it did back then—with 67 percent more customers.

Breaking off a deep love affair with lawns and other cultural changes brought about half the water savings. The other half has come from commercial users, including Concord. All over San Antonio, building superintendents and engineers such as Rex Poppy have made simple fixes to save huge amounts of water, in places their customers never would notice. Like this urban rooftop.

On sizzling summer days, giant commercial air conditioners crank up all over San Antonio, as they do all over the nation. Most of the big ACs are water chilled, sucking thousands of gallons a day into their cooling towers. Utilities pump this water—often from threatened sources such as the Edwards, the Colorado in the West, and the Chattahoochee in the East—and treat it for drinking at considerable costs, all passed on to customers. But there's no good reason to chill ACs with drinking water. We do it this way because, hypnotized by the illusion of water abundance, we've always done it this way.

Recycled water works just as well. AC units themselves generate a pretty steady supply in the form of condensate—the drip, drip, drip you sometimes see outside a home AC. Concord's seventy-ton units sweat off about ten thousand gallons a month—all water the company used to send down a drain pipe.

Rex Poppy changed that with one trip to the Home Depot.[6]

He rigged a system that captures the building's condensate and pumps it to the rooftop cooling towers. This relatively minor bit of re-piping doesn't generate all the water the towers need. But every year, it saves 120,000 gallons and knocks his company's water bill down by $1,200. Across town, San Antonio's River City Mall now collects 12 million gallons of water a year from its AC, after an upgrade that paid for itself in eight months.

Imagine the numbers if every building super in the country decided to save water this way, and you begin to get a picture of what the blue revolution will look like. But the numbers aren't the moral of the water story here. San Antonio is proof that an American metro that historically abused water can change—at many different levels of society. What sets San Antonio apart from other U.S. cities is a water consciousness unconfined to lonely sectors such as environmental groups or green builders. The water ethic has soaked in with the city-owned water utility, elected officials, residents, and private businesses such as Concord.

Before Frederick Law Olmsted designed New York City's Central Park, Boston's Emerald Necklace, or any of his other celebrated urban green spaces, the father of landscape architecture worked as a journalist. He had a vivid eye for people and, naturally, for places. In the mid-1850s, the *New York Times* commissioned him to write about slavery in the American South. His reporting took him to Texas, where Olmsted scribbled as much about land and water as the slave economy he so opposed.[7] In 1857, he published a book called *A Jour-*

ney through Texas, or, A Saddle-Trip on the Southwestern Frontier.
San Antonio, with its Spanish missions and "jumble of races," stands
out in the saddle-trip as one of Olmsted's favorite spots.[8] He was
enamored to find gushing water in one of the driest climates he'd
ever experienced:

> The San Antonio Spring may be classed as of the first water
> among the gems of the natural world. The whole river gushes
> up in one sparkling burst from the earth. It has all the beauti-
> ful accompaniments of a smaller spring, moss, pebbles, seclu-
> sion, sparkling sunbeams, and dense overhanging luxuriant
> foliage. The effect is overpowering. It is beyond your pos-
> sible conceptions of a spring. You cannot believe your eyes,
> and almost shrink from sudden metamorphosis by invaded
> nymphdom.[9]

Olmsted's fountain-spraying spring, along with several other large
artesian geysers and thousands of smaller ones, started their journey
to San Antonio as rainfall in the Texas Hill Country. The rain seeped
into the cavernous limestone of the Edwards Aquifer and flowed
south underground until it erupted in what is now the Alamo Heights
section of the city north of downtown, feeding the San Antonio River
and San Pedro Creek. Water coursed through the area with such
abundance that the Spanish were convinced to begin building missions here in 1718, including the legendary Alamo. Missionaries also
built *acequias*, or community water ditches, an extensive network
of canals and wells that brought the water to local crops and to the
Alamo itself.[10]

San Antonio had grown enough by 1866 that the ditches were
overflowing with waste, and a severe cholera outbreak sent leaders in search of a more modern system.[11] The San Antonio River's
headwaters were owned by Colonel George W. Brackenridge, a local
businessman and philanthropist who lived on the river and loved
the springs. He was the first to sink artesian wells into the aquifer
in 1889 and 1890 to supply water to the city. Photos from 1895 show
early wells shooting water 25 feet into the air.[12]

By 1900, all of the city's water came from wells dug into the Edwards. But by that year, too, San Antonio Springs had dried to a trickle. Brackenridge was devastated. He wrote that "the sinking of so many artesian wells" had dropped the water table enough to stop the flow of the springs. "The river is my child, and it is dying, and I cannot stay to see its last gasps."[13] Brackenridge sold 280 acres that included the San Antonio Springs to a religious order called the Sisters of Charity of the Incarnate Word, which had settled in the area in part to address the suffering caused by the cholera outbreaks. He sold the waterworks, including the wells, to another private water company; they were later acquired by city government. He also donated nearly 350 acres to the public for Brackenridge Park, as popular today as it was in the 1920s, when its rustic stone buildings and pathways were built.[14]

What's bewildering about the ravage of the Edwards and its springs more than a century ago was that Texans just kept pumping. In a Tragedy of the Commons acted out across the United States in the twentieth century, prescient warnings like Brackenridge's were drowned out by promoters growing cities in the sun.

Texas historically put no limits on groundwater, the use of which was governed by an English common law concept called the Rule of Capture.[15] In the nineteenth century, the rule applied to underground water in almost every state in the nation. The Ohio Supreme Court had given property owners the same absolute right to it as to rocks and minerals under their land, saying the water underground was so "secret, occult, and concealed" that any attempt to regulate it would be "practically impossible."[16] As the nineteenth century turned to the twentieth, groundwater movement was not so secret and the Rule of Capture became history in most of the country. But not in Texas. In 1904, the Texas Supreme Court affirmed the rule, also known as the Law of the Biggest Pump, giving landowners the right to suck up unlimited amounts of groundwater even if it hurt their neighbors.[17]

By 1934, withdrawals from the Edwards hit 100,000 acre-feet per year.[18] Pumping really revved up in the 1950s. In a mid-century drought, Comal Springs, not only the largest spring in the Edwards

but also the largest in the southwestern United States, stopped flowing altogether for nearly half of 1956.[19]

By 1981, nearly a quarter of the major freshwater springs of Texas
had failed due to groundwater withdrawals.[20] In 1989, pumping from
the Edwards reached a seemingly impossible peak of 542,400 acre-
feet.[21] The proverbial last straw was poked into the aquifer in 1991,
when a giant catfish farm called Living Waters Artesian Springs, fifteen miles southwest of San Antonio, began to suck up forty million
gallons of water a day—one-quarter of the entire city's daily draw.
Protected by the Rule of Capture, the fish farm slurped water out
from under neighbors, including some of the very pumpers who had
fought to preserve the rule. By taking the Law of the Biggest Pump
too literally, the catfish farm helped end the Rule of Capture for the
Edwards Aquifer.[22]

The case that ultimately toppled the Law of the Biggest Pump
and led to San Antonio's modern-day water ethic was *Sierra Club
v. Babbitt*. It began in 1991, when the Sierra Club filed a lawsuit
in defense of the federal Endangered Species Act against the U.S.
Department of the Interior and the U.S. Fish & Wildlife Service,
charging that relentless pumping doomed endangered fish, salaman-
ders, and wild rice that rely on the Edwards. Two years later, Judge
Lucius D. Bunton III told the Texas legislature it must come up with
a way to regulate pumping in the Edwards. While he was ruling on
the endangered-species case, Bunton set out a much larger vision for
a water ethic:

> Without a fundamental change in the value the region places
> on freshwater, a major effort to conserve and reuse Aquifer
> water, and implemented plans to import supplemental sup-
> plies of water, the region's quality of life and economic future
> are imperiled.[23]

Bunton's historic rulings led the Texas legislature to create the Edwards Aquifer Authority in 1993 to regulate groundwater withdrawals. In the midst of a severe drought in 1996, the Texas Supreme
Court overturned a state trial-court ruling that the authority was

unconstitutional. After the politically appointed authority (some of its members were fiercely opposed to its creation) declined to slow pumping during the drought, Bunton named a special master to create an emergency reduction plan. He was Todd Votteler, an environmental scientist who'd worked as a special assistant to the court during the Endangered Species Act litigation. Looking back, Votteler remembers that Texans across the region viewed Bunton's rulings "as the end of the world. They said, 'It can't be done.'"[24]

Twenty years later, it's clear they were wrong. San Antonians are still overreliant on the Edwards, says Votteler, now an executive with the Guadalupe-Blanco River Authority. But there is no question they've begun to undergo the "fundamental change in the value the region places on freshwater."[25]

Few people know that Bunton, a judge with a sense of humor who was known to brandish squirt guns in his courtroom when lawyers misbehaved, asked for updates on the Edwards until he died in 2001—even though the Endangered Species Act cases were no longer active.[26]

To this day, some landowners still battle in Texas courtrooms over the late judge's rulings and the groundwater protections they brought about. They're fighting to hold on to their right to the Biggest Pump as desperately as if they were back at the Alamo in 1836. But the odds, much like those at the Alamo, are near impossible that San Antonio, or any part of the United States in the twenty-first century, will ever return to the no-holds-barred pumping of the twentieth.

Take a drive around San Antonio, and it's clear that most people here have come to value water—in much the way Judge Bunton envisioned.

On a big-sun late afternoon in June, I head north of San Antonio's city limits to find the biggest communities behind the biggest gates in the suburbs. These are typically the places most wedded to their all-grass, all-green, all-the-time lawns, even during drought. I expect to discover that not everyone is doing their part to contribute to San Antonio's dramatic water reductions. I steer into Cibolo Canyons, a massive, master-planned community with a J. W. Marriott Resort & Spa and a TPC golf course, expecting it to glow green on the horizon like the Emerald City of Oz. Cibolo Canyons isn't glowing. Instead, it fits in earth-toned sync with the burnt-orange sky. The development's entrance is planted with Bermuda grass, straw colored in this dry period. Inside, the medians are landscaped with drought-tolerant clumps of muhly and Mexican feather grasses. Farther down the main thoroughfare, the developer left alone some hundreds of acres of native oak-juniper forest near the recharge zone of the Edwards Aquifer.

The wise water practices were negotiated with the San Antonio Water System, the public utility that handles water and wastewater for 1.3 million residents. Locals call the utility by its acronym, SAWS. The Alliance for Water Efficiency in Chicago describes SAWS's conservation efforts as the farthest reaching in the nation.

With legal limits looming on groundwater pumping from the Edwards, the city created SAWS in 1992 in a consolidation of traditional water boards and districts. Part of the idea was to make conservation a mainstream water-supply strategy. SAWS's conservation department, run by a former Texas A&M University Extension agent named Karen Guz, got a prominent position in the utility from the start. Its first conservation program, still ongoing, was called Plumbers to People: low-income residents with leaking pipes can call out a plumber to fix leaks for free. SAWS has spent about $1.7 million on the program since 1994, with a total water savings of more than 350 million gallons.

In 2005, SAWS led the city to pass an unprecedented water-conservation ordinance after a three-year collaboration that won the full support of stakeholders ranging from homeowners to the irrigation industry. The most unique part of the ordinance also makes the most sense: it's outright illegal to waste water in San Antonio—illegal to let water run off into a gutter or a ditch, illegal to have a gushing pipe and not call someone to fix it.

Other parts of the ordinance dictate that in restaurants, a glass of water comes by request only, and that charity car washes can be held only at actual car washes. (Full-service car washes are so efficient here that they use as little as eight gallons of water per car, with half of that recycled, compared with automatic car washes, which use up to ninety gallons per car.)

There are rules for everything from pools to power washing. The laws limit irrigated areas, restrict irrigation to between 8 p.m. and 10 a.m., and tell residents what type of grass they can plant around new homes and businesses. (They are grasses that will come back after a dry summer or a drought: any buffalo grass, many types of Bermuda, zoysia grass, and only one variety of St. Augustine, known as Floratam.[27]) New homes and businesses also have to install high-efficiency toilets and follow other conservation practices. Air-conditioning condensate turned out to be such a big source of savings that all new commercial businesses now have to capture it.

Overall, SAWS officials estimate that San Antonio has saved 121,000 acre-feet of water in the twenty-five years since it began in earnest to lay off the Edwards Aquifer.[28]

San Antonio is not the only city in the United States to have forged a water ethic. But a communitywide ethic is rare—the exception to the rule. Sarasota County, Florida, an upscale, art-loving community with bungalow-style homes and a subtropical climate, once had as many sod-carpeted lawns as any other city in the Southeast, and average daily water use of about 140 gallons. Two droughts ago, in 2002, it experienced its own blue revolution when the county's all-Republican commission passed one of the strictest lawn ordinances in the nation, with once-a-week irrigation and a requirement that new landscapes contain no more than 50 percent sod.[29]

Other local governments in the drought-ravaged Southeast also slapped down watering restrictions. But when the rain started falling again, almost all went back to letting residents soak their lawns. Commissioners in Sarasota didn't want to have to change their ordinances again next drought, so they kept them on the books. The combination of landscaping rules and conservation-rate pricing—customers who use a little water pay a little, those who use a lot pay a lot—has now lowered daily consumption to eighty gallons per person.

Shannon Staub, who's served on the Sarasota County Commission since 1998 and helped spearhead the ordinances, has watched an about-face as community developers, lawn-business owners, and others who once vilified the rules now tout them as assets. Anecdotal evidence has her convinced that drought-tolerant landscapes are more attractive to home buyers than water-hogging lawns. The county does have some of the most attractive yards in Florida. County government's action, too, made it easier for other local municipalities to act—when the Florida legislature has been unwilling to establish any sort of statewide conservation ethic. The water ethic "starts at the bottom and spreads," says Staub.[30]

Another shining exception is Monterey, California. The water-loving city, home to Fisherman's Wharf, Cannery Row, and the Monterey Bay Aquarium, has reduced its daily draw to among the lowest in the nation: seventy gallons per person. Under private utility California American Water's rate structure, anyone who uses more than a basic amount of water indoors, and practically any water outdoors, pays significantly higher prices. The utility and the Monterey Peninsula Water Management District offer rebates to customers who tear out lawns and replace them with synthetic turf—at $1.25 per square foot. They also rebate rainwater-catchment systems and other water-saving technologies. Parent company American Water, the largest publicly traded water company in the United States, saw 5 percent annual revenue growth between 2007 and 2009 even as its customers conserved more water than ever before.[31]

At SAWS, Chief Financial Officer Doug Evanson also does not decry water saved as lost revenue. Just the opposite. He calculates that by saving 120,000 acre-feet over the past quarter century, the city has deferred spending $3.3 billion on alternative water-supply projects. Less water used also means less running into the sewers. Conserving the 120,000 acre-feet has saved the city an additional $1.1 billion in wastewater treatment and storage costs, Evanson estimates.[32]

Every drop a utility sells costs something. And like all water utilities, SAWS's future water costs will be increasingly expensive. For example, the annual cost of one acre-foot of water from the Carrizo Aquifer, from which SAWS now pumps about 2 percent of its total supply, is $1,175. A permanent water right from the Edwards costs nearly $5,000. The yearly cost of an acre-foot of desalinated seawater, which SAWS hasn't yet tapped but may have to, would be $2,822.[33]

SAWS looks at conservation as acquiring new water—at $400 an acre-foot or less. "If you have a growing population and your primary source of water is not growing with you, conservation will save money," says Guz. "New supplies are incredibly expensive."[34]

One of the best ways SAWS officials have come upon to buy conserved water is a commercial-rebate program for business, industry, and other large institutions. Businesses that install water-saving equipment, from low-flow toilets to systems that capture AC condensate, are reimbursed by SAWS at half the cost or $400 an acre-foot saved over ten years. The businesses get below-cost upgrades, and SAWS gets much cheaper water.

Take Frito-Lay, the snack-chip maker whose Fritos started off in a San Antonio kitchen in 1932. In 2000, the company, now a division of PepsiCo, became one of the first major manufacturers to take advantage of SAWS's commercial rebate program. Frito-Lay spent $1.4 million on water-saving upgrades at its potato chip plant on the city's east side, including recovering steam condensate and switching out various manufacturing nozzles and washers. SAWS kicked in a rebate of $264,207. All told, the changes save forty-three million gallons of water every year. That's enough to supply 460 city households annually. And the company saves $138,000 a year on its water bill.[35]

Necessity has led to invention in many cases. Severe drought in 2006 brought emergency water restrictions, such as the shut-off of any fountains fed with potable water. Engineers like Rex Poppy at Concord quickly figured out how to reroute AC condensate to keep water features running. "We're charging our retail tenants money, and they don't like it when their amenities are shut off," says Poppy. "When I can keep the grass green and keep the fountains running *and* not have to pay for water—what's the downside?"[36] In a cost-sharing agreement with SAWS, San Antonio retrofitted its extensive downtown fountain park to run recycled water as well, buying the utility thirty million gallons of new water per year.[37]

In twelve years, the commercial rebate program has paid off in more than 580 million gallons saved in manufacturing plants, hospitals, laundries, hotels, and lots of other businesses you wouldn't imagine. A local granite company figured out a way to recycle the water used in its wet saw, which saved 2.3 million gallons per year. Other local stonecutters now have followed suit. A dentist realized that old "dental vac" machines wasted an inordinate amount of water compared to newer models that SAWS would help pay for. Other dentists are now switching. Hotel managers have booked some of the biggest savings, switching out thousands of showerheads and toilets around the city.

The water ethic has flowed across San Antonio this way—granite cutter by granite cutter, dentist by dentist, hotel manager by hotel manager. In the spirit of the Extension agent she once was, Karen Guz is convinced that water consciousness catches as it spreads, becoming a belief system that is just as important as rules and rebates to building a communitywide ethic.[38]

People in San Antonio don't let water run down the sidewalk anymore. The average person is interested enough in the health of the Edwards Aquifer that groundwater levels run every morning in the local newspaper, every evening on the television news. Even in older neighborhoods built during the heyday of the green lawn, yards seem to run only about one-third grass.

These days, SAWS relies on the Edwards for 60 percent of its water supply. Recycled water accounts for another 20 percent. Aquifer storage and recovery makes up another 15 percent, and the rest comes from three smaller aquifers. Alexander Briseño, the former city manager who is now SAWS chairman, says the utility is planning for diversified infrastructure projects that are sure to be costly. "But we have changed as much as anyone," he says. "We now start the conversation by asking, 'How can we conserve more?'"[39]

The Aquavores

If, like me, you've ever scratched your head over why Texans are so in love with their dry, cactus-filled, monotonous state, a drive through the Hill Country will clear up the mystery. The sky is outsized, as big as Australia's. The two-lane highways wind through wildflower valleys and oak-forest hills. They occasionally cross a glass-green river moving over a rocky bed. Less frequently, they hit a small, vintage cowboy town like Johnson City, where the welcome sign boasts "Hometown of President Lyndon B. Johnson."

More than a hundred miles pass without one golden arch, just the lonely iron arches that announce the names of ranches.

A few miles east of Johnson City on Highway 290, a patch of brightly painted domes appears on the horizon, out of place with the earth-toned ranchlands that have dominated for miles. The iron arch is here, but it doesn't announce a Flying L or a Running R. Instead, it says,

TANK TOWN
WORLD HEADQUARTERS
RAINWATER STUFF

The domes are rainwater tanks, of all sizes and colors: a funky blue, a mint green, a pale peach, a lavender ringer for the fragrant herb that grows here in bunches. Up the dusty driveway, a red-and-black ladybug tank crouches in the weeds. A wide, green sea turtle tank seems to enjoy the shady oak trees.

Tank Town is just one of a half dozen rainwater harvesting companies in the tiny town of Dripping Springs, about twenty-five miles outside Austin. There's also Lakota Water Company, Rain Man Waterworks, Sky Water Systems, Rainwater Collection Over Texas, and others. I've come here at the recommendation of Billy Kniffen, who may know more about rainwater harvesting than anyone else in the United States.

Kniffen, a weathered native who looks as if he's never squeezed a tube of sunscreen, is a water-resource specialist for Texas A&M

University's Biological and Agricultural Engineering Department. Kniffen and his wife, Mary, live in a log cabin supplied 100 percent by rain, with a catchment system that also irrigates their lush native landscape and got them through one of the worst droughts in Texas history with water to spare.

A longtime Extension agent, Kniffen has spent the past sixteen years returning the forgotten art of rainwater harvesting to communities across Texas and, more recently, other parts of the country. Hays County, home to Dripping Springs, is the trailblazer. "If there's one spot that was the first in the nation for large-scale rainwater harvesting, and has built an economy around rainwater harvesting," Kniffen told me, "it's Dripping Springs, Texas."[40]

Make that modern-day rainwater harvesting. Most every civilization in human history has captured rain. Some of the ancients survived on it. During the Hellenistic period, water supply in many Greek cities was entirely dependent on rainfall. The Greeks collected rainwater from their roofs, yards, and other open spaces.[41] Early Americans did, too, in both countryside and city. When New York City was founded as New Amsterdam in the 1600s, with little water flowing through the town proper, residents often captured rain in cisterns.[42] The city began to build public cisterns in 1811. In his book *Water for Gotham*, Gerard Koeppel describes the twin 200-hogshead stone cisterns built that year at the wings of City Hall, fed by rainwater from the roof. By 1830, forty-three public cisterns had been built throughout Manhattan. But rainwater lost favor after it proved inadequate to douse the Bowery Theatre fire and other blazes that raged in the city during the era.[43] It didn't help that the cisterns froze solid in winter, useless for drinking and firefighting alike.

Nineteenth-century America gave up widespread use of cisterns, along with urban wells, as public and private utilities took over water supply in response to fires, cholera outbreaks, and other maladies. But in the twenty-first century, a rainwater resurgence is under way. Drying aquifers and drought are part of the impetus. Counterintuitive as it is, during drought, rainfall can be more reliable than groundwater in areas such as Texas where aquifers are overpumped. Even drought-plagued areas get a little rain. Though a little rain isn't enough to fill the aquifer, it's enough to fill your rain tank, especially if your catchment area, usually the roof, is large enough. Another driver is stormwater management; regulators have learned that rainwater harvesting keeps stress off sewer systems during a downpour.[44]

But perhaps the most powerful reason for the rainwater revival is the same one inspiring Americans to install solar panels and plant backyard produce: rainwater is local. Its harvesting represents a step in the decentralization of our unsustainable water-supply regimen. It's a small step, but an important one, because you can take it right in your backyard. Capturing your own water gives a sense of self-sufficiency and control in uncertain times. It's a way to write a smaller check to the water utility each month, a way to stock some water in case of emergency. "More than anything, catching rainwater raises consciousness," says Kniffen. "Even the simplest rain barrel does wonders for teaching people to value water."[45]

When he moved to Dripping Springs from Palo Alto, California, twenty years ago, Richard Heinichen did not set out to make his fortune from the clouds. His love affair with rain began shortly after he relocated here to build a house in Hill Country. Heinichen (the name is pronounced just like Heineken beer's) and his wife, Suzy Banks, sank a well. It pumped up mineral-laden water they found horrid for drinking, harsh for bathing. Their well water, Banks deadpans, "turned our hair into fright wigs and our blue jeans into cardboard."[46]

Heinichen and Banks had two crummy options: spend thousands more dollars on huge water softeners, or hook up to a private supplier and pay a water bill every month for the rest of their lives. They had a third option they were ambivalent about—rainwater collection—but they chose ambivalence over crummy. When they guttered the house and bought their first tank, they felt they were settling for rainwater. Once they started drinking it and washing in it, they considered it gold. (Rainwater contains few if any minerals, so it tastes clean and creates a good lather. I found Heinichen's water delicious, but no more so than the chilled tap water in my own refrigerator.)

In 1994, the couple opened Tank Town, a 17-acre compound from which they design tanks and install systems ranging from 5,000 to 50,000 gallons throughout Hill Country. Their business, which also sells rainwater-harvesting paraphernalia online, hit $5 million in sales in 2009. Heinichen also bottles rainwater and sells it in Austin restaurants and groceries under the label Richard's Rainwater. "The taste," he says, "is the gold standard for water."[47]

But to many in Hill Country, the rainwater boon isn't so much about taste as it is about reliability in a region where hundreds of wells dried up in the last drought. When Heinichen first opened Tank Town, his customers tended toward the countercultural. They were "old hippies and conspiracy theorists," he says, who saw rainwater harvesting as a way to cut themselves off from government, live off the grid, or prepare for Armageddon.[48]

These days, harvesting is viewed in the region as a mainstream alternative to the devastating impacts of overpumping the Trinity and Edwards aquifers, which are connected and provide most of the water consumed here. Heinichen's clients nowadays are professionals, retirees, and others building dream homes in Hill Country. The Dripping Springs Community Library features one of Heinichen's 5,000-gallon sea turtle tanks. The Hays County Commission has a large tank, too, but more significantly, offers rainwater-collection rebates and urges developers and residents to capture rainwater instead of poking new holes in the Trinity and the Edwards.

The American Rainwater Catchment Systems Association estimates that thousands of Hill Country homes and businesses now have rainwater systems that are helping reduce groundwater pumping. The trend has caught on in Austin, where the city offers rebates of up to $500 for large catchment systems. Austin also has given away more than 12,000 rain barrels to residents in a program officials estimate has dropped daily citywide water demand by more than 300,000 gallons.[49]

On the other side of Dripping Springs, in Kendall County, economic developers took up rainwater as a way to save the aquifer and build a new industry that would bring small businesses and jobs. The county's newest high school, Boerne Champion, boasts a 300,000-gallon system that captures rain from all its rooftops and irrigates the grounds and playing fields.[50] In Bergheim, volunteer firefighters now fill their hoses with rainwater, thanks to a catchment system at the new firehouse. The station has a well, too, but, says fire chief Jeff Hoffstadt, "you don't want to go to that tap too often because it could run dry."[51]

To do the math on rainwater harvesting, figure that every one thousand square feet of roof catches about six hundred gallons of water in one inch of rain. The rain flows into gutters that send it to storage tanks above or below the ground. So-called first-flush devices can make sure the rain that hits the roof first is flushed away, in case it came in contact with contaminants. If the rainwater is for drinking, it next gets filtered and zapped with ultraviolet rays. Rainwater systems that supply the entirety of a home's water can be expensive— about $15,000, comparable to a well. Homeowners who want a system for irrigation alone can spend less than $1,000 and rely on gravity. (Or plunk down around $30 for a simple rain barrel.) In Menard, where Kniffen lives, the local library collects two thousand gallons at a time in a tank that in turn irrigates fifty plots of lush native plants, grasses, and wildflowers in an educational garden, all with no pump and no electricity. Kniffen built the system for less than $1,500.

The rainwater revival may be flooding Texas, but for most of the nation, it's been held back to a trickle. Kniffen blames America's conventional water wisdom, which favors centralized solutions. But slowly, common sense is eroding old-line water policies carved in stone more than a hundred years ago. In western states such as Colorado, even minimal rainwater harvesting was illegal until recently, based on century-old water rights that assigned ownership to every drop.[52] Science is helping convince western lawmakers that rain catching doesn't rob water from downstream owners. For example, a 2007 study found that in an average year, 97 percent of the precipitation that fell in Douglas County, Colorado, evaporated, never making it to a stream.[53]

That study helped convince Colorado to legalize rain harvesting in 2009, but only for residents who draw their own water from a well—not for utility customers. Environmental regulators in Washington clarified that state's policy in 2009 to say residents could harvest rain without a water right.[54] Utah's legislature in 2010 also made collection legal without a water right, although anyone who wants to take advantage of the new law has to register with the state Division of Water Rights.[55]

In eastern states, more than thirty inches of rainfall a year means most residents could survive entirely on rainfall. But many local governments still frown on any indoor use of rainwater, even for toilet flushing, because of health concerns. (Health departments that do allow rain-flushed toilets usually require warning signs over each commode. Apparently addressing those Americans who go around sticking drinking straws into toilets, the warnings advise that the water is "Non potable! Not for human consumption!" But at least they allow the toilets.)

In recent years, Kniffen has come across regulators who called for rainwater to be chlorinated, and who required an engineer to sign off on any rainwater project. The latter would not have been so bad, Kniffen says, had not a Virginia-based engineer refused to sign off on a livestock catchment system, claiming rainwater wouldn't be safe for cattle, and that his client needed an expensive filtration system. Kniffen was eventually able to show him otherwise. "There's no incentive for regulators to think outside the box," he says.[56]

Health officials worry that cistern water could contain contaminants. Rain may fall through car emissions or other pollutants, or pick up pesticides, fertilizers, and dust from the roof. But few published studies or data justify those concerns, say researchers in Australia, where rainwater harvesting is much more common. "Indeed, over three million Australians currently use rainwater from tanks for drinking in urban and rural regions with no reported epidemics or widespread health effects," write Peter Coombes and George Kuczera, engineering professors at the University of Newcastle.[57]

According to the Australian Bureau of Statistics, 11 percent of Australians, mostly in rural areas, rely on untreated rainwater for drinking. Over the past decade, Australia's mega-drought has sparked a rainwater revival in cities as well. More than one-third of citizens in Adelaide drink rainwater. An increasing number of households in Australia's larger cities now irrigate with rainwater, after generous government incentives funded tanks during the big drought.[58]

"Anywhere along the eastern coast of Australia that has an abundant supply of rainwater can get 25 to 50 percent, if not more, of its water literally from our rooftops—one of the greatest assets we have," says Charles Essery, a water consultant and professor at the University of Western Sydney who was formerly principal scientist at Sydney Water. "We shouldn't even think about it anymore. We should ensure every house has a rainwater tank."[59]

Coombes and Kuczera trace historic misconceptions about the quality of rainwater in Australia to central water suppliers whose economic viability was threatened by the popularity of rainwater tanks. Water purveyors convinced Parliament in the 1800s to require all urban dwellers to hook up to central supplies even if they didn't use the water.[60] Such laws also are common in the United States, even in those parts of the country encouraging rainwater collection. In Bandera, Texas, for example, a local businesswoman faced criminal charges and $90,000 in fines for refusing to hook up to municipal water after installing a rainwater catchment system in her real estate office. City officials finally forced her into a settlement, claiming "the utility's financial health depends on residents and business owners being rate-payers."[61]

But rainwater catchment, just like grass, doesn't have to be an either/or. It's one way of using a lot less potable water, particularly if rain replaces delivered water for irrigation. Those parts of the United States that have lived through the worst of the water crisis understand the folly of short-term water sales over the long-term health of aquifers and rivers. They are the places encouraging the capture of rain. Santa Fe County, New Mexico, was the first local government in the United States to pass a law that requires any new building larger than 2,500 square feet to have a rainwater-harvesting system.

Tucson, Arizona, is now pushing rainwater as a larger-scale solution to water shortages as well. Beginning in 2010, new businesses in the city must use rainwater for at least half their landscaping needs. If all of the city's rainwater could be collected, it would amount to about 75 percent of all the water delivered to homes and businesses each year, says University of Arizona hydrologist Jim Riley.[62]

Also in 2010—after Judge Paul Magnuson's Lake Lanier ruling—Georgia's legislature approved tax credits of up to $2,500 for homes and businesses that install rainwater-collection systems. North Carolina's state assembly passed tax credits for cisterns in a law that also prohibits local governments from standing in the way of rainwater systems for toilet flushing or irrigation. Rainy Oregon also has approved rainwater-harvesting alternatives to the state building code, including for drinking-water supply, and makes it relatively easy for citizens to learn about and land approval to harvest rain.[63]

Richard Heinichen calls it cloud juice—made between heaven and Earth. Back in San Antonio, the water ethic is spreading farther with a little help from heaven, too.

Today, the spring that Frederick Law Olmsted described so ebulliently in 1857 is hidden behind an octagonal stone wall in a quiet, 60-acre forest in the middle of the city. The spring can no longer be called a "sparkling burst." In fact, it is often dry. Rains bring it back sometimes, creating a beautiful azure pool down in the stone. Now known as Blue Hole, the spring and surrounding grounds remain in the private ownership of the Sisters of Charity of the Incarnate Word—the same order that bought the property from Colonel George W. Brackenridge more than a hundred years ago.

Three young French nuns founded the Sisters of Charity in 1866. They came to Texas to answer an urgent call for help from Bishop Claude Marie Dubuis. The bishop, also from France, was overwhelmed by the illness, disease, and poverty he'd found throughout Texas, including the cholera outbreaks in San Antonio. The Sisters founded the first Catholic hospital in Texas, now a major health system. They established an orphanage to care for the many children who lost their parents to cholera and yellow fever. Over the years, the Sisters also built a global Catholic university—San Antonio's University of the Incarnate Word—as well as transitional facilities for the homeless, a high school, elementary schools, and significant international ministries targeting countries ranging from Guatemala to Zambia.

In fact, the human suffering they worked to end in Texas and around the world was so vast that the Sisters never put their considerable skills into what was ailing the enchanting springs and headwaters of the San Antonio River, which they owned. In the 1970s and '80s, they turned a large part of the spring shed into athletic fields toward a goal to bring more male students to the University of the Incarnate Word.[64] They were doing what they thought best for the university, but they took a lot of hits from the community, as well as their own students and faculty members.

The Sisters' lack of attention to the water flowing—or not flowing, as it were—beneath their feet finally changed in 2002. For the first time, the congregation, the largest women's religious organization in Texas, officially committed itself to ecological work, including water.[65] University professors and students, who had been pushing for more attention to the headwaters since the early 1970s, were part of the impetus. The Sisters also were inspired by fellow nuns who'd established ecological orders around the country. They visited the Santuario Sisterfarm in nearby Boerne, Texas, where nuns are creating a "living lightly on Earth" model to showcase sustainable agriculture.[66]

But most significantly, the Sisters of Charity changed along with Catholic social teaching. In 1990, Pope John Paul II delivered the first papal document devoted entirely to ecology. In *The Ecological Crisis: A Common Responsibility*, John Paul II said the need for ecological responsibility had become "urgent." He called for "a genuine conversion in ways of thought and behavior." In the years since, the Vatican has often promoted an ethical approach to water in papal documents and testimony at international meetings.[67] Bishops from around the world have worked to bring the theme home to their regions. In 2001, U.S. and Canadian members of the Catholic Bishops of the Columbia Watershed Region came out with a document proclaiming that area Catholics had a "responsibility to God" to protect the Columbia River and its tributaries. The eight bishops collectively lead 1.2 million Catholic parishioners spread over 260,000 square miles in the western United States and Canada.[68] They worked for five years on the document, which makes the argument that God intended the region's rivers and streams to remain "living water: bountiful and healthy providers for the common good. The water itself is to be a clear sign of the Creator's presence."[69]

The Sisters of Charity got their start in San Antonio in the first place because of water: the abuse of the San Antonio River as a sewer gave rise to the epidemics that called the Sisters to care for suffering people. More than one hundred years later, they've come full circle, to see care of the river and its headwaters as a religious call as well. They created a nonprofit organization called the Headwaters Coalition, donated more than fifty acres at the river's headwaters, and funded a full-time employee to work on water stewardship locally, as well as in Zambia and at the Sisters' other ministries around the world.

The Sisters' changing view of their responsibility to the headwaters is a microcosm of the larger changing Christian view, which also points to a gradual shift in the American culture. Many Christian evangelical groups, and civic organizations, especially Rotary International, are active in the cause of bringing clean water to developing countries. Until recently, that ethic did not often extend to their own hometowns. But now, influential people in cities such as Atlanta who never paid attention to water want to know what went wrong and how to fix it. As outsiders to the water-industrial complex, they are open to new answers.

Of course, this group has its share of doomsayers, too. Americans have devoured postapocalyptic novels and movies for half a century, but none so much as the current Left Behind series, by Tim LaHaye and Jerry Jenkins. In the books, millions of true Christians vanish from the globe in an instant. Those left behind must endure a grim seven-year tribulation overseen by the Antichrist. The heroes in the series turn into believers and battle the Antichrist (who, incidentally, has taken the form of *People* magazine's Sexiest Man Alive).

Throughout the series, the repentant good guys are denied the most basic necessities of life on Earth, including water. But for La-Haye, Jenkins, and millions of their readers, the idea that we're living in the end times is not fiction, and the water crisis is part of their proof. Outside their novels, LaHaye and Jenkins point to the planet's ongoing droughts, water shortages, and water pollution, even to our turn toward desalination, as proof that the tribulations surrounding the second coming of Christ have begun.[70]

Perhaps it is easier to surrender, and declare that the end is near, than to struggle to change problems that seem so massive. But I think the Sisters are on the right track, reaching out in their humble way to other parts of the world and working on the global crisis as they help bring about a blue revolution at home.

CHAPTER 12

Local Water

One Sunday afternoon outside Charlotte, North Carolina, in the middle of July, the sticky heat clung to me the way it does in the South, the way that makes you feel you'll never, ever cool off again until you go for a swim. I'd spent the day on the Catawba River, checking out its lakes, dams, power plants, and endless housing developments. Now that my work was finished, I looked forward to jumping in.

I drove alongside the river with my GPS, searching for a possible spot. As with a lot of American rivers, even when you're adjacent to the Catawba, you wouldn't know of its proximity without a map—except for the clues in the subdivision names: Riverdale, Riverpointe, Norman Shores. Surely, these river residents would not appreciate a stranger showing up with bathing suit and towel. Instead, I steered to a 1,350-acre Mecklenburg County park that I'd heard was worth seeing, Latta Plantation.

Latta, one of many cotton plantations that stretched along the Catawba River in the 1800s, is the only one remaining open to the public. The plantation was originally home to the James Latta family and fifty slaves. By the Civil War, the William Azmon Sample family lived here. All four of the sons were called to fight with the 53rd North Carolina Troops, Company B. All four survived.[1]

It was just my luck that the Sunday afternoon I sought a quiet swim, the park had scheduled a special Civil War reenactment. I dodged scraggy-bearded Confederate soldiers as I drove by the plantation house, but I finally made my way beyond the battle to the riverfront section of the park. It had grassy play areas and grills, hiking trails and a fishing pier, and—hurrah!—a beach. Given the record temperatures and humidity, I was surprised how few families were gathered here at the waterfront, compared with the massive crowd at the reenactment.

Then I saw the signs: NO SWIMMING/PROHIBIDO NADAR.

A three-generation Hispanic family was gathered at the shore. Two parents and two grandparents were squeezed onto one side of a picnic table, facing out to watch three boys under ten playing on the beach. The boys poked sticks into the Catawba's reddish mud and waded up to their calves. Beyond them in the open water, speedboats zoomed back and forth, towing water skiers and kids in tubes.

"Why aren't we allowed to swim?" I asked the parents. "Is there something wrong with the water?"

"We don't know," the dad said. "We're not from here—we're on vacation."

An athletic, older man sitting at another picnic table came over with a look of disgust. He said he was a park volunteer up at Latta's Carolina Raptor Center. "I'll tell you why you can't swim," he said. "It's liability—blame the lawyers." The volunteer explained no swimming was allowed in any of Mecklenburg County's parks along the river.

Now, the mom had something to say. "It's privilege," she announced, pointing to the squealing kids zooming back and forth behind the motorboats. "You're allowed to swim if you have a boat, not if you don't have a boat."

That looked to be true, but it couldn't be, I thought. So I made my way back to the plantation house to ask a park ranger. The reenactment was just breaking up. Parents and children swarmed the gift shop. They loaded up on honey candy, toy canteens, and wooden muskets in two colors—black or hot pink. A sign near the cash register said that for $2 extra, kids "will have the opportunity to march with the soldiers and learn how to hold their muskets and respond to military commands!" I also read about the plantation's Civil War

Soldier Camps, where "boys and girls ages 8–12 can relive the Civil War for a week."

I felt sorry for the young woman behind the register, dressed for the nineteenth century with a long, gingham dress and headscarf that looked stifling. But she was the only one I could find to ask, "Um, is it true you're not allowed to swim here, at the park beach, but it's okay to swim if you come by boat?"

"Yes, that's right," she said with an apologetic smile.

"But isn't this supposed to be an authentic historical experience?" I asked. "Don't you think kids swam in the river in the 1800s?"

"Yes," she said, still polite, but now wary. "I'm sorry, but it's a county rule." She appeared to be steeling herself for some sort of criticism of her plantation role-playing. But I had no beef with her way of teaching American history. I just wanted to swim.

Later, I found out the no-swimming rule is even more compli-cated than blaming the lawyers. Mecklenburg County banned swim-ming at all its lakefront parks in the 1970s, after three drownings in one year. Local elected officials and parks staff have been working to lift the ban. But the budget-squeezed county has to find hundreds of thousands of dollars to build facilities and hire lifeguards for each beach opened. Meanwhile, Duke Energy has so much of the river tied up in power generation that the county also must secure per-mission under the company's years-long Federal Energy Regulatory Commission permit process, still ongoing.[2]

So, for the time being, Mecklenburg County kids can go to sol-dier camp, choose to fight for the Gray or the Blue, and experience "strategic battle planning." But they cannot swim from the public beaches of their local river.

Of all that's broken with America's approach to freshwater, the most harmful break is that of the ancient bond between people and water. Humans have always needed rivers, lakes, and streams not only to stay alive but also to *live*, like adventuresome boys drawn to the sea in the opening pages of *Moby-Dick*. Indeed, Herman Melville did not begin his novel with the great whale. The pages that immediately follow "Call me Ishmael" are a love letter to water, specifically its allure to humankind. "There is magic in it," says Ishmael. The wise narrator sees water as much more than a necessity for drinking, cleaning, and growing crops. As perfectly as water quenches the throat and the field, it soothes the harried, inspires the artist, and heals the troubled.

The nation's waters also mirror who we are, as clearly as our national gem Crater Lake reflects mountain peaks on a windless day. We see ourselves "in all rivers and oceans," writes Melville as Ishmael. "It is the image of the ungraspable phantom of life; and this is the key to it all."[3]

Water *is* the key to it all. The ancients knew this long before modern science could tell us that our bodies are 75 percent H_2O and before the catchphrase "Water is life" entered the lexicon.

But if water is a cultural reflection, Americans look alarmingly like Narcissus (son, incidentally, of the river god, Cephisus). We love our lakes and springs. Our reverence for rivers has increased, as more families enjoy paddling vacations and more river cities revitalize their best asset with waterfront boardwalks, cafés, and parks. But ours is a superficial love that doesn't acknowledge frailty. We gaze at the surface and we are enamored, but we don't go deep. We see a reflection of apparent abundance that will always meet our basic needs, with plenty left over for show and for soul quenching. But, like children, we don't understand what's underneath: where water comes from, how it flows out of the faucet like magic, what's in it, who's in charge of it, what it really costs, where it goes after we use it.

We've lost what we knew when we relied on a local river to run the grist mill. We've lost the sense of place we had when kids' boundaries were defined by streams rather than by concrete culverts. We've lost the connection between the water we bathe in and the last little patch of wetlands surviving in the neighborhood.

A natural water body somewhere feeds every tap and toilet in the nation. But most people couldn't identify their water source. So, how would they know if it's in trouble?

◆   ◆   ◆

No one wants to return to the time when we had to schlep our own water and worry about its cleanliness. But the aquavores in Texas Hill Country were onto something when they noticed their intimately local water supply helping build a communitywide ethic.

At the Pacific Institute for Studies in Environment and Security, in Oakland, California, cofounder and president Peter H. Gleick has spent a career pondering water challenges on the global scale. But he's recently called for thinking about water in a much smaller way: a "local water movement."[4] We make an effort to buy local goods to support community businesses. We try to eat locally grown food to help the farmers and economies where we live, and to save on the fuel and packaging needed to haul produce across the country or the world. (Not to mention that the food tastes better.) Local water reflects the same idea—with water from nearby rivers, streams, or aquifers treated and managed by local, rather than unseen and distant, authorities.

"Local water" may not be what you want to hear if you live in Las Vegas, which relies on a shrinking Lake Mead for 90 percent of its water supply. Just like it's not always convenient to "eat local," local water won't always be possible. Major metropolitan areas such as New York City and Los Angeles outgrew their ability to provide local water years ago, in the same way they do not grow enough food—for the time being, anyway—to support populations of millions.[5] But, as urban agriculture is helping return locally grown crops to major metropolitan areas, so the blue revolution will help local water make a comeback in communities that cannot imagine it today.

Gleick isn't saying cities should shrink, or cut off water transferred from neighboring watersheds. Rather, a local movement would seek out every drop on hand before looking afield, treating and reusing water to the greatest extent possible. Las Vegas would reimagine the way it uses water now before tapping groundwater from rural Nevada and Utah. Communities that rely on local water supplies would try to keep it that way, boosting efficiency and reusing water for lawns and gardens, clothes washers and toilets.

During the rare deluge in Los Angeles, enough water pours off the streets and into the massive storm-drain system to quench the needs of more than 130,000 homes for a year. With relatively simple water-harvesting techniques in new construction and redevelopments—installing cisterns and designing landscapes that allow water to seep back into the ground—some estimates show LA could increase local supplies to half its annual demand.[6]

In the mid-1980s, Boston faced the archetypal American water crunch: a growing population slurped and flushed so much potable water that demand would soon outstrip the city's primary supply— the thirty-nine-square-mile Quabbin Reservoir, one of the largest human-made public water supplies in the nation.[7]

Boston water officials looked to the familiar path of big infrastructure. They wanted to build a pipeline to the Quabbin from New England's largest river, the Connecticut, which stretches from northern New Hampshire four hundred miles south to Long Island Sound. Area residents and environmental groups were strongly opposed. They insisted the region could more easily reduce demand, an option better for taxpayers as well as the Atlantic salmon in the Connecticut River.[8]

Yielding to public opinion, the Massachusetts Water Resources Authority, a water wholesaler for 2.5 million residents and more than 5,500 large industries, began an aggressive conservation program in 1986. It went after leaks and repaired community pipes. It retrofitted 370,000 homes with low-flow plumbing fixtures. It raised water rates. It worked with area businesses, governments, and nonprofit organizations to cut water use in large operations.[9]

Despite population growth, total water use has dropped 43 percent from the 1980 peak of 126 billion gallons to 71 billion in 2009. Today, the Connecticut River diversion is long off the table, says Sandra Postel, of the Global Water Policy Project. The water authority's current controversy? What to do with a "surplus" in the Quabbin Reservoir.[10]

On the flood-control side, local water means communities shape their own projects rather than having them dictated by federal agencies. Nearly twenty years ago, citizens of Napa County, California, helped convince the U.S. Army Corps of Engineers to overhaul a flood-control project that would have carved channels through downtown and lined them with concrete, a disaster for both the City of Napa's central business district and the Napa River. In 1998, county voters approved a half-cent sales tax to share the costs of an ambitious "living river" flood-control project. The local tax, augmented with federal money and private grants, bought up more than 800 acres that had been drained for agriculture and industry. Today, those once-neglected lands are shimmering saltwater and freshwater wetlands drawing numbers of fish and birds unseen in recent decades. Along another stretch of the river, some of Napa County's major vineyard owners banded together and donated productive cropland to restore five more miles of the watershed.[11]

Local water leads to wiser, more ethical use, and makes us good neighbors. But it is also key to the blue revolution for closing the distance between Americans and their water. It reconnects us to water and watersheds—the land that drains to streams and rivers—in the same way Saturday-morning farmers' markets have reconnected us to local produce and the men and women who grow it. In Napa, so many citizens wanted to help save the river that policy makers and scientists were able to hand over important monitoring jobs to volunteers. Citizens measure water quality, flow, velocity, and rainfall. Their data has proved critical to computer-modeling programs that generate flood warnings and other reports. Volunteers also map and keep track of wildlife and vegetation, and they survey fish populations, all projects for which most governments rely on scientists—and forgo when agency budgets shrink. Community college students are a formal part of the monitoring, too; children and teenagers, meanwhile, visit streams, identify native plants, and discuss pollution through grade school and high school watershed curricula.[12]

Ask American kids to describe their neighborhood, and most will tell you the names of the streets they live near, the schools, the Kroger, Walmart, or Chuck E. Cheese's. Imagine if they also knew the name of their local watershed. Imagine if they could see more of its lifeblood flowing—in creeks and streams and restored wetlands, rather than behind chain-linked storm drains.

Children in Napa know their Napa River Watershed. Those in Portland, Oregon, know the Bull Run Watershed, which they tour on daylong field trips. Boston kids converge on their historic harbor to learn about the five rivers that flow into it. By building a constituency for local water in this generation, these communities are building a water ethic for the next.

I have an environmental-historian friend who is skeptical that Americans will embrace a water ethic in his lifetime. Yet, having witnessed revolutionary change in the behavior of the entire nation in one generation, he holds out hope that his five-year-old daughter will see the ethic. He cites the transformation in America's littering habits. Forty years ago, it was fairly common to see people fling empty cigarette packs, fast food bags, and other trash out car windows while driving down the highway at top speeds. It's not something you see anymore.

Litter research confirms a dramatic turnaround. In 1969, the Keep America Beautiful organization conducted a major study of littering in the United States and found that exactly half the Americans surveyed had littered in the past month. The organization replicated its study forty years later, in 2009, and found an astonishing drop, with only 15 percent of respondents having littered. In their analysis of actual trash in public places, researchers found 61 percent less litter in 2009 than in 1969.[13]

Principal investigator P. Wesley Schultz, a professor of psychology at California State University, San Marcos, ties the decrease in part to widespread educational campaigns, ongoing clean-up efforts, and big changes by American business—primarily in packaging, such as the elimination of soda-can pull-off tops. But *most* responsible for the turnaround was a personal obligation to not litter—an ethical belief that littering is wrong. Fines and threats of punishment didn't matter much. In fact, recent psychological research suggests threats can actually trigger undesirable behavior because they act as a reminder.[14] When you pass by that large billboard scolding that you're allowed to water only two times a week, it might just serve to remind you that your grass is looking a little peaked.

Schultz, who, it must be said, never litters but does water his California lawn, now happens to be studying water waste—liquid litter.

Besides the fact that personal obligation is more meaningful than any number of water cops, what strikes him about the results for both littering and watering is where the obligation, or ethic, comes from. It's driven more by physical and social settings than by internal compass. In other words, if you're at a public park where garbage is heaped all over the ground, you're likely to leave your picnic detritus behind, too. But picnicking at a sparkling, pristine place, your personal obligation kicks in and keeps you from littering. It's the same with lawn watering. "The norm, in most places, is still to have grass and to use a lot of water," says Schultz. "So you look at your neighbors and your community and your city, and you see green grass as a sign of success. You don't want to be different. You don't want to be deviant. You don't want to be the only one with the cactus and the rocks."[15]

Someday, you may not want to be the only one with bright green grass. The aesthetic—not in favor of cactus and rocks, but preferring the beautiful natives that defined our local landscapes before imported turfgrass replaced them—has already emerged in some parts of the United States as communities forge their own water ethic. No two will look the same. In Philadelphia, the ethic looks like green roofs. In Seattle, it looks like 90,000 acres of wild watershed preserved along the Cedar River—a commitment made a century ago and completed by city government in the 1990s. In the Klamath River Basin, it is a long-time-coming agreement to tear down dams and save both fish and local agriculture. In Kansas City, it looks like Ten Thousand Rain Gardens. That's the name of a massive horticultural effort launched by Kansas City mayor Kay Barnes in 2005 that deployed citizens instead of big new stormwater pipes to reduce runoff and clean up water pollution. In the Sacramento–San Joaquin Delta of California and in the Everglades of Florida, it will look like greater investment in the large-scale restoration of wetlands and less spent on the kinds of uncertain, big-tech fixes that helped ruin the ecosystems. New economic models that put a tangible dollar value on restoration, adding up benefits from clean drinking water to flood safety to recreation, will help build support rather than suspicion.[16]

Likewise, no other country's water ethic is just right for the United States. Americans wouldn't tolerate the level of government control in Singapore. Hurricane Katrina made clear that we are too large, diverse, and regionalized for even the worst water calamity to bring us together in a national "Never again" pledge like the Dutch. And unlike in Australia, where the entire continent can be battered by drought or by flood, our water problems are intensely local: the Southeast can be swamped with hurricane waters at the same time the Southwest is scorched in drought.

But if the Netherlands, Singapore, and Australia have one thing in common, it is the ongoing conversation among citizens, government, and industry about water and its value. In Perth, the daily newspaper runs charts showing water levels in the dams right alongside the weather forecast. Sue Murphy is on the speaker's circuit, challenging citizens and college students "to design a future which is our own—resilient to our changing climate."[17] The Dutch are spending billions of euros to adapt to the water challenges of climate change, relocating or buying out farmers and in some cases building communities to float.

Children, notably, are part of the conversation. Children's water museums in Singapore and the Netherlands are jam-packed with elementary-school-age students. On a school day in Singapore, kids run through the halls in tidy uniforms, furiously filling out water worksheets assigned by their teachers. During spring break in the Netherlands, kids still cram the Watermuseum, built inside and under a thirteenth-century mill in a national park called Sonsbeek. Heidi Van Zwieten watches her son, six, and daughter, four, jump on a scale that showed how much of their weight was water. Most Dutch kids, she says, seem to know as much about water scarcity as they do about their country's flood menace.

The local water board runs the museum and provides water curriculum to the Arnhem schools. Museum director Jos van den Mosselaar tells me there is good reason why his exhibits are oriented more toward conservation than toward Dutch flood history.

"Our history makes children angry with water," he says, "and we don't want them to be angry.

"We want them to know the history. But we really want them to know how lucky they are to have a drink."

◆   ◆   ◆

The blue revolution is a reconnection to water. It gives children more natural waters to play in—flowing springs and rivers. It alters the way our communities look: More meandering streams, less concrete. More natural wetlands thronged by living things, fewer chain-linked retention ponds. More green roofs, less asphalt. More shade trees, less open lawn. More plant buffers to filter rain, fewer stagnant storm-water basins. More community farms, less industrial irrigation.

As much as this revolution is a physical change in landscape, a turn away from super-sized infrastructure and toward local water, it is also a mental shift—a water consciousness. It is a water ethic for America.

More lyrical voices have tried to sound this call. The Global Water Policy Project's Sandra Postel defines the essence of a water ethic as making "protection of freshwater ecosystems a central goal in all that we do."[18] Oregon writer and ethicist Kathleen Dean Moore makes the moral argument that "taking whatever we need from the world to support our comfortable lives, and leaving for the future only degraded rivers, unreliable freshwater supplies, impoverished oceans, and an unstable climate *is not worthy of us as moral beings.*"[19]

Aldo Leopold's biographer, Curt Meine, connects water to the health of the land as a whole, underscoring his subject's belief that such an ethic "entails responsibility for the healthy functioning of the entire biotic community."[20]

Leopold described his land ethic as a "community instinct-in-the-making." His hydrologist son, Luna, applied his father's concept specifically to water. Luna articulated a water ethic as a set of "guiding beliefs" for citizens, large water users, and government. Most important, for him, was the warm and spiritual "reverence for rivers." But the lyricism and the reverence are not enough. He expressed the cold realities, too: Technology cannot fix all our water problems. Indefinite expansion of our water supplies is not possible. With nature's lessons in mind, we can find the balance point at which our water use today doesn't jeopardize fresh, clean water for our children tomorrow.

Water laws, water politics, water funding, and even water science can bend in all sorts of strange ways. A shared water ethic is the only straight guide we have to know whether water decisions are right for future generations. All our choices about water come down to the ethic: from the biggest, whether to transfer the Mississippi River west, to the smallest, whether to create English gardens and quench them with potable water.

After all my searching, from the NEWater plant in Singapore to Simon Bar Sinister's Big Dipper plot in *Underdog*, I thought Luna Leopold had come closest to articulating a water ethic for America. I sketched out one of my own, outlining common goals with the raindrop reminder that they are fluid—able to "evolve in the minds of the thinking community"[21]:

♦ Americans value water, from appreciating local streams to pricing water right.
♦ We work together to use less and less—rather than fight each other to grab more and more.
♦ We try to keep water local.
♦ We avoid the two big mistakes of our history: overtapping aquifers and surface waters and overrelying on the costliest fixes that bring unintended consequences to future generations.
♦ We leave as much as prudently possible in nature—aquifers, wetlands, and rivers—so that our children and grandchildren, with benefit of time and evolving knowledge, can make their *own* decisions about water.

Getting there will take political will, what Luna called "the acid test of leadership."[22] It also will require courage. It takes courage to be the first person on the block to transition from a bright-green lawn to your own, water-wise definition of beauty. It takes courage to be the one faculty member in the Extension office to question whether practices are really helping or hurting water. It takes courage to be the one engineer in the firm who defies pressure to donate to political campaigns. To be the member of Congress who speaks out against irrigation subsidies. To be the local elected official to stand up for higher water rates and recognize the value of this national treasure.

The water ethic begins with that one, brave steward. Then, it spreads out into the community, building collective courage among citizens, businesspeople, church members, political leaders. Just like ripples of children playing in a wide, free river.

Acknowledgments

This morning, Christmas, the gift I was burning to open was the one from my children, Will and Ilana Hoover, currently nine and six. I knew it was a book. They had gone into the bookstore and asked the clerk to help them find a certain author. They chose a title by this mysterious author and had it gift-wrapped in cat-and-dog paper.

I have never seen them so excited about a present. They kept giving me one, intriguing hint: "Mom, you talk about this writer *every single day!*" I racked my brain. I could not imagine any one writer who had dominated my thoughts, much less my conversations with my kids.

When I carefully opened the cat-and-dog paper, I was amazed to find *A Sand County Almanac,* by Aldo Leopold. Before that sweet moment, I had not realized how big a place in our family *Blue Revolution* had taken up since our summer vacation in 2009, when we enjoyed trips to Leopold's shack *and* the biggest water park in America. Six months later, Will cast a special Harry Potter spell on me to land a book contract—complete with local water and a cat whisker—and it worked. (Thanks to my literary agents, Sandra Dijkstra and Elise Capron, for the real magic.)

I thank Will and Ilana for putting up with this other, demanding baby with such good sportsmanship—indeed, with such exuberance. I also thank them for opening my eyes to the importance of free-flowing water in the lives of children. They have shown me how perfectly a river rocks a baby to sleep in the bottom of her canoe-cradle, how mastering a rope swing builds confidence in a small boy.

I am often asked how, with these kids, I can write books and juggle a full-time job and many other pursuits. My running joke is, "I married a superhero." But it's not really a joke. You would not be holding this book if not for the superhero, Aaron Hoover. Aaron is a talented speechwriter who edits my work before anyone else, saving me much embarrassment. He proved equally adept at full-time parenting, caring well for our children for weeks at a time so that I could tour far-off rivers and water plants for *Blue*. Aaron's love and support keeps me buoyed during even the confidence-bashed times in every author's life.

Next, I am ever grateful for my writing friendship with Jack E. Davis. The environmental historian who is author of *An Everglades Providence*, the biography of Marjory Stoneman Douglas, writes as cleverly as his subject. I have the great fortune to be able to e-mail Jack a metaphor at 3 a.m. and know by 5 a.m. whether I should trash it or keep at it. Jack helped shape *Blue* from the big picture to the small bottle: I thank him and his daughter, Willa, for finding the Big Dipper episode while mining *Underdog* cartoons.

I also could not have written *Blue* without the support of Mark Howard, my editor for thirteen years at *Florida Trend* magazine. Mark, along with *Trend* publisher Andy Corty and Paul Tash, chairman and CEO of Times Publishing Co., has kept *Trend* a deep-thinking publication and a meaningful place to work despite the crisis in our profession. I thank them for my book leave, and thank John Annunziata, Michael Vogel, Amy Keller, and Art Levy for picking up my work *and* being such inspirational colleagues.

Another group of generous colleagues are those I got to know during my Knight-Wallace Fellowship at the University of Michigan in 2004–2005. I thank KW director Charles Eisendrath for his continuing assistance, and '05 fellows Bill Duryea, Scott Elliott, and Jason Tanz for invaluable feedback on early chapters. In another KW–Ann Arbor bond, I thank University of Michigan Press director Philip Pochoda, who published my first book, then generously connected me to the Sandra Dijkstra Literary Agency so I could find a trade press for my second.

For their helpful feedback on drafts and other support, I thank Mindy Blum, Mary Frances Campana, Michael Campana, Ronnie Cochran, David Colburn, Robin Craig, John Garrison, Paul Hoover, Pierce Jones, Christine Klein, Robert Knight, Barbra Larson, Stuart Leavenworth, Jennifer Leubbe, Jacki Levine, Michael Maidenberg, Karl Meyer, Bob Mooney, Jim Owens, Bill Pine, Ros Sadlier, Tom Swihart, Billy Townsend, Clive Wynne, and David Zetland. Karen Arnold, Julie Garrett, Kathy Grantham, Stephanie Milch, Claude Owens, Sonya Rudenstine, Judy Smith, and Jane Toby also contributed to *Blue* and its author in myriad ways, as did Louise OFarrell and Larry Leshan, Mike and Gracy Castine, Mary and Charles Furman, Diana and Dhanesh Samarasan, and Steven Doherty and Sydney Prince.

I thank my mom, Gerry Garrison, for her big heaps of confidence, and for the small water-news items she faithfully clips from her local newspaper and sends me in the mail. I tried to make this book equal parts pipeline and poetry. The duality may stem from my stepfather, Dr. Joe Garrison, who is science oriented, and my father, Rusty Barnett, who is more poetic. I thank each of them for their perspectives. My brother, Brett Garrison, gets a special medal for helping with both *Blue* and the children. Destined to be one of those superhero guys, Brett can organize campaign contributions in Excel and bake chocolate chip cookies topped with sea salt for his niece and nephew all in the same day.

I thank the Collins Center for Public Policy in Florida and President Rod Petrey for the journalist's travel grant that funded my reporting trips to Australia and Singapore. Further, the Collins Center vigorously promoted the vision for a Florida water ethic that I brought back from those trips. I am especially grateful to the center's Steve Seibert for seeing the promise of a water ethic, and for being one of the big thinkers in my native state.

Likewise I am grateful to the Florida Earth Foundation and Executive Director Stan Bronson for seeing what important lessons the Netherlands holds for Florida, Louisiana, and other flood-prone parts of the United States, and for bringing me along on one of their eye-opening Florida-Holland Connection trips.

In Delft, the UNESCO Institute for Water Education and Dr.

Schalk Jan van Andel were especially helpful. I also thank Ria Geluk, a survivor of the 1957 storm, and the Watersnoodmuseum (Flood Museum) in Zeeland she helped make a reality, for helping me understand the disaster. In Singapore, I thank my knowledgeable guide Teo Yin Yin. Phil Kneebone and Clare Lugar helped make my trip to Australia a smooth and productive one.

Here at home, I repeat the thanks I made in my first book to what may be the two most underappreciated professions in America: librarians and environmental reporters. I am particularly grateful for the existence of Carnegie Libraries—inspirational spaces that gave me quiet corners to write in Cumberland, Wisconsin, and in Catskill, New York, during ostensible family vacations. I am grateful, too, for my productive hours at the University of Florida's Library West and at the Savannah College of Art and Design's dramatic Jen Library.

While I had the luxury of pondering water over the life of this project, I relied on the quick-turnaround work and wisdom of reporters including Matt Weiser at the *Sacramento Bee*, Craig Pittman at the *St. Petersburg Times*, Mark Schleifstein at the *Times-Picayune* in New Orleans, Michael Grunwald at *Time* magazine, John Fleck at the *Albuquerque Journal*, and Osha Gray Davidson at the *Phoenix Sun*, along with the amazing water scribes Emily Green, in Southern California, and Peter Annin, the longtime Great Lakes journalist recently named managing director of the University of Notre Dame's Environmental Change Initiative. The journalists at the international consortium Circle of Blue have done a particularly good job filling the dearth of water reporting left by contraction in the newspaper industry. I am especially grateful to Bruce Ritchie at Florida Environments.com, not only for his important water reporting but also for our friendship that has now lasted a quarter century.

Deep thanks are due Curt Meine at the Center for Humans and Nature, author of the powerful biography *Aldo Leopold: His Life and Work*, for providing such helpful background on Aldo and Luna Leopold and water-ethic scholarship. I thank Dominican sister Pat Siemen of the Center for Earth Jurisprudence and Sister of St. Joseph of Peace Suzanne Golas for their patient introduction to the ideas of

Christian stewardship for water. Likewise, I thank artists Annie Pais and Stewart Thomas for continuing to show me the role that art and culture play in environmental stewardship. I am thankful to them, too, for their tireless promotion of my first book, *Mirage*, as part of their One Region/One Book project and in many other venues. I am forever indebted to the hundreds of citizens who came to my talks about *Mirage*, gave me their support, and led me to *Blue* with their questions about America's water. *Blue* was conceived following one of those talks, at the Cedar Key kitchen table of Mary Stone and Hans Van Meer.

The original metaphor for this book was not the blue revolution but the gentler blue path. I thank my editor at Beacon Press, Alexis Rizzuto, for kicking me off the path and onto the revolution. Her push here—and there, and there—made *Blue* much better. Alexis embodies every author's top wish for an editor: one who cares deeply about the book and its subject. Also at Beacon Press, I thank Mandi Bleidorn for designing a book jacket worthy of the revolution, Sarah Laxton for its beautiful production, and Caitlin Meyer for her work on publicity. I am grateful to copy editor Mark Nichol for his excellent catches and to Tim Meyer for his eagle-eyed proofread.

The blue path endures, thanks to Annie and Stewart, who have turned that phrase into the name of a campaign to protect the springs of north Florida. I wish them success in saving the largest concentration of freshwater springs in the world. Every water author seems to have a special place that connects to childhood and inspires their work. Mine are the Suwannee River and those pane-clear springs. It seems fitting to end at one of them.

I wrote much of *Blue* at a silent retreat overlooking a springhead of Gum Slough, a jungly tributary of the Withlacoochee River. A family that wishes to remain anonymous owns more than eight hundred acres along the slough, including seven of fifteen feeder springs. They could have made multiple millions selling the property in any one of Florida's housing booms. Instead, they placed these beautiful lands, wetlands, and springs in a series of conservation easements to protect the watershed in perpetuity. Everything they do on the property—from giving quiet inspiration to a harried book author to bringing in grad students to research the little-touched springs—is deliberately aimed at trying to save the planet.

I thank the family, and I thank the place, which I came to call Muse Spring. I began each writing day diving into its blue embrace. The resulting clarity led to my favorite parts of this book—and yet one more reason to save America's freshwaters.

Christmas Day 2010
Savannah, Georgia

Notes

Chapter 1 The Illusion of Water Abundance

1. Jeff Wiltse, *Contested Waters: A Social History of Swimming Pools in America* (Chapel Hill: University of North Carolina Press, 2007), 198–200.
2. Cynthia Barnett, "Liquidity," *Florida Trend*, July 2004.
3. Marybeth Bizjak, "Green Thumbs," *Sacramento* magazine, March 2007.
4. Matt Weiser, "Capital Gushes Wasted Water: Metropolitan Region's Per-Capita Daily Use Tops U.S. Average as Conservation Pledges Go Unmet," *Sacramento Bee*, June 19, 2008. Weiser, whose analysis relied on the U.S. Geological Survey for California per capita rates, reports 287 gallons per person in the greater metropolitan region and 494 gallons per person in Granite Bay.
5. States News Service, "Boat Removal Beginning at Reclamation's Folsom Lake Due to Dry-Year Reservoir Conditions," U.S. Bureau of Reclamation, August 5, 2009.
6. San Juan Water District, "Current Water Conservation Warning: Stage 3—Voluntary Reductions Now Requested," *Water Gram*, May/June 2009, 1.
7. U.S. Department of Energy, "Top Ten Utility Green Power Programs." The Sacramento Municipal Utility District had the fourth-highest participation rate in the nation. See "Customer Participation Rate," December 2009, http://apps3.eere.energy.gov/greenpower/resources/tables/topten.shtml.
8. Residents of Aspen, Colorado, may actually use more than anyone else on the planet, according to statistics from Pitkin County that show an average of 1,851 gallons per person each day. See Bruce Finley, "As Water Use Falls in Front Range, It Explodes Elsewhere in Colorado," *Denver Post*, December 21, 2009.
9. Weiser, "Capital Gushes Wasted Water."
10. Water Corporation of Western Australia, 2010 data; London State of the Environment Report, 2010; Vewin water-supply statistics for the Netherlands compiled for 2007.
11. Nancy Vogel, "Sacramento May Finally Go with Flow, Get Water Meters," *Los Angeles Times*, May 6, 2003.

12. Sacramento Department of Utilities, "Water Meters Coming to Sacramento," http://www.cityofsacramento.org/utilities/water/water-meters.cfm.

13. Andrew Maddocks, "Freshwater Crisis Not Included in Final Copenhagen Accord Despite Calls for Action," Circle of Blue, January 4, 2010, http://www.circleofblue.org/waternews/2010/world/freshwater-crisis-not-included-in-final-copenhagen-accord-despite-calls-for-action/.

14. Author interview with Tom Gohring, July 15, 2009.

15. T. P. Barnett and D.W. Pierce, "When Will Lake Mead Go Dry?," Water Resources Research 44 (March 2008): 4.

16. Robert Kunzig, "Drying of the West," National Geographic, February 2008.

17. Glen M. MacDonald, "Water, Climate Change, and Sustainability in the Southwest," part of "Climate Change and Water in Southwestern North America Special Feature," Proceedings of the National Academy of Sciences 107, no. 50 (December 14, 2010): 21259.

18. Kunzig, "Drying of the West."

19. Barnett and Pierce, "When Will Lake Mead Go Dry?," 9.

20. Timothy Egan, The Worst Hard Time: The Untold Story of Those Who Survived the Great American Dustbowl (New York: Mariner Books, 2006), 310.

21. B. Rajagopalan and others, "Water Supply Risk on the Colorado River: Can Management Mitigate?," Water Resources Research, August 21, 2009.

22. Joan F. Kenny and others, "Estimated Use of Water in the United States in 2005: U.S. Geological Survey Circular 1344," 2009, http://pubs.usgs.gov/circ/1344/.

23. U.S. Department of Energy, "Energy Demands on Water Resources: Report to Congress on the Interdependency of Energy and Water" (December 2006): 30, http://www.sandia.gov/energy-water/docs/121-RptToCongress-EWwEIAcomments-FINAL.pdf.

24. Robert F. Service, "Another Biofuels Drawback—the Demand for Irrigation," Science 326, no. 5952 (October 2009): 516–17.

25. According to the California Water Plan, 2005 edition, agriculture uses about 75 percent of all the developed water in the state; http://www.waterplan.water.ca.gov/.

26. Thomas Friedman, Hot, Flat, and Crowded: Why We Need a Green Revolution—and How It Can Renew America (New York: Farrar, Straus and Giroux, 2008), 22.

27. Some of these ideas are from "Green Infrastructure Projects in 25 States Would Create Jobs, Stimulate Economy," press release, American Rivers, December 17, 2008.

28. Luna B. Leopold, A View of the River (Cambridge, MA: Harvard University Press, 1994), 2.

29. Bevan Griffiths-Sattenspiel and Wendy Wilson, "The Carbon Footprint of Water," River Network, May 2009, http://www.rivernetwork.org/resource-library/carbon-footprint-water/.

30. F. Herbert Bormann, Diana Balmori, and Gordon T. Geballe, Redesigning the American Lawn (New Haven, CT: Yale University Press, 2001), 54.

31. Author interview with Cristina Milesi, August 5, 2009.

32. P.W. Mayer and others, Residential End Uses of Water (Denver: AWWA Research Foundation and American Water Works Association, 1999).

33. Records from the City of West Palm Beach public utility, which supplies water to the island of Palm Beach, show that Trump's 2007–08 fiscal-year average monthly

consumption was 2,053,663 gallons and his average monthly bill was $9,826.33. The only two utility customers that used more than Trump were the Breakers, a 540-room resort, and the Four Seasons Ocean Grand, a 210-room resort. In July 2008, Trump sold the estate to Russian fertilizer billionaire Dmitry Rybolovlev.

34. Robert Frank, "What Drought? Palm Beach Is an Island of Green," *Wall Street Journal*, November 16, 2007.

35. Rachel Simmonsen, "Singer Dion Splashiest of Treasure Coast's Big Water Users," *Palm Beach Post*, May 24, 2008.

36. Henry Brean, "Not a Drop in the Bucket: Top 100 Users Consume Enough Water to Supply 1,950 Homes, But That's Only Half the Story," *Las Vegas Review-Journal*, March 22, 2009.

37. Simmonsen, "Singer Dion Splashiest of Treasure Coast's Big Water Users," and Brean, "Not a Drop in the Bucket."

38. Georgina Littlejohn, "First Look at Celine Dion's $20 Million Florida Waterpark Mansion That Boasts Slides, Bridges, and Even a Lazy River," *Daily Mail* (UK), June 8, 2010.

39. Marty Toohey, "No Dry Days at These Homes," *Austin American-Statesman*, August 15, 2008.

40. The Wisconsin Historical Society has the most well-documented argument, at http://www.wisconsinhistory.org/topics/wisconsin-name/.

41. Aldo Leopold, *A Sand County Almanac* (New York: Ballantine Books, 1970; originally published by Oxford University Press, 1949), 246.

42. Ibid.

43. Author interview with Curt Meine, director of the Center for Humans and Nature and author of *Aldo Leopold: His Life and Work* (Madison: University of Wisconsin Press, 1988), August 14, 2009.

44. All data courtesy of Noah's Ark Water Park.

45. Laura Ingalls Wilder, *Little House on the Prairie* (New York: HarperCollins, First Harper Trophy edition, 1971), 160.

46. Lien Hoang, "Minnehaha Falls Now a Waterfall in Name Only," *St. Paul Pioneer Press*, July 30, 2009.

47. Total daily water withdrawals in the United States were about a hundred billion gallons per day in 1950 and about four hundred billion gallons per day in 2000, according to the U.S. Geological Survey, "Estimated Use of Water in the United States 2000."

48. Brad Linder, "Philadelphia Tackles Rainwater Runoff Pollution," National Public Radio, September 29, 2006, npr.org.

49. Christopher Thacker, *The History of Gardens* (Berkeley: University of California Press, 1985), 154.

50. The $680 billion figure is from Datamonitor's *Construction & Engineering—North America (NAFTA) Industry Guide* (August 2009), http://www.mindbranch.com/catalog/print_product_page.jsp?code=R313-53048.

Chapter 2   Reclamation to Restoration

1. Samuel P. Shaw and C. Gordon Fredine, *Wetlands of the United States: Their Extent and Their Value to Waterfowl and Other Wildlife* (Department of the Interior, Cir-

cular 39, 1956), available online at http://www.npwrc.usgs.gov/resource/wetlands/uswetlan/.

2. T. E. Reilly and others, "Ground-Water Availability in the United States: U.S. Geological Survey" (Circular 1323, 2008), 6, http://pubs.usgs.gov/circ/1323/.

3. H. L. Jelks and others, "Conservation Status of Imperiled North American Freshwater and Diadromous Fishes," *Fisheries* 33, no. 8 (2008): 372–407.

4. Patrick McCully, *Silenced Rivers: The Ecology and Politics of Large Dams* (London: Zed Books, 1996), 7.

5. Wendell R. Haag, "Past and Future Patterns of Freshwater Mussel Extinctions in North America During the Holocene," in Samuel T. Turvey, ed., *Holocene Extinctions* (New York: Oxford University Press, 2009), 107–28.

6. Jelks and others, "Conservation Status of Imperiled North American Freshwater and Diadromous Fishes."

7. Karl Blankenship, "Atlantic Sturgeon Under Consideration for Endangered Species List," *Chesapeake Bay Journal*, February 2010.

8. Ibid.

9. Michael Grunwald, "An Everglades Saga," *Forum* [Florida Humanities Council] 33, no. 3 (Fall 2009): 5.

10. U.S. Army Corps of Engineers and the Central and Southern Florida Flood Control District, *Waters of Destiny*, International Sound Films, Atlanta, 1955.

11. Jack E. Davis, *An Everglades Providence: Marjory Stoneman Douglas and the American Environmental Century* (Athens: University of Georgia Press, 2009), 299.

12. Michael Grunwald, *The Swamp: The Everglades, Florida and the Politics of Paradise* (New York: Simon & Schuster, 2006), 193.

13. Zora Neale Hurston, *Their Eyes Were Watching God* (Urbana: University of Illinois Press, Illini Books edition 1978; originally published 1937), 234–39.

14. U.S. Army Corps of Engineers and the Central and Southern Florida Flood Control District, *Waters of Destiny*.

15. "Kissimmee River," South Florida Water Management District, http://my.sfwmd .gov/portal/page/portal/levelthree/kissimmee%20river.

16. Robert P. King, "Pollution Still Threatens Everglades," *Palm Beach Post*, September 19, 2007.

17. Andy Reid, "Coasts Soar to Clean Pollution, Fix Lake Okeechobee Dike," *South Florida Sun-Sentinel*, March 3, 2007.

18. Robert P. King, "Lake O Releases Stir Up Regrets as Drought Lasts," *Palm Beach Post*, May 28, 2007.

19. Associated Press, "Drought Forces Water Limits in South Florida," April 12, 2007.

20. King, "Lake O Releases Stir Up Regrets as Drought Lasts."

21. Jay Lund and others, *Envisioning Futures for the Sacramento–San Joaquin Delta* (San Francisco: Public Policy Institute of California, 2007), 2; and Deltapark Neeltje Jans, "The Delta Project: Preserving the Environment and Securing Zeeland Against Flooding" (report, 2009).

22. Lund and others, *Envisioning Futures for the Sacramento–San Joaquin Delta*, 2.

23. S. E. Ingebritsen and others, "Delta Subsidence in California: The Sinking Heart of the State," U.S. Geological Survey, http://ca.water.usgs.gov/archive/reports/fs00500/fs00500.pdf.

24. Peter B. Moyle and others, "Changing Ecosystems: A Brief Ecological History of the Delta," February 2010, http://watershed.ucdavis.edu/pdf/Moyle-et-al-Delta_history-WP.pdf.

25. Author interview with Jeffrey Mount, founding director, UC Davis Center for Watershed Sciences, November 19, 2010; and Jeffrey Mount, presentation, "Hell and High Water in the Delta: The Fate of California's Water Supply Hub," UC Davis Center for Watershed Science, Water Resources Center Archives (WRCA) California Colloquium on Water, February 14, 2006.

26. David Lewis Feldman, *Water Policy for Sustainable Development* (Baltimore: Johns Hopkins University Press, 2007), 155–56.

27. Aldo Leopold, *A Sand County Almanac* (New York: Ballantine Books, 1970; originally published by Oxford University Press, 1949), 262.

28. Luther J. Carter, "The Leopolds: A Family of Naturalists," *Science* 207, no. 4435 (March 7, 1980): 1051–55.

29. Ibid., 1051.

30. Author interview with Curt Meine, director of the Center for Humans and Nature and author of *Aldo Leopold: His Life and Work* (Madison: University of Wisconsin Press, 1988), August 14, 2009.

31. Ibid.

32. Carter, "The Leopolds," 1053.

33. Jeremy Pearce, "Luna Leopold, River Researcher, Is Dead at 90," *New York Times*, March 20, 2006.

34. Davis, *An Everglades Providence*, 457–90.

35. Author interview with Meine.

36. Luna B. Leopold, *A View of the River* (Cambridge, MA: Harvard University Press, 1994).

37. Carter, "The Leopolds," 1054.

38. Two key speeches in which Leopold calls for a water ethic are Luna B. Leopold, "A Reverence for Rivers," keynote address, the Governor's Conference on the California Drought, Los Angeles, California, 1977, and Luna B. Leopold, "Ethos, Equity, and the Water Resource," Abel Woman Distinguished Lecture, U.S. National Research Council of the U.S. National Academy of Sciences, 1990.

39. Mark Arax and Rick Wartzman, *The King of California: J. G. Boswell and the Making of a Secret American Empire* (New York: Perseus Books, 2003), 350–51.

40. Norris Hundley Jr., *The Great Thirst: Californians and Water: A History*, rev. ed. (Berkeley: University of California Press, 2001), 322–23.

41. Ibid.

42. Luna Leopold, "A Reverence for Rivers."

43. Ibid.

44. Hundley, *The Great Thirst*, 373–74.

45. Davis, *An Everglades Providence*, 523.

46. Elizabeth Royte, "A Tall, Cool Drink of . . . Sewage?," *New York Times Magazine*, August 8, 2008.

47. Florida Department of Environmental Protection, "2009 Annual Reuse Inventory," http://www.dep.state.fl.us/water/reuse/inventory.htm.

48. Marc Reisner, *Cadillac Desert: The American West and Its Disappearing Water*, rev. ed. (New York: Penguin Books, 1993), 510.

49. Hundley, *The Great Thirst*, 373.

50. Lund and others, *Envisioning Futures for the Sacramento–San Joaquin Delta*, vi.

51. Jelks and others, "Conservation Status of Imperiled North American Freshwater and Diadromous Fishes."

52. Haag, "Past and Future Patterns of Freshwater Mussel Extinctions in North America During the Holocene," 127–28.

53. The $8.7 billion figure is from Hundley, *The Great Thirst*, 420.

54. Lund and others, *Envisioning Futures for the Sacramento–San Joaquin Delta*, 87–93.

55. Grunwald, "An Everglades Saga," 6.

56. Grunwald, *The Swamp*, 1–3.

57. Committee on Independent Scientific Review of Everglades Restoration Progress, National Research Council of the National Academies, *Progress Toward Restoring the Everglades: The Second Biennial Review*—2008 (Washington, DC: National Academies Press, 2008), 1–2.

58. South Florida Water Management District, "Governor Bush Breaks Ground on Massive Reservoir to Restore America's Everglades," press release, August 2, 2006.

59. Jennifer Steinhauer, "California Tries to Solve Water Woes," *New York Times*, October 13, 2009.

60. Hundley, *The Great Thirst*, 330.

61. Office of Governor Arnold Schwarzenegger, "2009 Comprehensive Water Package Special Session Policy Bills and Bond Summary," November 2009.

62. Juliet Christian-Smith and others, "The 2010 California Water Bond: What Does It Say and Do?," Pacific Institute, August 2010, http://www.pacinst.org/reports/water_bond/2010_water_bond_report.pdf.

63. Southern California Water Committee, "California's Water Crisis: Developing Solutions," Microsoft PowerPoint presentation, March 26, 2010.

64. Curtis Morgan, "Charlie Crist's Downsized U.S. Sugar Deal under Siege," *Miami Herald*, March 7, 2010.

Chapter 3 The Netherlands: Deluge, Dams, and the Dutch Miracle

1. BBC Weather, "1953 East Coast Floods," http://www.bbc.co.uk/weather/features/understanding/1953_flood.shtml.

2. Greg McKevitt, "Ferry Disaster Victims Remembered," January 30, 2003, http://news.bbc.co.uk/2/hi/uk_news/northern_ireland/2705901.stm.

3. Ibid.

4. Ilan Kelman, "1953 Storm Surge Deaths: UK," ver. 5, August 17, 2009, IlanKelman.org, http://www.ilankelman.org/disasterdeaths/1953DeathsUK.doc.

5. Kelman, 7.

6. Deltapark Neeltje Jans, "The Delta Project: Preserving the Environment and Securing Zeeland against Flooding" (report, 2009), 2.

7. Most of the details about the North Sea flood of 1953 and its impact on the Netherlands are from the author's visit to the Watersnoodmuseum (the Flood Museum) in Zeeland, May 12, 2010, and from the museum's website, http://www.watersnoodmuseum.nl.

8. Instituut voor Sociaal Onderzoek van het Nederlandse Volk and U.S. National Research Council Committee on Disaster Studies, *Studies in Holland Flood Disaster 1953*, 1 (1955): 49.

9. Deltawerken, "The Flood of 1953: Climatic Circumstances," http://www.delta werken.com/Climatic-circumstances/483.html.

10. Herman Gerritsen, "What Happened in 1953? The Big Flood in the Netherlands in Retrospect," *Philosophical Transactions of the Royal Society A*, 363, no. 1831 (2005): 1271–91.

11. Author visit to Watersnoodmuseum.

12. Author interview with Jan Luijendijk, head of hydroinformatics at UNESCO-IHE, May 12, 2010.

13. Ibid.

14. Author visit to Watersnoodmuseum.

15. Ibid.

16. Kenneth C. Davis, *Don't Know Much About Mythology* (New York: HarperCollins, 2005), 123, 157. See also Steven Solomon, *Water: The Epic Struggle for Wealth, Power, and Civilization* (New York: HarperCollins, 2010), 39–42.

17. Davis, *Don't Know Much About Mythology*, 333.

18. Ibid., 456.

19. See William Ryan and Walter Pitman, *Noah's Flood: The New Scientific Discoveries about the Event That Changed History* (New York: Simon & Schuster, 1999).

20. Davis, *Don't Know Much About Mythology*, 159.

21. Deltapark Neeltje Jans, *The Delta Project: Preserving the Environment and Securing Zeeland Against Flooding* (The Hague: Ministry of Transport and Public Works, 2009), 4.

22. "Survey Shows Americans Too Confident in Flood, Hurricane Preparedness," *Civil Engineering News*, May 24, 2010, http://www.cenews.com/news-survey_shows_americans_too_confident_in_flood__hurricane_preparedness-946 .html.

23. Author visit to Watersnoodmuseum.

24. Deltawerken, "The Flood of 1953: Rescue and Consequences," http://www .deltawerken.com/Rescue-and-consequences1309.html.

25. Douglas Brinkley, *The Great Deluge: Hurricane Katrina, New Orleans, and the Mississippi Gulf Coast* (New York: William Morrow, 2006), 79–80.

26. Ibid., 108.

27. U.S. House of Representatives, "A Failure of Initiative: Final Report of the Select Bipartisan Committee to Investigate the Preparation for and Response to Hurricane Katrina," 109th Congress, February 15, 2006, 3. The report uses the word *paralyzed* seven times, first in the executive summary on page 3, http://www.gpoaccess.gov/ katrinareport/fullreport.pdf.

28. Brinkley, *The Great Deluge*, 343. Adequate help and supplies did not arrive until the morning of Friday, September 2.

29. Richard D. Knabb and others, "Tropical Cyclone Report: Hurricane Katrina" (National Hurricane Center, updated August 10, 2006), 11, http://www.nhc.noaa.gov/ pdf/TCR-AL122005_Katrina.pdf.

30. Brinkley, *The Great Deluge*, 424.

31. Ibid., 618.

32. Gerritsen, "What Happened in 1953?," 1284.

33. Rijkswaterstaat, "The Delta: Rich and Robust," November 2007, 16. See also Deltawerken, "Water, Nature, People, Technology," 3, http://www.deltaworks.org/downloads/summaries/PDF/english_pdf_deltaworks.org.pdf.

34. Gert van Engelen, review of *World Famous But Unknown*, *Delft Integraal*, http://www.delftintegraal.tudelft.nl/info/index736a.html?hoofdstuk=Artikel&ArtID=5108.

35. Hans Sijberden, *Coast and Sea: Inspiration for Innovative Developments* (Breda, Netherlands: Arttechnick, 2010), 36–37; and Gerritsen, "What Happened in 1953?," 1285.

36. Deltapark Neeltje Jans, *The Delta Project*, 6.

37. Ibid.

38. Ibid., 7.

39. Walter H. Waggoner, "New Lands From Old," *New York Times*, November 9, 1958.

40. Deltawerken, "Water, Nature, People, Technology," 8, http://www.deltaworks.org/downloads/summaries/PDF/english_pdf_deltaworks.org.pdf. The current Delta Commission estimates that the total cost of the Delta Works was about $5 billion Euros.

41. The Port of Rotterdam has long been the top port in Europe by many measures, including gross annual weight and number of containers moved. "Port Statistics 2009," Top 20 European Ports, 2009–2006, 2, http://www.portofrotterdam.com/en/Port/port-statistics/Documents/Port_Statistics_2009_tcm26-64785.pdf.

42. John McQuaid, "Give & Take: The Dutch Found Out the Hard Way: Flood Control Can Cause as Many Problems as It Solves," *Times-Picayune* (New Orleans), November 15, 2005.

43. Rijkswaterstaat, "The Delta," 16.

44. Frank P. Hallie and Richard E. Jorissen, "Protection Against Flooding: A New Delta Plan in the Netherlands," *Destructive Water: Water-Caused Natural Disasters, Their Abatement and Control*, International Association of Hydrological Sciences, publication nos. 239 (1997): 362–63.

45. Sijberden, *Coast and Sea*, 18.

46. Rijkswaterstaat, "The Delta," 16.

47. Deltawerken, "Nature," http://www.deltawerken.com/Nature/421.html.

48. Huib de Vriend, "The Eastern Scheldt Barrier: Environmentally Friendly Engineering?," *Proceedings of the Second International Conference of Civil Engineering, Planning and the Environment* (September 2004): 1271.

49. Rijkswaterstaat, *Design Plan Oosterschelde Storm-Surge Barrier: Overall Design and Design Philosophy* (Rotterdam: Balkema, 1994), 5.

50. Deltawerken, "Oosterschelde Storm Surge Barrier/Construction," http://www.deltawerken.com.

51. Author interview with a longtime water engineer in Zeeland.

52. Huib de Vriend, "The Eastern Scheldt Barrier," 1280.

53. Sander Wijnhoven and others, "The Decline and Restoration of a Coastal Lagoon (Lake Veere) in the Dutch Delta," *Estuaries and Coasts* (November 2009): 16.

54. Catherine Osborne, *Presocratic Philosophy: A Very Short Introduction* (New York: Oxford University Press, 2004), 87.

Chapter 4   Powerful Thirst

1. Mitch Weiss, "Drought Could Force Nuclear-Plant Shut-Downs," Associated Press, January 24, 2008.

2. Joan F. Kenny and others, "Estimated Use of Water in the United States in 2005: U.S. Geological Survey Circular 1344," 2009, http://pubs.usgs.gov/circ/1344/.

3. Ibid.

4. Eric Pooley, *The Climate War: True Believers, Power Brokers, and the Fight to Save the Earth* (New York: Hyperion, 2010), 143.

5. Benjamin K. Sovacool and Kelly E. Sovacool, "Preventing National Electricity-Water Crisis Areas in the United States," *Columbia Journal of Environmental Law* 34, no. 2 (Summer 2009): 365.

6. Robert F. Durden, *Bold Entrepreneur: A Life of James B. Duke* (Durham, NC: Carolina Academic Press, 2003), 96.

7. Ibid., 43 and 97.

8. Ibid., 63.

9. Duke Farms Foundation, "Hydropower," http://www.dukefarms.org/History/Landscape/Hydropower/.

10. Durden, *Bold Entrepreneur*, 63.

11. Ibid., 65.

12. Duke Farms Foundation, "Hydropower."

13. Durden, *Bold Entrepreneur*, 100–101.

14. Ibid., 120.

15. Catawba Riverkeeper, "About the Catawba-Wateree River," http://www.catawbariverkeeper.org/about-the-catawba/catawba-wateree-facts/.

16. Durden, *Bold Entrepreneur*, 120.

17. Ibid., 136.

18. Ibid., 122.

19. Ibid., 123–24.

20. Ibid., 124–26.

21. Ibid., 133–34.

22. Steven Solomon, *Water: The Epic Struggle for Wealth, Power, and Civilization* (New York: HarperCollins, 2010), 286–87.

23. Ibid., 287.

24. Elizabeth Leland, "Cry for the Catawba, Part 1: Drought and Development Threaten the Source of Life for Our Cities," *Charlotte Observer*, October 28, 2007.

25. Amy Baldwin, "Duke Makes Deal for Crescent," *Charlotte Observer*, September 9, 2006.

26. Crescent Resources, http://www.crescent-resources.com/.

27. Baldwin, "Duke Makes Deal for Crescent."

28. The 785-million-gallon-per-day figure is from Duke's filings with the Federal Energy Regulatory Commission, but the filing says it is more than 80 million gallons higher during times of drought, when Duke has to pump more to keep the river cooler, FERC document 20080801–5227, 41.

29. Duke Energy, "How Do Coal-Fired Plants Work?," http://www.duke-energy.com/about-energy/generating-electricity/coal-fired-how.asp/.

30. Victoria Morton, "Electric Power Plant Water Use in North Carolina: Forced Evaporation and Emission Controls" (master's project, Nichols School of the Environment, Duke University, 2010).

31. U.S. Department of Energy, "Energy Demands on Water Resources: Report to Congress on the Interdependency of Energy and Water" (December 2006), 30, http://www.sandia.gov/energy-water/docs/121-RptToCongress-EWwEIAcomments-FINAL.pdf; and Sovacool and Sovacool, "Preventing National Electricity-Water Crisis Areas in the United States," 360.

32. State of North Carolina Department of Environment and Natural Resources, Division of Water Quality, "Permit to Discharge Wastewater Under the National Pollutant Discharge Elimination System," Permit # NC0004979, pg. 3.

33. State of North Carolina Department of Environment and Natural Resources, Division of Water Quality, Permit Notice, Allen Steam Station, April 28, 2010.

34. John Downey, "Duke Energy, State Monitoring Lake Norman Fish Deaths," *Charlotte Observer*, July 23, 2010.

35. Sue Sturgis, "Disaster in East Tennessee," *Southern Exposure* (Institute for Southern Studies), May 2010, http://www.southernstudies.org/2010/05/disaster-in-east-tennessee.html.

36. Electric Light & Power, "Duke Energy Moving into New Corporate Headquarters," July 22, 2010, http://www.elp.com/index/display/article-display/0623439481/articles/electric-light-power/generation/2010/07/Duke_Energy_moving_into_new_corporate_headquarters.html.

37. Pooley, *The Climate War*, 352.

38. Democracy North Carolina, "Special-Interest PACS Guard Tax Loopholes," research report, June 16, 2009, 4.

39. Clive Thompson, "A Green Coal Baron?" *New York Times Magazine*, June 22, 2008.

40. Jim Rogers, "Why Nuclear Power Is Part of Our Future," *Wall Street Journal*, August 4, 2009.

41. Sovacool and Sovacool, "Preventing National Electricity-Water Crisis Areas in the United States," 340.

42. U.S. Energy Information Administration, "Frequently Asked Questions: Electricity," http://www.eia.doe.gov/ask/electricity_faqs.asp/.

43. U.S. Department of Energy, "Energy Demands on Water Resources: Report to Congress on the Interdependency of Energy and Water" (December 2006), v, http://www.sandia.gov/energy-water/docs/121-RptToCongress-EWwEIAcomments-FINAL.pdf.

44. Weiss, "Drought Could Force Nuclear-Plant Shut-Downs."

45. Dave Flessner, "Hot River Forces Costly Cutback for TVA," *Chattanooga Times Free Press*, August 23, 2010.

46. Michael Hightower, "Energy Security—Addressing the Water Footprint," *Ground Water* 47, no. 6 (November–December 2009): 765–66.

47. Phil McKenna, "Measuring Corn Ethanol's Thirst for Water," *MIT Technology Review*, April 14, 2009.

48. Shaun McKinnon, "Amid State's Push for Solar Power, Water-Supply Worries Arise," *Arizona Republic*, January 17, 2010.

49. Colin Sullivan, "California Regulators Ask Genesis Solar to Revise Water-Use Proposal," *Energy & Environment News*, June 17, 2010.

50. American Wind Energy Association, http://www.awea.org/.

51. Reuters, "U.S. Wind Power Growing Fast But Still Lags," *CNET News*, March 19, 2010.

52. Duke Energy, "2009 Net Megawatt Hour Generation," *Duke Energy 2009–2010 Sustainability Report*, Environmental Metrics, http://sustainabilityreport.duke-energy .com/environmental/metrics.asp/.

53. David Owen, "The Inventor's Dilemma," *New Yorker*, May 17, 2010.

54. Natural Resources Defense Council and Pacific Institute, "Energy Down the Drain: The Hidden Costs of California's Water Supply," August 2004, 2, http://www.nrdc .org/water/conservation/edrain/edrain.pdf.

55. State of South Carolina v. State of North Carolina, no. 138, original, June 7, 2007.

56. Ibid.

57. David H. Getches, *Water Law in a Nutshell* (St. Paul, MN: West, 1997), 397.

58. Kevin Colburn, "Catawba Analysis Released, Meetings Planned," American Whitewater (March 20, 2009), http://www.americanwhitewater.org/content/Article/view/ articleid/30316/display/full/.

59. State of South Carolina v. State of North Carolina, no. 138, October 13, 2009: 35.

60. Ibid., 24.

61. Duke Energy, "Water: A Shared Resource," *Duke Energy 2009–2010 Sustainability Report*, Environmental Footprint, http://sustainabilityreport.duke-energy.com/ environmental/water-shared-resource.asp; and Edward D. Bruce, "Developing a Protocol for Water Use During a Drought," Hydroworld.com 27, no. 1.

62. "The Duke Mansion: Built in 1915, Saved in 1998, The History of Charlotte's Grandest Home," Duke Mansion brochure.

Chapter 5   Taproot of the Crisis

1. Craig Pittman and Jessica Vander Velde, "30 Percent of Florida Crops Damaged by Freeze; 22 Sinkholes Open After Fields Sprayed," *St. Petersburg Times*, January 14, 2010; and Freeze Event Workshop, Southwest Florida Water Management District, February 17, 2010, Plant City, Florida.

2. Ibid.

3. James A. Miller, "The Floridan Aquifer System," in *Ground Water Atlas of the United States: Alabama, Florida, Georgia, South Carolina*, HA 730-G, 1990, http://pubs .usgs.gov/ha/ha730/ch_g/G-text6.html.

4. Cynthia Barnett, *Mirage: Florida and the Vanishing Water of the Eastern U.S.* (Ann Arbor: University of Michigan Press, 2007), 1.

5. This is the Southwest Florida Water Management District's official figure.

6. Hillsborough County Schools, "Work Set to Begin at Trapnell Elementary," press release, Hillsborough County Schools, February 2, 2010.

7. Donna Koehn, "Sinkhole Politics: Who Gets Heard?," *Tampa Tribune*, January 17, 2010.

8. Ibid.

9. Barry Newman, "This Town Is Going Down, and Strawberries Share the Blame," *Wall Street Journal*, April 19, 2010.

10. "Determining the Need for a Cap on Groundwater Use for Freeze Protection," Southwest Florida Water Management District presentation, technical work session, Tampa, Florida, April 21, 2010, http://www.swfwmd.state.fl.us/emergency/frost-freeze/04–21–10_PDF-Introduction-Overview.pdf.

11. "Workshop Summary," Southwest Florida Water Management District, Public Workshop #1, Plant City, Florida, February 17, 2010, http://www.swfwmd.state.fl.us/emergency/frost-freeze/02–17–10_Workshop_Minutes.pdf.

12. Ibid.

13. Ibid.

14. Jerald L. Schnoor, "Water Sustainability in a Changing World," National Water Research Institute, 2010 Clarke Prize Lecture, Costa Mesa, California, July 15, 2010.

15. Joan F. Kenny and others, "Estimated Use of Water in the United States in 2005: U.S. Geological Survey Circular 1344," 2009, http://pubs.usgs.gov/circ/1344/.

16. John Opie, *Ogallala: Water for a Dry Land* (Lincoln: University of Nebraska Press, 2000), 7 and xvii.

17. Andrew Kimbrell, ed., *Fatal Harvest: The Tragedy of Industrial Agriculture* (Washington, DC: Island Press, 2002), 230.

18. Opie, *Ogallala*, 3–4. The High Plains, or Ogallala, Aquifer originally contained three billion acre-feet of water. In his book, published in 2000, Opie reported the total at two billion.

19. U.S. Geological Survey, "Land Subsidence in the United States," USGS Fact Sheet 165–00, December 2000.

20. U.S. Department of Agriculture, "Long Range Planning for Drought Management—the Groundwater Component," http://wmc.ar.nrcs.usda.gov/technical/GW/Drought.html.

21. Douglas Jehl, "Arkansas Rice Farmers Run Dry, and U.S. Remedy Sets Off Debate," *New York Times*, November 11, 2002. The 2015 projection is from the U.S. Army Corps of Engineers, Memphis District.

22. John B. Gates, "Groundwater Irrigation in the Development of the Grand Prairie Rice Industry, 1896–1950," University of Nebraska–Lincoln Department of Earth and Atmospheric Sciences, Papers in the Earth and Atmospheric Sciences, Year 2005, 412.

23. Ibid.

24. California Rice Commission, "Water Supply," http://calrice.thewebhounds.com/Environment/Balance+Sheet/Chapter+2+-+Water+Supply.htm.

25. Melinda Burns, "Trading 'Virtual' Water," Miller-McCune, June 10, 2009, http://www.miller-mccune.com/business-economics/trading-virtual-water-3650/.

26. Fred Pearce, *When the Rivers Run Dry: Water—the Defining Crisis of the Twenty-First Century* (Boston: Beacon Press, 2006), 5.

27. Nathan Childs and Janet Livezey, "Rice Backgrounder," U.S. Department of Agriculture, RCS-2006–01, December 2006, 8.

28. Robert Glennon, *Unquenchable: America's Water Crisis and What to Do About It* (Washington, DC: Island Press, 2009), 276.

29. Childs and Livezey, "Rice Backgrounder," 31.

30. Norman Myers and Jennifer Kent, *Perverse Subsidies: How Tax Dollars Can Undercut the Environment and the Economy* (Washington, DC: Island Press, 2001), 136–37.

31. David Lewis Feldman, *Water Policy for Sustainable Development* (Baltimore: Johns Hopkins University Press), 46.

32. Carolyn Dimitri and others, "The 20th Century Transformation of U.S. Agriculture and Farm Policy," U.S. Department of Agriculture Economic Research Service, Economic Information Bulletin no. 3 (June 2005): 2.

33. Lance Gunderson and others, *Barriers & Bridges to the Renewal of Ecosystems and Institutions* (New York: Columbia University Press, 1995), 114.

34. Bill Kovarik, "Henry Ford, Charles F. Kettering, and the Fuel of the Future," *Automotive History Review*, no. 32 (Spring 1998): 7–27, http://www.radford.edu/~wkovarik/papers/fuel.html.

35. Ibid.

36. Phil McKenna, "Measuring Corn Ethanol's Thirst for Water," *Technology Review*, April 14, 2009.

37. Ibid.

38. Mark Schleifstein, "Dead Zone as Big as Massachusetts Along Coast of Louisiana and Texas, Scientists Say," *Times-Picayune* (New Orleans), August 3, 2010.

39. Schnoor, "Water Sustainability in a Changing World."

40. Ibid.

41. Aldo Leopold, *A Sand County Almanac* (New York: Ballantine Books, 1970; originally published by Oxford University Press, 1949), 6.

42. Robert F. Sayre, "Aldo Leopold on Agriculture," Leopold Center for Sustainable Agriculture, Iowa State University, http://www.leopold.iastate.edu/pubs/other/aldoonag.htm.

43. Author interview with Frederick Kirschenmann, distinguished fellow at Iowa State University's Leopold Center for Sustainable Agriculture, September 21, 2010.

44. Author interview with Kirschenmann; and Frederick Kirschenmann, "Food in Dry Times: How to Grow Food with Less Water," *Yes* magazine, May 27, 2010.

45. Sayre, "Aldo Leopold on Agriculture"; and Leopold, *A Sand County Almanac*, 260.

46. Author interview with Kirschenmann; and Kirschenmann, "Food in Dry Times."

47. "Agriculture's Next Revolution—Perennial Grain—Within Sight," *Science News*, June 27, 2010.

48. Cynthia Barnett, "Squeezed: Does Big Citrus Have a Future in Florida?" *Florida Trend*, March 2003.

49. David Millar and others, "Quantification and Implications of Soil Losses from Commercial Sod Production," *Soil Science Society of America Journal* 74, no. 3 (February 2010): 892.

50. The $80 billion figure is what Global Industry Analysts Inc. project the landscaping-services market will reach in 2015.

51. C. Milesi and others, "A Strategy for Mapping and Modeling the Ecological Effects of U.S. Lawns," International Society of Photogrammetry and Remote Sensing, 3rd International Symposium Remote Sensing and Date Fusion Over Urban Areas, Tempe, AZ, March 2005.

52. Ibid.

53. The Texas story was recounted to me by employees of the San Antonio Water System. See also Jerry Needham, "Update Coming on Drought-Tolerant Grasses," *San Antonio Express-News*, December 31, 2006. The Florida story was recounted in news articles, including Janet Zink, "Fertilizer Restrictions Creating Turf Wars," *St. Petersburg Times*, December 6, 2009, which calculated that the turf industry had paid $505,000 for research projects at the University of Florida's Institute of Food and Agricultural Sciences since 2006. Comparisons of UF/IFAS publications since 2008 demonstrate increase in fertilizer-rate recommendations. There also has been an increase in the annual amount of nitrogen recommended for St. Augustine grass in much of Florida.

54. Steven C. Blank, "Sustainable Agriculture: Golf Courses, Nurseries and Turf Farms," in Blank, *The End of Agriculture in the American Portfolio* (Westport, CT: Greenwood Publishing Group, 1998).

55. Ibid., 117.

56. John E. Ikerd, *Crisis & Opportunity: Sustainability in American Agriculture* (Lincoln: University of Nebraska Press, 2008), 2–3.

57. Author interview with land planner Matthew "Quint" Redmond, September 21, 2010.

58. Kirschenmann, "Food in Dry Times."

59. Douglas C. Sackman, foreword to Carey McWilliams, *Factories in the Field* (Berkeley: University of California Press, 1999), ix–xv.

60. Arnold Schwarzenegger, speech at San Luis Reservoir, Los Banos, CA, April 17, 2009.

61. Malia Wollan, "Hundreds Protest Cuts in Water in California," *New York Times*, April 17, 2009.

62. Schwarzenegger speech, April 17, 2009.

63. Wollan, "Hundreds Protest Cuts in Water in California."

64. Ibid.

65. Myron Levin, "Smoker Group's Thick Wallet Raises Questions," *Los Angeles Times*, March 30, 1998; and Dan Morain, "Behind Fuming Bar Owners Is Savvy, Well-Heeled Group," *Los Angeles Times*, January 30, 1998.

66. Author interview with Stephen Levy, director and senior economist at the Center for Continuing Study of the California Economy, August 5, 2010. At the beginning of the recession, in December 2007, California had 850,800 construction jobs and 343,900 farm jobs. Fast forward to December 2009, and there were 564,500 construction jobs and 320,600 agricultural jobs.

67. Danielle E. Gains, "Merced County's Jobless Rate Holds Steady—At Awful," *Merced Sun-Star*, April 17, 2010.

68. Merced County, "2009 Annual Report on Agriculture," http://www.co.merced.ca.us/archives/36/2009_merced_ag_report.pdf.

69. The word was from agricultural lobbyist and dairyman George Soares, as quoted in Harry Cline, "California Water Crisis' Human Face," *Farm Press*, November 9, 2009.

70. George Skelton, "Trim Pork from Water Bond," *Los Angeles Times*, August 12, 2010.

71. E. J. Schultz, "Gov. Wants to Delay Vote on $11 Billion Water Bond," *Fresno Bee*, June 29, 2010.

72. South Florida Water Management District, "SFWMD Board Approves Affordable Plan for River of Grass Acquisition," news release, August 12, 2010.

73. Leopold, *A Sand County Almanac*, 245.

74. Author interview with Levy.

Chapter 6   The Water-Industrial Complex

1. Louis Uchitelle and others, "Steep Job Losses Add to Pressure for U.S. Stimulus," *New York Times*, December 6, 2008.

2. Adam Nagourney, "Obama Elected President as Racial Barrier Falls," *New York Times*, November 4, 2008.

3. James Surowiecki, "The Stimulus Strategy," *New Yorker*, February 25, 2008.

4. John M. Broder, "Proposal Ties Economic Stimulus to Energy Savings," *New York Times*, December 4, 2008.

5. The phrase is often attributed to former Alaska governor Sarah Palin, Republican presidential candidate John McCain's running mate. But it was first uttered at the 2008 Republican National Convention by Michael Steele, chairman of GOPAC, an influential party political action committee.

6. Gallup, "2009 Gallup Environment Survey," http://www.gallup.com/poll/117079/Water-Pollution-Americans-Top-Green-Concern.aspx/.

7. Ibid.

8. Author interview with Mary Ann Dickinson, executive director, Alliance for Water Efficiency, December 18, 2009.

9. Dan McCarthy, "Water Didn't Start the Fight," white paper, Black & Veatch Global Water Business, August 31, 2009.

10. Author interview with Dickinson.

11. Ibid.

12. American Rivers and Alliance for Water Efficiency, "Creating Jobs and Stimulating the Economy through Investment in Green Water Infrastructure," white paper, 2008, 3, 8.

13. Michael Grabell and Christopher Weaver, "The Stimulus Plan: A Detailed List of Spending," *ProPublica*, February 13, 2009, http://www.propublica.org/special/the-stimulus-plan-a-detailed-list-of-spending.

14. Sen. Bob Bennett, "Bennett: The Only Thing This Bill Will Stimulate Is the National Debt," press release, February 13, 2009.

15. *ProPublica*, "Bennett Gets $50 Million Utah Water Project in Stimulus Bill," *Salt Lake Tribune*, February 21, 2009.

16. American Society of Civil Engineers, "Drinking Water," http://www.infrastructure reportcard.org/fact-sheet/drinking-water/.

17. Valerie I. Nelson, "Truly Sustainable Water Infrastructure," *WE&T Magazine* [Water Environment Federation] 20, no. 9 (September 2008).

18. Author interview with Glen T. Daigger, president of the International Water Association, September 2, 2010; and Glen T. Daigger, "Evolving Urban Water and

Residuals Management Paradigms: Water Reclamation and Reuse, Decentraliza-tion, and Resource Recovery," *Water Environment Research* 81, no. 8 (August 2009): 809–23.

19. Daigger, "Evolving Urban Water and Residuals Management Paradigms."

20. Ibid.

21. Author interview with Valerie Nelson, director of the Massachusetts-based Coali-tion for Alternative Wastewater Treatment, September 13, 2010.

22. Center for Public Integrity, "The Top 100 Private Contractors in Iraq and Afghani-stan, 2004–2006," http://www.publicintegrity.org/tools/entry/122/.

23. "Uncertainty Clouds Recovery Picture," *Engineering News-Record*, April 26, 2010, 58.

24. Debra Rubin and others, "The Top 200 Environmental Firms," *Engineering News-Record* 263, no. 4 (August 3, 2009): 33.

25. Ibid.

26. Charles F. Wilkinson, *Crossing the Next Meridian: Land, Water, and the Future of the West* (Washington, DC: Island Press, 1992), 21.

27. Donald Worster, *Rivers of Empire: Water, Aridity, and the Growth of the American West* (New York: Pantheon Books, 1985), 5.

28. Katherine Baer, "American Rivers Helps Redefine Water Infrastructure," press re-lease, Aspen Institute, July 29, 2009.

29. TWDB agendas are archived at http://www.twdb.state.tx.us/BoardMembers/TWDBCurrentAgendas.asp/.

30. Eve Samples, "Public Eager to Be Heard on Lake O Discharges as Meeting Contin-ues Thursday," *Palm Beach Post*, May 12, 2010.

31. Jake Berry, "Level Playing Field Sought for Sewage," *Cape Cod Times*, April 30, 2010.

32. Federal campaign–contributions data courtesy of the Center for Responsive Poli-tics; Debra K. Rubin, "CH2M Hill's Ralph Peterson, Industry Icon, Dies at 64," *Engineering News-Record*, September 2, 2009.

33. Federal Elections Commission, 2009 PAC count; 4,611 registered PACs covering U.S. presidential and congressional races.

34. California Secretary of State's Office, Cal-Access campaign-finance database, con-tributions made by CH2M Hill Inc. Details for Proposition 50 are from California Resource Agency, "Summary of Programs in Proposition 50," http://www.resources.ca.gov/bond/Prop_50_Summary_of_Programs2.pdf.

35. Salton Sea Authority, "Salton Sea Restoration: Final Preferred Project Report," July 2004, 28.

36. California Secretary of State's Office, Cal-Access campaign-finance database, con-tributions made by Parsons.

37. California Secretary of State's Office, Cal-Access campaign-finance database, con-tributions made by CH2M Hill Inc.

38. Melanie Turner, "CH2M Hill Awarded $9.5 Million for Delta Plan," *Sacramento Business Journal*, May 6, 2010.

39. California Secretary of State's Office, Cal-Access campaign-finance database, con-tributions made by AECOM.

40. John Wildermuth, "Newsom Rakes in Double His Rival's Haul," *Chronicle* (San Francisco), May 30, 2010.

41. "AECOM Awarded U.S. $26 Million Construction-Management Contract for San Francisco Public Utilities Commission," press release, AECOM, April 15, 2010.

42. Bradley Olson, "Fundraising Shows Mayor's Race Is Open," *Houston Chronicle*, July 15, 2009.

43. Kacey Bacchus and others, "Playing the Game: Big Campaign Contributions and Political Influence in Houston," Campaigns for People, October 2003, 5, http://www.click2houston.com/pdf/playingthegame.pdf.

44. National Institute for Engineering Ethics, "Ethics Case Study 2: Political Contributions," http://www.niee.org/EthicsModule/Ethics2.htm.

45. Frances E. Griggs Jr., "New Look at the Code of Ethics," *Journal of Professional Issues in Engineering Education and Practice* (January 2009): 46.

46. Cynthia Barnett, "Culture of Trust," *Florida Trend*, March 2007.

47. Cynthia Barnett, "Stimulus Made Easy," *Florida Trend*, June 2009.

48. Barnett, "Culture of Trust."

49. Federal Elections Commission, MUR 5903, in the matter of PBSJ Corporation and others, "General Council's Report No. 2," September 22, 2009, 5.

50. Federal Elections Commission, "General Council's Report No. 2."

51. United States of America v. Richard A. Wickett, U.S. District Court, Southern District of Florida, March 8, 2007.

52. Federal Elections Commission, "General Council's Report No. 2," 3.

53. Ibid., 8.

54. USA v. Wickett.

55. Federal Elections Commission, "General Council's Report No. 2," 18.

56. USA v. Wickett.

57. Federal Elections Commission, "General Council's Report No. 2," 20–21.

58. Patrick Danner and Dan Christens, "Former Exec Avoids Prison," *Miami Herald*, May 10, 2008.

59. Author telephone conversation with Jorge Martinez, June 25, 2010.

60. Michael A. Fletcher, "Obama Leaves D.C. to Sign Stimulus Bill," *Washington Post*, February 18, 2009.

61. The Denver Museum of Nature & Science opened *Grand Canyon: River at Risk* in its Phipps IMAX Theater on February 13, 2009.

62. Ronnie Scheib, "Review: Grand Canyon Adventure: River at Risk," *Variety*, March 17, 2008, 30.

63. Lake Superior State University, "Lake Superior State University 2010 Banished Words List," http://www.lssu.edu/banished/.

64. Barnett, "Stimulus Made Easy."

65. "The Florida Trend 350: Private Companies," *Florida Trend*, June 2010.

66. Barnett, "Stimulus Made Easy." Government collectively accounts for more than 90 percent of PBSJ's income.

Chapter 7   Singapore: Of Songbirds and Sewage

1. Author interview with Linda Dorothy de Mello, deputy director of PUB's 3P Network Department, March 12, 2010.

2. United Nations, *The World at Six Billion*, table 9, "Population Densities of the

Countries of the World, 1999 and 2050," 28. Singapore had 5,699 people per square kilometer in 1999.

3. Salmah Zakaria and Zalilah Selamat, "Water Resources Management in Malaysia," National Institute for Land and Infrastructure Management, Japan, http://www .nilim.go.jp/lab/bcg/siryou/tnn/tnn0156pdf/ks0156013.pdf.

4. Peter H. Gleick, "Water Conflict Chronology," Pacific Institute for Studies in Development, Environment, and Security database, http://www.worldwater.org/conflict/ list/.

5. Tan Yong Soon, *Clean, Green, and Blue: Singapore's Journey Towards Environmental and Water Sustainability* (Singapore: Institute of Southeast Asian Studies Publishing, 2009), 70.

6. Author interview with Tan Seng Chai, vice president for water projects in the Asia Pacific region for Black & Veatch, March 11, 2010.

7. Lee Kuan Yew, *From Third World to First: The Singapore Story: 1965 to 2000* (New York: HarperCollins, 2000); see chapter 13, "Greening Singapore," especially pp. 173–75.

8. Ibid, 173–74.

9. Goh Chok Tong, speech for the official launch of NEWater, NEWater Visitor Centre, Singapore, February 21, 2003, http://app.mfa.gov.sg/data/2006/press/water/ SpeechPM.html.

10. Soon, *Clean, Green, and Blue*, 71–72.

11. Ibid., 72.

12. Ibid., 73.

13. Ibid., 73–74.

14. U.S. Department of Commerce, http://www.buyusa.gov/asianow/soilgas.html.

15. Assif Shameen, "Singapore, the New Switzerland," *Barron's*, January 14, 2008, http://online.barrons.com/article/SB120009958593085271.html.

16. U.S. Department of State, Background Note: Singapore, http://www.state.gov/r/pa/ ei/bgn/2798.htm#econ.

17. Unemployment rates from 2009 are from the U.S. Bureau of Labor Statistics, http:// data.bls.gov/PDQ/servlet/SurveyOutputServlet?data_tool=latest_numbers&series_ id=LNS14000000, and the government of Singapore, http://www.singstat.gov.sg/.

18. World Bank, "Gross National Income Per Capita 2008," http://siteresources.world bank.org/DATASTATISTICS/Resources/GNIPC.pdf.

19. Travel and Leisure Southeast Asia, Ion Orchard, http://www.travelandleisureasia .com/destinations/singapore/singapore-shopping/359338/ion_orchard.html.

20. Lee, *From Third World to First*, 180.

21. "State of the Family in Singapore," Singapore Ministry of Community Development, Youth, and Sports, General Household Survey from 2005; see fertility rate, 7.

22. Mui Teng Yap, "Singapore's 'Three or More' Policy: The First Five Years," *Asia-Pacific Population Journal* 10, no. 4 (1005): 39–52, http://www.un.org/Depts/escap/ pop/journal/v10n4a3.htm.

23. Lee, *From Third World to First*, 183–84.

24. Author interview with Harry Seah, director of the Technology and Water Quality Office at Singapore's Public Utility Board (PUB), March 11, 2010.

25. *From Third World to First*, 178.

26. Ibid., 180.

27. As just one example, see Cecilia Tortajada, "Water Management in Singapore," *International Journal of Water Resources Development* 22, no. 2 (June 2006): 227–40.

28. Rural Community Assistance Corporation, http://www.rcac.org/.

29. U.S. Environmental Protection Agency, "U.S. Census Data on Small Community Housing and Wastewater Disposal and Plumbing Practices," http://www.epa.gov/owm/mab/smcomm/factsheets/census/index.htm.

30. Author interview with Seah; and Teo Yin Yin at PUB, March 11, 2010.

31. Ibid.

32. Author interview with Teo, March 11, 2010.

33. A LexisNexis search turned up 215 stories about NEWater between January 2001 and February 2003.

34. Dominic Nathan, "NEWater, It's Mind over Matter," *Straits Times*, July 20, 2002.

35. Natalie Soh, "Cheers! to 37 years . . . and Newater," *Straits Times*, August 10, 2002.

36. Author interview with Seah.

37. Tan, *Clean, Green, and Blue*, 74.

38. The number of fish is from Tan Heok Hui and others, "Fishes of the Marina Basin, Singapore, Before Erection of the Marina Barrage," *Raffles Bulletin of Zoology* 58, no. 1 (February 28, 2010): 137–44.

39. Hui, "Fishes of the Marina Basin, Singapore, Before Erection of the Marina Barrage," 138.

40. Author interview with Seah.

41. Ibid.

42. Author interview with Yong Wei Hin, assistant director, Changi Water Reclamation Plant, March 12, 2010.

43. Ibid.

44. Tan, *Clean, Green, and Blue*, 162.

45. All per capita numbers were provided by the Public Utilities Board.

46. The quote is from the Public Utilities Board's "ABC Waters" brochure.

47. Author interview with de Mello.

48. American Rivers, "River Facts," http://www.americanrivers.org/library/river-facts/river-facts.html.

49. U.S. Environmental Protection Agency, "Great Lakes, Basic Information," http://www.epa.gov/glnpo/basicinfo.html.

50. T. E. Reilly and others, "Ground-Water Availability in the United States: U.S. Geological Survey Circular 1323," 2008, 6, http://pubs.usgs.gov/circ/1323/.

Chapter 8   The Big Dipper

1. Felicity Barringer, "Las Vegas's Worried Water Czar," *New York Times* online, *Green* blog, September 28, 2010.

2. Emily Green, "The Chosen One," *Las Vegas Sun*, June 8, 2008.

3. Michael E. Campana, "Mulroy as Moses," *Aquadoc* blog, http://aquadoc.typepad.com/waterwired/2009/08/mulroy-as-moses.html.

4. Hal Rothman and Mike Davis, *The Grit Beneath the Glitter: Tales from the Real Las Vegas* (Berkeley: University of California Press, 2002), 116.

5. Green, "The Chosen One."

6. Ibid.

7. Ibid.

8. Laura Parker, "Las Vegas Breaks Growth Bank, Census Says It Expanded by 40.9%," *USA Today*, January 2, 1998.

9. Author interview with Patricia Mulroy, chief of the Southern Nevada Water Authority, September 29, 2010.

10. Green, "The Chosen One."

11. Ibid.

12. Rothman and Davis, *The Grit Beneath the Glitter*, 117.

13. Mort Rosenblum, *Escaping Plato's Cave: How America's Blindness to the Rest of the World Threatens Our Survival* (New York: St. Martin's Press, 2007), 89.

14. Joe Gelt, "Drop 2—End-of-the-Line Reservoir Salvages Colorado River Water," *Arizona Water Resource Journal* 16, no. 5 (May–June 2008).

15. John Lippert and Jim Efstathiou Jr., "Las Vegas Running Out of Water Means Dimming Los Angeles Lights," *Bloomberg News*, February 26, 2009.

16. Author interview with Mulroy.

17. Brett Walton, "The Price of Water: A Comparison of Water Rates, Usage in 30 U.S. Cities," Circle of Blue, April 26, 2010, http://www.circleofblue.org/waternews/2010/world/the-price-of-water-a-comparison-of-water-rates-usage-in-30-u-s-cities/. Prices cited are for a family that uses an average of one hundred gallons daily per capita.

18. Solomon, *Water*, 350; see chapter 4, note 22.

19. Rosenblum, *Escaping Plato's Cave*, 89.

20. Matt Jenkins, "Vegas Forges Ahead on Pipeline Plan," *High Country News*, October 12, 2009.

21. Associated Press, "Vegas Water Pipeline Foes Seek Nevada Court Hearing," *Salt Lake Tribune*, August 21, 2010.

22. Jenkins, "Vegas Forges Ahead on Pipeline Plan."

23. Henry Brean, "Mulroy Advice for Obama: Tap Mississippi Floodwaters," *Las Vegas Review-Journal*, January 12, 2009.

24. Robert Glennon, *Unquenchable: America's Water Crisis and What to Do About It* (Washington, DC: Island Press, 2009), 15.

25. Solomon, *Water*, 348.

26. Peter Annin, *The Great Lakes Water Wars* (Washington, DC: Island Press, 2006), 68.

27. Ibid., and personal communication with Jonathan Bulkley.

28. Brean, "Mulroy Advice for Obama."

29. Peter G. Brown, "Are There Any Natural Resources?" in *Water Ethics: Foundational Readings for Students and Professionals*, eds. Peter G. Brown and Jeremy J. Schmidt (Washington, DC: Island Press, 2010), 203–18.

30. The Pew Forum on Religion and Public Life, "Major Religious Traditions in the U.S.," http://religions.pewforum.org/reports. According to the 2007 report, 78.4 percent of Americans identified with a Christian faith and 16 percent said they had no religious affiliation.

31. Gary Chamberlain, *Troubled Waters: Religion, Ethics, and the Global Water Crisis* (Lanham, MD: Rowman & Littlefield, 2008), 40.

32. Naser I. Faruqui and others, eds., *Water Management in Islam* (Japan: United Nations University Press, 2001), 1.

33. Ibid.; and Howard Schwartz, *Tree of Souls: The Mythology of Judaism* (New York: Oxford University Press, 2004), 94.

34. Rajendra Pradhan and Ruth Meinzen-Dick, "Which Rights Are Right? Water Rights, Culture, and Underlying Values," in *Water Ethics*, eds. Brown and Schmidt, 48.

35. Sidney Lanier, "Song of the Chattahoochee," in *Yale Book of American Verse*, ed. Thomas R. Lounsbury (New Haven, CT: Yale University Press, 1912), 480.

36. Cynthia Barnett, "Shortage in the Land of Plenty," in *Water Matters*, ed. Tara Lohan (San Francisco: Alternet Books, 2010), 26.

37. According to the Florida Department of Environmental Protection, Florida paid $15.5 million in legal fees on the tristate water conflict between November 2001 and May 2010, with $11.7 million of that to lawyers at Hogan Lovells offices in Miami and Washington, DC. According to the Georgia Attorney General's Office, Georgia had spent $7.7 million through May 2010, $6.9 million of that to McKenna Long & Aldridge. The Atlanta Regional Commission reports that it paid another $7 million in legal fees, most to King & Spalding. The $30 million total does not include other cities or Alabama, whose governor's and attorney general's offices did not respond to public-records requests.

38. ABC News, video, "Georgians Pray for Rain—Literally," November 13, 2007.

39. Ibid. Perdue is quoting Psalm 65 of the New King James version of the Bible, lines 9–10.

40. U.S. district judge Paul A. Magnuson, Memorandum and Order in re Tri-State Water Rights Litigation, Case No. 3:07-md-01, U.S. District Court, Middle District of Florida, 94.

41. "Governor Perdue Reflects on Years in Office," *Channel 2 Action News*, Atlanta, December 28, 2010.

42. "Petition for Reconsideration of Endangerment and Cause or Contribute Findings for Greenhouse Gases Under Section 202 (a) of the Clean Air Act," EPA Docket No. EPA-HQ-OAR-2009–0171, December 23, 2009.

43. Harris Blackwood, "Are More Dams on the Flint the Answer?" *Gainesville Times*, May 4, 2008.

44. Georgia Water Coalition, "Water for All Georgia" (commercial, available on You Tube at http://www.youtube.com/watch?v=uezMV9ri-LY/).

45. Shaila Dewan, "Georgia Claims a Sliver of the Tennessee River," *New York Times*, February 22, 2008.

46. Earth Covenant Ministry, "River of Life Project," http://www.earthcovenantministry .org/RiverOfLife/index.htm.

47. Author interview with Joe Cook, Riverkeeper of the Upper Coosa River, December 23, 2010.

48. Cynthia Barnett, *Mirage: Florida and the Vanishing Water of the Eastern U.S.* (Ann Arbor: University of Michigan Press, 2007), 123.

49. Ibid., 105.

50. Bobby MacGill, "Aaron Million Tweaks His Water Project," *Coloradoan*, December 24, 2010.

51. Pearce, *When the Rivers Run Dry*, 227.
52. "NAWAPA: Water for Life"; see this video and a series of videoconferences at http://www.larouchepac.com/node/15570/.
53. Annin, *The Great Lakes Water Wars*, 193.
54. U.S. Environmental Protection Agency, "The Great Lakes: An Environmental Atlas and Resource Book," http://www.epa.gov/glnpo/atlas/index.html.
55. Annin, *The Great Lakes Water Wars*, 23.
56. Ibid., 23–28.
57. Author interview with Mulroy.
58. Solomon, *Water*, 350–51.
59. Barnett and Pierce, "When Will Lake Mead Go Dry?," 19.
60. Author interview with Mulroy.

Chapter 9   The Business of Blue

1. Rich Rovito, "The Pied Piper of Milwaukee: Meeusen Speaks Up to Get the Job Done," *Milwaukee Business Journal*, May 22, 2009.
2. "The Greener Side of Blue," Badger Meter Inc. Annual Report 2008, 2.
3. Author interview with Richard Meeusen, chairman, president, and CEO of Badger Meter Inc., November 30, 2010.
4. Joe Barrett, "Water Plan Aims to Help Jobs Flow," *Wall Street Journal*, November 30, 2009.
5. John G. Craig Jr. "Out of the Ashes," *Milwaukee Journal-Sentinel*, May 16, 2009.
6. Elizabeth Cutright, "Green Fever Blues," *Water Efficiency*, March 2008.
7. Tristan Roberts, "Your Guide to the New Draft of LEED," *Environmental Building News*, November 8, 2010.
8. CapitalEND, "The Water Opportunity for Ontario," March 2010.
9. "Water Use in Buildings: Achieving Business Performance Benefits through Efficiency," McGraw-Hill Construction, June 2009.
10. IBM. "Smarter Water for a Smarter Planet," IBM Conversations for a Smarter Planet Series #14.
11. Schnoor, "Water Sustainability in a Changing World."
12. The Alliance for Water Efficiency, "Water Sense and Green Jobs" (white paper, 2010), http://www.allianceforwaterefficiency.org/.
13. Karen Herzog, "Perch Return to Local Waters—in an Old Factory," *Milwaukee Journal-Sentinel*, February 5, 2010.
14. Brett Walton, "The Price of Water" (see chapter 8, note 17).
15. Data courtesy of Milwaukee Water Works.
16. Author interview with economist David Zetland, May 20, 2010.
17. Office of Governor Arnold Schwarzenegger, "Gov. Schwarzenegger Announces Appointments to Water Commission, Sacramento–San Joaquin Delta Conservancy," May 14, 2010.
18. *Economist*, "For Want of a Drink," May 22, 2010, 5.
19. International Development Research Center, "Water and Islam," http://www.idrc.ca/en/ev-66732-201-1-DO_TOPIC.html.

20. Maude Barlow, "Our Water Commons: Toward a New Freshwater Narrative," http://www.canadians.org/water/publications/water%20commons/water%20 commons%20-%20web.pdf, 2.

21. Data from the United Nations and the Council of Canadians.

22. Peter H. Gleick, *Bottled & Sold: The Story Behind Our Obsession with Bottled Water* (Washington, DC: Island Press, 2010), 4–5.

23. Joan F. Kenny and others, "Estimated Use of Water in the United States in 2005: U.S. Geological Survey Circular 1344," 2009, http://pubs.usgs.gov/circ/1344/.

24. Author interview with Zetland.

25. U.S. Government Accountability Office, "Bureau of Reclamation Information on Allocation and Repayment of Costs of Constructing Water Projects" (report, July 2006).

26. Author interview with Zetland.

27. Douglas Jehl, "As Cities Move to Privatize Water, Atlanta Steps Back," *New York Times*, February 10, 2003.

28. Cynthia Barnett, *Mirage: Florida and the Vanishing Water of the Eastern U.S.* (Ann Arbor: University of Michigan Press, 2007), 166.

29. Zetland has been working on a book called *The End of Abundance: A Guide to the New Economics of Water Scarcity.*

30. Andy Newman, "City Proposes Water Rate Increase of Nearly 13%," *New York Times*, April 9, 2010.

31. Author interview with Zetland.

32. Tan Yong Soon, *Clean, Green, and Blue*, 165–67.

33. Australian Government, "The Cost-Effectiveness of Rainwater Tanks in Urban Australia," March 2007, table 2, ES viii. http://www.nwc.gov.au/www/html/605-waterlines-1.asp?intSiteID=1.

34. U.S. Census Bureau data for the period between July 2007 and July 2008.

35. Author interview with Dean Amhaus, director of the Milwaukee Water Council, September 15, 2010.

36. Anne Davies, "Sydney's Future Eaten: The Flannery Prophecy," *Sydney Morning Herald*, May 19, 2004.

Chapter 10   Australia: Dry Down Under

1. Antipodes maps allow users to see the other side of the world; see, for example, http://www.antipodemap.com/.

2. Australian Bureau of Statistics, National Regional Profile, Perth, http://www.abs .gov.au/ausstats/abs@.nsf/9fdb8b444ff1e8e2ca25709c0081a8f9/648af544ef27bc13c a25771300181857!OpenDocument/.

3. Marnie Leybourne and Andrea Gaynor, *Water: Histories, Cultures, Ecologies* (Perth: University of Western Australia Publishing, 2006), 122–30.

4. M. Donaldson, "The End of Time? Aboriginal Temporality and the British Invasion of Australia" (Faculty of Arts Papers, University of Wollongong, Wollongong, Australia, 1996), 5.

5. Pamela Statham-Drew, *James Stirling: Admiral and Founding Governor of Western Australia* (Crawley: University of Western Australia, 2003), 77.

6. Ibid., 124–25.

7. Ibid., 79.

8. Government House, http://www.govhouse.wa.gov.au/garden.htm.

9. E.A. Pearce and C.G. Smith, *The World Weather Guide* (London: Hutchinson, 1984), 304.

10. The Australian Bureau of Statistics reports that Western Australia's population doubled between 1970 and 2001. The Government of Western Australia Department of State reports average GDP growth at 5.21 percent during the first ten years of the new century, outperforming nationwide GDP growth of 4.34 percent. http://www.dsd.wa.gov.au/7159.aspx.

11. Water Corporation of Western Australia. Perth's 2001 per capita use was 185 kiloliters per year, according to the utility. That's 506 liters per person per day, or about 135 U.S. liquid gallons per person each day.

12. See note 10.

13. Craig James, "Australian Homes Are Biggest in the World" (November 2009). Western Australian home sizes averaged 243.9 square meters in the 2008–2009 fiscal year, compared to 201.5 square meters in the United States. http://images.comsec.com.au/ipo/UploadedImages/craigjames3f6189175551497fada1a4769f74d09c.pdf.

14. Michael McKernan, *Drought: The Red Marauder* (Crows Nest, New South Wales: Allen & Unwin, 2005), 23.

15. Australian Government Bureau of Meteorology, "The 'Federation Drought,' 1895 to 1902," http://www.bom.gov.au/lam/climate/levelthree/c20thc/drought1.htm.

16. McKernan, *Drought*, 15.

17. Michael Cathcart, *The Water Dreamers: The Remarkable History of Our Dry Continent* (Melbourne, Victoria: Text Publishing, 2009), 2.

18. Frank Welsh, *Australia: A New History of the Great Southern Land* (Woodstock, NY: Overlook Press, 2004), 250 (for first irrigation schemes and U.S. model); 392–93 (for some results).

19. Ibid., 392–93.

20. Cathcart, *The Water Dreamers*, 206–7.

21. William J. Coughlin, "Into the Outback: How a Young Herbert Hoover Made His Name—and His Fortune—in Australia," *Stanford Magazine*, http://www.stanfordalumni.org/news/magazine/2000/marapr/articles/hoover.html.

22. Murray River Tourism Proprietary Ltd., "About the Murray River," http://www.murrayriver.com.au/about-the-murray/.

23. National Archives of Australia, Water Dreaming, exhibit guide, document 5. http://www.naa.gov.au/images/waterdreaming_tcm2-2981.pdf.

24. National Heritage Trust, "Water Resources in Australia," (2000), 8.

25. Wentworth Group of Concerned Scientists, "Australia's Climate Is Changing Australia," http://www.wentworthgroup.org/uploads/3.%20Aust.Climate_is_Changing_Australia.pdf.

26. Deborah Cameron, "Wheat Imports Loom as Drought Bites," *Sydney Morning Herald*, November 15, 2006.

27. R.J. Fensham and R.J. Fairfax, "Drought-Related Tree Death of Savannah Eucalypts," *Journal of Vegetation Science*, January 1, 2007.

28. Australian Broadcasting Corporation, *Brisbane Evening News*, March 7, 2010.

29. Water Services Association of Australia, "WSSA Report Card 2007–2008: Performance of the Australian Water Services Industry and Projections for the Future," 4, https://www.wsaa.asn.au/Publications/Documents/WSAA%20Report%20Card%202007–08.pdf.

30. John Vidal, "Australia Suffers Worst Drought in 1,000 Years," *Guardian*, November 8, 2006.

31. Ibid.

32. Water Services Association of Australia, "WSSA Report Card 2008–2009: Performance of the Australian Water Services Industry and Projections for the Future," 5, https://www.wsaa.asn.au/Publications/Documents/WSAA%20Report%20Card%202008–09.pdf.

33. Ibid., 4–5.

34. Terry Murphy and Phil Kneebone, *Water Story: The Battle to Keep Perth Green*, Leederville, Western Australia: Water Corporation, 2007, 30. The quote "Winter did not come" is from planning engineer Keith Barrett.

35. Murphy and Kneebone, *Water Story*.

36. Author interview with Jim Gill, former CEO of the Water Corporation of Western Australia, March 15, 2010.

37. The population-growth figures are from the Australian Bureau of Statistics, http://www.dsd.wa.gov.au/7159.aspx.

38. Murphy and Kneebone, *Water Story*, 6.

39. Richard Weller, *Boomtown 2050: Scenarios for a Rapidly Growing City* (Perth: University of Western Australia Publishing, 2009), xxvii.

40. Greens Western Australia, "Urban Bushland" (background paper), http://wa.greens.org.au/Policy/UrbanBushland/.

41. Government of Western Australia, Environmental Protection Authority, "Environmental Protection of Wetlands Position Paper No. 4" (November 2004) 2, http://www.epa.wa.gov.au/docs/1034_PS4.pdf.

42. Government of Western Australia, "Reasons to Invest in Western Australia," http://www.dsd.wa.gov.au/7159.aspx.

43. Murphy and Kneebone, *Water Story*, 4.

44. Greg Stewart, "Australia Case Study: Residential Irrigation in Perth," (presentation, WaterSmart Innovations 2009, Las Vegas, Nevada, October 7, 2009). Stewart's presentation is what first got me interested in looking into Perth's water ethic.

45. Murphy and Kneebone, *Water Story*, 2.

46. Author interview with Chari Pattiaratchi, professor of coastal oceanography at the University of Western Australia, March 15, 2010.

47. Commonwealth Scientific and Industrial Research Organisation and Australian Bureau of Meteorology, "Climate Change in Australia: Technical Report 2007" (2007), 21, http://www.climatechangeinaustralia.gov.au/documents/resources/TR_Web_Ch2.pdf.

48. Ibid.

49. Author e-mail correspondence with Richard Weller, April 18, 2010.

50. Greg Stewart, "Australia Case Study."

51. Kim MacDonald, Eloise Dortch, and Monica Videnieks, "Water Chaos as Leaders Split on Sprinkler Ban," *West Australian*, February 2, 2005.

52. Amanda Banks and Graham Mason, "Scientists Attack Plan to Tap SW Aquifer," *West Australian*, March 26, 2007.

53. Murphy and Kneebone, *Water Story*, 58.

54. "IWSS Water Efficiency Program Business Case" (consultant's report, October 2009), 1.

55. Author interview with Sue Murphy, CEO of the Water Corporation of Western Australia, March 15, 2010.

56. Water Corporation, "Corporate Snapshot 2009–10" (report, October 2009), 5.

57. Water Corporation of Western Australia. Perth's 2001 per capita use was 185 kiloliters a year, according to the utility. That's 506 liters per person per day, or about 135 U.S. liquid gallons per person each day. In 2009, it had dropped to 147 kiloliters per year. That's 397 liters, or about 100 U.S. liquid gallons, per day.

58. Water Corporation, "Water Forever: Towards Climate Resilience" (report, October 2009), 40. http://www.watercorporation.com.au/_files/.../Water_Forever_50_Year_Plan.pdf.

59. Joanne Chong and others, "Review of Water Restrictions," Institute for Sustainable Futures, University of Technology Sydney, 2009. http://utsescholarship.lib.uts.edu.au/iresearch/scholarly-works/handle/2100/906.

60. Author interview with Murphy.

61. As just one example, see "Water Restrictions Eased, Two Extra Hours," *Adelaide Now*, April 12, 2010, http://www.adelaidenow.com.au/water-restrictions-eased-two-extra-hours/story-e6frea6u-1225852350467.

62. Author e-mail correspondence with Richard Weller, April 18, 2010.

63. Author interview with Murphy.

64. Ibid.

65. Ibid.

66. National Science Foundation, "Employed Scientists and Engineers, by Occupation, Highest Degree Level, and Sex: 2006," http://www.nsf.gov/statistics/wmpd/pdf/tabh-5.pdf. The NSF reported that of 1,621,000 engineers working nationwide in 2006, 187,000 were women.

67. National Science Foundation, "Women, Minorities, and Persons with Disabilities in Science and Engineering" (table B-9, "Undergraduate enrollment in engineering programs by sex, race/ethnicity, and citizenship: 1995–2008"), http://www.nsf.gov/statistics/wmpd/pdf/tabb-9.pdf. In 1995, women made up 67,286 out of 363,315 engineering undergraduates. In 2005, the proportion was 70,579 out of 409,326.

68. U.S. Bureau of Labor Statistics, "Employed Persons by Detailed Industry, Sex, Race, and Hispanic or Latino Ethnicity," 2009, http://www.bls.gov/cps/cpsaat18.pdf. The BLS reported 231,000 employees working specifically in the water utility sector, 23,000 of them women.

69. Jack E. Davis, ed., *The Wide Brim: Early Poems and Ponders of Marjory Stoneman Douglas* (Gainesville: University Press of Florida, 2002), 95–96.

70. Jack E. Davis, *An Everglades Providence: Marjory Stoneman Douglas and the American Environmental Century* (Athens: University of Georgia Press, 2009), 518.

71. Davis, *The Wide Brim*, 115.

72. UDaily, "Electric Power Executive Talks About Turmoil, Transition in U.S. Energy Sector," April 15, 2010, http://www.udel.edu/udaily/2010/apr/electricpower041510.html.

73. Kathy Robb, "On the Heads of Women," in *Written in Water: Messages of Hope for Earth's Most Precious Resource*, ed. Irena Salina (Washington, DC: National Geographic Society, 2010), 255–56.

74. United Nations, "Water for Life, 2005–1015" (fact sheet), http://www.un.org/water forlifedecade/factsheet.html.

75. The workforce age estimates are from the Conference Board, "America's Aging Workforce Posing New Opportunities and Challenges for Companies," 2005, http://www.conference-board.org/utilities/pressDetail.cfm?press_ID=2709. The phrase "announce and defend" comes from an anonymous Water Corporation engineer. See Terry Murphy and Phil Kneebone, "Water Story: The Battle to Keep Perth Green" (Water Corporation of Western Australia, June 2007), 7.

76. Author interview with Murphy.

77. Mundaring and Hills Historical Society, http://www.mhhs.org.au/MHHS-Mundaring-Weir-Settlement.htm.

78. Frank Batini, lead scientist on the trial, provided these species, numbers, and results in an e-mail correspondence with the author, April 25, 2010.

79. Tom Wolfe, *The Right Stuff* (New York: Farrar, Straus, and Giroux, 1979), 258–60.

80. Ibid., 260.

Chapter 11 An American Water Ethic

1. Steve Campbell, "Texas Has Half the Big Cities with the Greatest Population Growth," *Fort Worth Star-Telegram*, June 22, 2010.

2. U.S. Census, "Annual Estimates of the Resident Population for Incorporated Places over 100,000" (2009 update), http://www.census.gov/popest/cities/tables/SUB-EST 2009-01.xls.

3. Author interview with Alexander Briseño, chairman of the board of trustees of the San Antonio Water System, June 21, 2010.

4. *Sierra Club v. Babbitt*, MO-91-CA-069, 1993.

5. Author interview with Briseño.

6. Author interview with Rex Poppy, chief building engineer for Concord Property Corporation, June 24, 2010.

7. Lewis W. Newton, "Olmsted, Frederick Law," http://www.tshaonline.org/handbook/online/articles/OO/fol5.html.

8. Frederick Law Olmsted, *A Journey Through Texas, or, A Saddle-Trip on the Southwestern Frontier* (Boston: Mason Brothers, 1860), 150. (An initial version, now out of print, was published in 1857.)

9. Ibid., 156–57.

10. Dana Nichols, "The *Acequias* of San Antonio and the Beginnings of a Modern Water System," in *Environmental and Water Resources: Milestones in Engineering History*, ed. Jerry R. Rogers (Baltimore: ASCE Publications, 2007), 79–80.

11. Ibid., 81.

12. Gregg Eckhardt, "Introduction to the Edwards Aquifer," http://www.edwardsaquifer.net/intro.html.

13. Gregg Eckhardt, "San Antonio Springs and Brackenridge Park," http://www.edwardsaquifer.net/saspring.html.

14. Maria Pfeiffer, "Brackenridge Park: An In-Depth Historical Review," http://www
    .sanantonio.gov/sapar/brackhistory.asp?res=1280&ver=true/.

15. Todd H. Votteler, "Raiders of the Lost Aquifer? Or, the Beginning of the End to
    Fifty Years of Conflict over the Texas Edwards Aquifer," *Tulane Environmental Law
    Journal* 15 (August 2004), 269.

16. Todd H. Votteler, "Water from a Stone: The Limits of the Sustainable Development
    of the Texas Edwards Aquifer," PhD diss., Southwest Texas University, February 23,
    2000, 80. The Ohio case was *Frazier v. Brown*, 12 Ohio St. 294, 311 (1861).

17. Barnett, *Mirage*, 96 (see chapter 8, note 48).

18. Votteler, "Raiders of the Lost Aquifer?," 261.

19. Ibid., 268.

20. Votteler, *Water from a Stone*, 31.

21. Votteler, "Raiders of the Lost Aquifer?," 261.

22. Todd H. Votteler, "The Little Fish That Roared: The Endangered Species Act,
    State Groundwater Law, and Private Property Rights Collide Over the Texas Ed-
    wards Aquifer" (paper, Northwestern University School of Law, Chicago, 1998),
    855.

23. *Sierra Club v. Babbitt*.

24. Author interview with Todd Votteler, an executive with the Guadalupe-Blanco River
    Authority, July 14, 2010.

25. Ibid.

26. Ibid.

27. San Antonio Water System, "Drought-Tolerant Grass" (2005), http://www.saws.org/
    conservation/Ordinance/TurfGrass/index.shtml.

28. Author interview with Karen Guz, director of conservation, and Phil Weynand,
    manager of indoor programs, at the San Antonio Water System, June 22, 2010.

29. Author interview with Shannon Staub, a Sarasota County, Florida, commissioner,
    July 26, 2010.

30. Ibid.

31. See American Water, http://www.amwater.com/.

32. Doug Evanson, "2010 Rate Structure Update," PowerPoint presentation, San Anto-
    nio City Council, March 17, 2010.

33. Author interview with Guz.

34. Ibid.

35. Author interview with Weynand.

36. Author interview with Poppy.

37. Author interview with Weynand.

38. Author interview with Guz.

39. Author interview with Briseño.

40. Author interview with Billy Kniffen, water-resource specialist for Texas A&M Uni-
    versity's Biological and Agricultural Engineering Department, June 23, 2010.

41. Larry W. Mays, ed., *Ancient Water Technologies* (New York: Springer, 2010), 15.

42. Gerard T. Koeppel, *Water for Gotham: A History* (Princeton, NJ: Princeton Univer-
    sity Press, 2001), 13.

43. Ibid., 124–25.

44. Lyn Corum, "A New Old Water Source," *Water Efficiency* (July/August 2010), 28.

45. Author interview with Kniffen.

46. Suzy Banks with Richard Heinichen, *Rainwater Collection for the Mechanically Challenged* (Austin, TX: Tank Town Publishing, 2008), 10.

47. Author interview with Richard Heinichen, co-owner of Tank Town, June 23, 2010.

48. Ibid.

49. Corum, "A New Old Water Source," 30.

50. Zeke MacCormack, "Kendall Looks at Water as a Cash Crop," *San Antonio Express-News*, August 1, 2009.

51. Ibid.

52. Kirk Johnson, "It's Now Legal to Catch a Raindrop in Colorado," *New York Times*, June 28, 2009.

53. Ibid.

54. Washington Division of Ecology, "Rainwater Collection in Washington State," http://www.ecy.wa.gov/programs/wr/hq/rwh.html.

55. Utah Division of Water Rights, "Rainwater Harvesting," http://nrwrt1.nr.state .ut.us/.

56. Interview with Kniffen.

57. Peter J. Coombes and George Kuczera, "Integrated Urban Water Cycle Management: Moving Towards Systems Understanding" (2nd National Conference on Water Sensitive Urban Design, Brisbane, Australia, 2002).

58. Karen McGhee, "Bring in the Tanks," *Australian Geographic* 89 (January–March 2008): 120–27.

59. Ibid.

60. Coombes and Kuczera, "Integrated Urban Water Cycle Management," 5–6.

61. Zeke MacCormack, "Bandera Settles with Business Refusing Water," *San Antonio Express-News*, February 6, 2010.

62. UPI, "Rain Harvesting Saves Tucson Water," December 28, 2009.

63. See Portland Department of Consumer and Business Services, "Oregon Smart Guide: Rainwater Harvesting," http://www.cbs.state.or.us/external/bcd/pdf/3660.pdf.

64. Sister Margaret Patrice Slattery, "Promises to Keep: A History of the Sisters of Charity of the Incarnate Word, San Antonio, Texas" (vol. 2, Alumni Office, University of the Incarnate Word, 1999), 39.

65. Bob Connelly and others, "The Birth of the Incarnate Word Headwaters Project," *The Eclectic Edition* (University of the Incarnate Word faculty anthology, 2004), 66–76.

66. Ibid.

67. Roger S. Gottlieb, ed., *The Oxford Handbook of Religion and Ecology* (New York: Oxford University Press, 2006), 82.

68. Jim Robbins, "Ideas and Trends: God and Nature; Saving Souls and Salmon," *New York Times*, October 22, 2000.

69. Catholic Bishops of the Watershed Region, "The Columbia River Watershed: Caring for Creation and Common Good" Columbia River Pastoral Letter Project, 2001.

70. Tim LaHaye and Jerry B. Jenkins, *Are We Living in the End Times?* (Carol Stream, IL: Tyndale House, 1999), 187–88. Here, the authors discuss the second and third "trumpets" that will precede the Rapture. First a third of the sea and then a third of the rivers and springs become poisoned and unlivable.

Chapter 12   Local Water

1.   Latta Plantation, "Teachers Resource Guide" (Civil War Soldier's Life Program), 13, http://www.lattaplantation.org/LATTAFILES/Adobe%20PDF%20Files/Civil%20War%20Soldier%27s%20Life%20Program.pdf.

2.   Greg Jackson, "Beach Swimming Recommendation," Mecklenburg County memorandum, May 26, 2009.

3.   Herman Melville, *Moby-Dick* (New York: Bobbs-Merrill, 1964, Library of Literature edition), 26.

4.   Author interview with Peter H. Gleick, cofounder and president of the Pacific Institute for Studies in Environment and Security, August 26, 2010; see also, Peter H. Gleick, "Call for a 'Local Water Movement' and a New Way of Thinking About Water," *Huffington Post*, July 14, 2010.

5.   Gleick, "Call for a 'Local Water Movement' and a New Way of Thinking About Water."

6.   Bettina Boxall, "In a Region That Imports Water, Much Goes to Waste," *Los Angeles Times*, December 24, 2010.

7.   Sandra L. Postel, "Lessons from the Field—Boston Conservation" (National Geographic Water Conservation Series), http://environment.nationalgeographic.com/environment/freshwater/lessons-boston-conservation/.

8.   Ibid.

9.   Massachusetts Water Supply Authority, "Water Supply and Demand," http://www.mwra.state.ma.us/04water/html/wsupdate.htm.

10. Postel, "Lessons from the Field—Boston Conservation."

11. Kevin Courtney, "Birds and Fish Are Big Winners as Napa River Is Restored," *Napa Valley Register*, September 5, 2010.

12. Watershed Management Council, "Watershed Stewardship in Napa Valley," http://www.watershed.org/?q=node/239/.

13. P. Wesley Schultz, "Littering Behavior in America: Results of a National Study," January 2009, http://www.kab.org/site/DocServer/KAB_Report_Final_2.pdf?docID=4581/.

14. Ibid.

15. Author interview with P. Wesley Schultz, professor of psychology at California State University, San Marcos, September 9, 2010.

16. Author interview with John Arthur Marshall, Angelique Giraud, Ed Pritchard, Dylan Scott, Adrienne Smith, and Jim Wally of the Arthur R. Marshall Foundation on their work on ecosystem valuation in the Everglades, July 7, 2010.

17. Sue Murphy, "Water, Fundamental to a Sense of Place," 2010 George Seddon Lecture, University of Western Australia, Perth, June 16, 2010.

18. Sandra L. Postel, "Why We Need a Water Ethic," in *Water Matters*, ed. Tara Lohan (San Francisco: Alternet Books, 2010), 183.

19. Kathleen Dean Moore, "Water: Do We Have a Moral Obligation to the Future?," lecture, Oregon State University, December 2, 2009. See also Kathleen Dean Moore and Michael P. Nelson, eds., *Moral Ground: Ethical Action for a Planet in Peril* (San Antonio: Trinity University Press, 2010).

20. Curt Meine, "Ripples of a Water Ethic in Wisconsin" Marquette University Law

School Public Service Conference on Water and People, Milwaukee, Wisconsin, February 26, 2010.

21. Aldo Leopold, *A Sand County Almanac* (New York: Ballantine Books, 1970; originally published by Oxford University Press, 1949), 263.

22. Luna B. Leopold, "A Reverence for Rivers," keynote address, Governor's Conference on the California Drought, Los Angeles, 1977.

Index